HEROIC FAILURE AND THE BRITISH

PREFACE AND ACKNOWLEDGEMENTS

THIS BOOK ORIGINATED from a conversation with Heather MacCallum of Yale University Press at the Anglo-American Conference in London in the summer of 2010. I was meeting with her to discuss the publication of my then current project, on country houses and their relationship to the British Empire. That project did not fit Yale's roster of titles (it soon found a home at Manchester University Press), but in the course of our conversation I mentioned a long-standing but as yet ill-defined idea I had to explore the reasons for the prevalence of heroic failure in British culture. I first encountered heroic failure while writing about Captain Scott's death in the Antarctic in 1912 and had been struck by two things: first, many British people assumed that heroic failure was something they celebrated more than other cultures; and second, their opinions as to whether this was something positive or negative were divided. Some Britons felt that their nation's best qualities emerged in its moments of greatest duress, and that the celebration of heroic failure reflected an admirable embrace of perseverance, resilience and stoicism,

CONTENTS

For information about this and other Yale University Press publications, please contact:
U.S. Office: sales.press@yale.edu   www.yalebooks.com
Europe Office: sales@yaleup.co.uk   www.yalebooks.co.uk

Typeset in Adobe Caslon Pro by IDSUK (DataConnection) Ltd
Printed in Great Britain by TJ International Ltd, Padstow, Cornwall

Library of Congress Cataloging-in-Publication Data

Barczewski, Stephanie L., author.
  Heroic failure : the British / Stephanie Barczewski.
  New Haven : Yale University Press, 2016.
  2015023660 | ISBN 9780300180060 (cl : alk. paper)
  National characteristics, British. | Failure (Psychology)—Great Britain—History. |
Heroes—Great Britain—History. | Great Britain—Civilization.
  LCC DA118 .B29 2016 | DDC 941—dc23
  LC record available at http://lccn.loc.gov/2015023660

A catalogue record for this book is available from the British Library.

10 9 8 7 6 5 4 3 2 1

STEPHANIE BARCZEWSKI

HEROIC FAILURE

AND THE BRITISH

YALE UNIVERSITY PRESS
NEW HAVEN AND LONDON

conquest of, and political authority over, hundreds of millions of non-white peoples was not, however, the one that most Britons imagined or wanted. Though India has received by far the most scholarly attention among Britain's nineteenth-century colonies, and though the scramble for Africa remains the thing that most people associate with the late Victorian age of high imperialism, it was the colonies of white settlement (Canada, Australia, New Zealand and, to a certain extent but in a more complicated fashion, South Africa) that embodied the ideal form of empire for most people, political leaders and ordinary Britons alike. This was because Britons imagined an empire not of conquest of, and authority over, alien, subjugated peoples, but an empire of 'little Britains' through which British people, culture and political ideals would be spread over the world.

But this was not the empire that they actually had. After the American Revolution, the populations of Britain's colonies were overwhelmingly non-white. Nor did the indigenous peoples welcome the British with open arms, making it difficult to pretend that the gifts of civilization, Christianity and economic modernization were being bestowed on grateful and happy recipients. In this context, it was helpful to create stories of imperialism that de-emphasized might and promoted the notion that the British were sacrificing themselves for the good of their colonial possessions. Here, then, is what engendered the embrace of heroic failure.

The latter emerged from two specific contexts: exploration and military action. The exploration of dangerous places such as the interior of Africa, the Arctic and the Antarctic allowed the British to see themselves as selfless pursuers of scientific and geographical knowledge. Images of lone, isolated explorers facing hostile indigenous peoples and harsh natural environments helped transcending a mere thirst for victory and success. Others, however, thought that the British had come too readily to tolerate defeat, and that the elevation of so many failures to heroic status was a sign of cultural malaise and a contributory factor in Britain's decline as a great power in the twentieth century.

Five years ago, I did not know which, or if either, of these views was correct. But, with the support of Yale University Press, I was sufficiently intrigued to explore them further. This was my third book project on Victorian and Edwardian heroes, and I already knew enough about the subject to suspect that the celebration of heroic failure had deep roots in British culture, roots that stretched back further than the postwar era of economic decline and the loss of the empire. I believed that the idea of heroic failure had emerged in the nineteenth century, when the British Empire was at its peak, not during its post-1945 decline. I thus wanted to understand why failure had been celebrated so enthusiastically by a nation that was enjoying so much success in expanding its territorial and economic reach to all corners of the globe.

The answer to that puzzle, as this book sets out, lay in Britons' desire to see their empire as just, benevolent and moral. The nineteenth century abounded with moments in which the sheer might of British power made this difficult. The Royal Navy was virtually unchallenged as the most formidable fighting force in the world for most of the century, and the head start the nation enjoyed in industrialization created economic advantages that did not begin to dissipate until the 1870s. The latter factor not only played a role in expanding Britain's 'informal' sway over distant markets, but brought advances in military technology that made the conquest of territory in Asia, Africa and elsewhere rapid – and bloody – for those who attempted to resist. An empire based on military to counterbalance notions of the British as all-powerful. When these heroes failed, and died, their self-sacrifice could be highlighted. Images of brave soldiers standing against overwhelming numbers of indigenous foes performed much the same function. British losses in battles such as Aliwal, Chillianwallah, Isandlwana and Maiwand helped to offset the massive technological advantages that Britain enjoyed on the battlefield. They served to occlude Britain's military might and to shift attention away from extremely lopsided battles that were more akin to slaughters. I will thus argue in this book that heroic failure emerged as a means to help the British feel good about the uglier aspects of imperialism in the nineteenth century. To be sure, it then evolved into a coping mechanism for imperial decline in the twentieth, but this is not why it originally became so prominent.

As is the case with every book, I have accumulated numerous debts in writing this one. Much of the research support has come from the Department of History, the College of Art, Architecture and Humanities and the National Scholars Program at Clemson University. My Clemson colleagues continue to serve as bastions of professional and personal support; special thanks go to Elizabeth Carney, Steve Marks, Michael Meng, Rachel Moore, Megan Shockley, Christa Smith and, particularly, James Burns, who read my sections on South Africa and helped me sufficiently to nuance its complex history as a British colony. The research was carried out at over a dozen archives in the United Kingdom and United States; all were extremely helpful and delightful places in which to work. I would like to thank in particular Anne Martin of the David Livingstone Centre; Edward Smith of the National Army Museum; Juline Baird of the Scottish Borders Archive; Roberta Goldwater of the Tyne and Wear Archive; and Naomi Bonham of the Scott Polar Research Institute at the University of Cambridge. In a broader sense, I would like to thank Sir David Cannadine, Linda Colley, Dane Kennedy and John MacKenzie for their continuing professional support and inspiration; an hour of conversation with any of those distinguished scholars is invaluable. I first put the argument that is the primary focus of this book on public display at the British Scholar Conference in Newcastle in June 2014, and so I thank the organizers and the audience for giving me the opportunity to do so and for offering so much useful feedback. I would also like to thank Ed, Claire and William Moisson for making my research trips to London so much more enjoyable. This book would never have existed without Heather McCallum and Yale University Press. And finally, my husband and colleague, Michael Silvestri, has once again patiently edited the manuscript and even more patiently helped me to answer numerous questions and solve numerous problems in seeing it through to completion. He knows better than anyone that living with a fellow British historian means that you live with their work as well.

INTRODUCTION

L ONDON IS NOT a city of grand ceremonial avenues and squares like its fellow capitals Paris and Washington, DC. Urban planning of this kind has historically been minimal; only in a few places does the celebration of British heroes take precedence over the need for spaces in which people can live, work and play. Waterloo Place, located at the bottom of Regent Street, is one of those rare sites. Linking Piccadilly Circus to the Mall, the space was first developed in the years after 1815 as part of John Nash's scheme to create a royal processional route from the new Regent's Park to Buckingham Palace. In keeping with this royal purpose, Waterloo Place's earliest monument was Sir Richard Westmacott's 120-foot-high (36.5 m) column honouring Prince Frederick, Duke of York, George III's second son and commander-in-chief of the British forces during the Napoleonic Wars.

In the mid-nineteenth century, however, Waterloo Place evolved from a celebration of royalism to a celebration of heroism. This was not, to be sure, due to any conscious desire on the part of the British government to carry out commemorative projects on

1

that particular spot, but because it was one of the few sites in London that was not controlled by the Office of Works, which was extremely stingy about granting permission for monuments to be erected in public spaces. Instead, Waterloo Place was under the jurisdiction of the less stringent Office of Woods and Forests. This led to a collection of monuments and memorials being placed there between the 1860s and the 1920s. In 1861, John Bell's memorial to the 2,162 men from the Brigade of Guards who fell in the Crimean War, with its three figures of guardsmen on the front cast from captured Russian guns, was unveiled. In 1914, John Henry Foley's statue of Lord Herbert of Lea, secretary at war during the Crimean conflict, was moved to the space in front of Bell's memorial. Dating from 1866, it originally stood in front of the War Office on Whitehall. Relocated to Waterloo Place, it was soon joined by a new statue of Florence Nightingale by Arthur George Walker in order to create a Crimean group. (See Figure 1.)

The Crimean monuments occupy the central area of Waterloo Place, while a clutch of other monuments lines its perimeter. In 1866, Matthew Noble's statue of the Arctic explorer Sir John Franklin was installed on the western edge, followed a year later by Carlo Marochetti's statue of Colin Campbell, Lord Clyde, on the opposite side. Another Crimean hero, Clyde had fought in the Napoleonic Wars, the War of 1812, the First Opium War and the Second Anglo-Sikh War prior to commanding the Highland Brigade in the Crimea. His 'thin red line' of Sutherland Highlanders famously repulsed a Russian attack at the Battle of Balaclava in October 1854. In 1874, Sir Joseph Edgar Boehm's statue of yet another Crimean veteran, Field Marshal John Fox Burgoyne, who had served as an official advisor to the commander-in-chief of British forces, Lord Raglan, was erected next to that of Franklin.

Eight years later, Boehm's statue of the prominent Indian adminis-
trator Lord Lawrence joined Campbell on the east side of Waterloo
Place. A long gap then ensued; no further statues were added until
1914, when Walker's statue of Florence Nightingale and Foley's of
Lord Herbert were placed in front of the Crimean War Memorial.
The following year, a statue of the Antarctic explorer Captain Robert
Falcon Scott by his widow, Kathleen, was erected to the north of
Lord Clyde. Finally, in 1924, an equestrian figure of Edward VII by
the Australian sculptor Bernard Mackennal was placed to the north
of the Crimean group, thereby bringing Waterloo Place full circle
back to its origins as a royal commemorative space.[1]

Encompassing three-quarters of a century of statuary, Waterloo
Place provides an opportunity to examine the evolution of British
conceptions of heroism from the early nineteenth to the early
twentieth century. The most prominent commemorative impulse
was provided by the Crimean War, with five of the ten statues (the
memorial to the Brigade of Guards, Herbert, Nightingale, Clyde
and Burgoyne) relating to it. Though the British emerged victorious in the Crimea, the war was most frequently remembered for
the difficulties of the War Office in supplying troops, which
resulted in the deaths of thousands of men during the winter of
1854–55, and for the debacle of the Charge of the Light Brigade
at Balaclava, in which a misinterpreted order resulted in an unsupported cavalry charge being made into a valley that was surrounded
on three sides by Russian artillery. Of the remaining five monuments, one was imperial (Lawrence), two were royal (the duke of
York's column and Edward VII) and two were polar explorers
(Franklin and Scott). Both of the latter men died in the course of
their explorations. Franklin, along with 128 of his men, perished
in the search for the Northwest Passage in the late 1840s in what

3

remains as by far the worst disaster in British exploration history. Scott died with four of his companions in 1912 on the return journey from the South Pole, after having been beaten by the Norwegian explorer Roald Amundsen in the race to become the first person to reach it. Waterloo Place thus represents not only a rare use of London's urban space for commemorative purposes, but a strange one. Most of its monuments recall events – the Crimean War and the polar expeditions of Franklin and Scott – that were widely perceived by the British public as failures rather than triumphs. Why, one might ask, would such a prominent and precious space in London be used to commemorate these particular events and persons?

The answer relates to a strain in British culture that embraces the nobility of suffering, defeat and heroism in the face of disaster over triumphalism and the glory of victory. In this conception of heroism, effort, perseverance, pluck and grace under pressure are seen as more important than winning. In his autobiography, the comedian John Cleese recalls how his entire school was taken to see the Ealing Studios film *Scott of the Antarctic* in 1948:

> We were all deeply impressed by Scott's uncomplaining acceptance of suffering. But you couldn't help feeling that the message of the film was not just that the highest form of English heroism is stoicism in the face of failure, but that in Scott's case a whiff of success might have tarnished the gallantry of his silent endurance of misery. After all, he and his men all froze to death while losing the gold medal to the Norwegians, in the same way that the magnificence of the Charge of the Light Brigade was enhanced by its utter futility, and General Gordon's being calmly hacked to death was all the more impressive

because it occurred during the complete annihilation of his forces at Khartoum. On the other hand, Lord Nelson's and General Wolfe's heroism may have lost a little of the sparkle by the close association with two all-important victories, even if they did get extra marks for being killed at the moment of their triumph. I think Americans must suspect that General Custer may have been of English descent.[2]

Here, Cleese goes through a roster of the greatest hits of British heroic failure: the Charge of the Light Brigade, Gordon at Khartoum and Scott of the Antarctic, and asserts that they occupy a more prominent place in the national psyche than heroes who actually succeeded.

The British love of heroic failure that Cleese describes manifests itself in various ways. In polls asking Britons to name their favourite poem, Rudyard Kipling's 'If' regularly comes out on top. The work was inspired by Leander Starr Jameson, the leader of the eponymous raid that failed to provoke the British population of the Transvaal into a rebellion against the Boer government in 1895. It has enjoyed a special place in the affections of the public, if not of literary critics, ever since its publication in 1910, due to its celebration of stiff-upper-lip stoicism. When Captain Scott, another heroic failure, died in the Antarctic in 1912, the clergyman who gave the memorial sermon at the Royal Naval College in Dartmouth quoted lines from 'If' and then added: 'If you can thus show the sportsman spirit – the Christian spirit – then your final victory will date from the day when somebody said of you, kindly or unkindly, "He has failed"; when you said to yourself, "Things have come out against me".' This was, according to the clergyman, 'the blessing of failure'.[3] The poem became so popular that even Kipling grew sick of it. In his autobiography, *Something of Myself* (1937), he wrote:

> Among the verses in *Rewards* was one set called 'If', which escaped from the book, and for a while ran about the world ... Once started, the mechanization of the age made them snowball themselves in a way that startled me. Schools, and places where they teach, took them for the suffering Young – which did me no good with the Young when I met them later. ('Why did you write that stuff? I've had to write it out twice as an impot [British public school slang for a written task used as a punishment].'). They were printed as cards to hang up in offices and bedrooms; illuminated text-wise and anthologized to weariness. Twenty-seven of the Nations of the Earth translated them into their seven-and-twenty tongues, and printed them on every sort of fabric.[4]

The popularity of 'If' today shows the continuing importance of magnanimity, fortitude and calm in the face of disaster as a British cultural ideal.

These days, British sports teams can hardly step on the field of play without heroic failure being invoked. Every four years at World Cup time, the England football squad comes in for its customary round of diminished expectations and nostalgic invocations of the never-to-be-seen-again glory days of 1966. 'We will get to the quarter-finals or semi-finals and lose on penalties to Argentina or Germany like we always do,' said the DJ and musician Norman Cook (a.k.a. Fatboy Slim) before England's first match in 2010. 'I think the English football team are always doomed to be heroic failures.'[5] In tennis, meanwhile, 'heroic failure' was frequently used to describe the fate of British male competitors at Wimbledon in the decades after Fred Perry's victory in 1936, until Andy Murray ended the seventy-seven-year drought in 2013. And there was 'Eddie the Eagle' Edwards, the hapless ski-jumper from the 1988 Winter Olympics in Calgary, whom the *Daily Telegraph* described in 2012 as 'a man who made a living from being an heroic failure'.[6]

What is responsible for this preference for losers over winners and defeats over victories? Some commentators have suggested that it is a product of Britain's decline as a world power in the twentieth century. The *Sunday Telegraph* columnist Matthew d'Ancona asserted in 2013 that the celebration of failure is 'part of a postwar, postcolonial Britishness – the idea that all we had left was a sense of irony about inevitable decline'.[7] Some historians have concurred with this view. In his 1985 dual biography of Robert Falcon Scott and Roald Amundsen, Roland Huntford, in seeking an explanation for why the British had elevated Scott as a hero when he had so manifestly failed, argued that Scott was 'a suitable hero for a nation in decline'.[8] Some scholars have even gone so far as to *blame* the celebration of heroic failure, or at least the values with which it is associated, for Britain's decline. In *The Collapse of British Power* (1972), Correlli Barnett attacked what he saw as the toxic effect of the British public-school ethos, which emphasized complacency, mediocrity and moral idealism over pragmatism, hard work and self-interest. In Victorian Britain, he argued, displaying a gentlemanly character became more important than manufacturing goods or winning wars.[9] In 1981, Martin Wiener argued in *English Culture and the Decline of the Industrial Spirit* that Britain's economic decline could be attributed to the persistence of aristocratic, anti-capitalist, anti-entrepreneurial values from the late nineteenth century onwards.[10]

Barnett and Wiener were responding to the economic and cultural malaise of the 1970s, in which the loss of the empire and of industrial competitiveness seemed to doom Britain to permanent second-rate status as a world power. In the political context of the decade that followed, their arguments enjoyed considerable influence, as they perfectly suited the Thatcherite view that British decline had been a consequence of failure of will, not of anti-colonial challenges to empire or of an aging industrial infrastructure. Keith Joseph, who served as secretary of state for industry and secretary of state for education and science under Margaret Thatcher, and whose economic views were crucial in shaping hers, admired both Barnett and Wiener's works, and even gave copies of *English Culture and the Decline of the Industrial Spirit* to other members of the Cabinet. Michael Heseltine later did the same with one of Barnett's books. When failure became embedded as an ideal in the national consciousness, these supporters of 'declinism' argued that it had a corrosive effect.[11]

If the celebration of heroic failure was actually a prominent part of British culture long before decline began, however, then the argument that it played an active role in that decline makes little sense. This leads to two questions. First, when did the celebration of heroic failure begin? This book will show that it started around 1800, when explorers such as Mungo Park and soldiers like Rollo Gillespie and Edward Pakenham were early exemplars. By the 1840s and 1850s, when Sir John Franklin and 128 of his men disappeared in the Canadian Arctic and the Light Brigade charged at Balaclava, heroic failure was well established as a model for assessing the actions of British explorers and military leaders. This brings us to the second question: when did British decline begin? This has been much debated, but the participating scholars generally sort themselves into two camps. First, there are those who point to a *relative* decline that began after 1870, when other nations, most notably the United States and Germany, began to surpass Britain's industrial productivity in key areas such as coal and steel. Second, there are those who argue that what really matters is not relative but *absolute* decline, or that the diminution of British productivity in statistical terms and the significant erosion of Britain's status as a dominant global power, did not begin until the interwar period.[12]

Either way, if the celebration of heroic failure began in the early nineteenth century, then it could neither have arisen as a coping mechanism for, nor have been a causal factor in, Britain's decline. This book will instead argue that the celebration of heroic failure emerged not from Britain's decline, but rather from its political, military, imperial and economic dominance in the nineteenth century. In that era, there were two main arenas in which it appeared as an ideal in British culture: the exploration of, and the military conflicts in, distant parts of the world. Heroic failure thus originated from an imperial context; its exemplars established their heroic reputations in Africa, Asia, and even the Arctic and Antarctic, while they were engaged in imperial endeavours. We should therefore stop thinking of heroic failure as being associated with the imperial decline of the twentieth century and start thinking of it as a product of the imperial expansion of the nineteenth.

On the surface, arguing that failure as a cultural ideal was bred from Britain's success as a global power in the nineteenth century seems paradoxical. Comprehending this connection requires an understanding of the history of the ideology that underlay the British Empire. That ideology was riven with contradictions. From the sixteenth century onwards, Britons sought to distinguish their empire from both its historical precedents and its contemporary rivals. The Spanish Empire was, or was imagined to be, based on military force and the subjugation of indigenous peoples; the British Empire, by contrast, would be based on commerce and liberty, and would benefit the colonized as well as the colonizer. The British Empire, as one critic of the government's attempts to impose its authority on the unruly American colonies in the 1760s asserted, was 'a dominion founded on freedom', not one based on 'an uncontrolled power over slaves'; it had not been 'founded for the purposes of ambition and vain glory of a monarch', but 'for the establishment and extension of the commerce of the British dominions'.[13]

But liberty and imperial power do not easily coexist.[14] If many Britons succeeded in ignoring their country's prominent role in the slave trade and the presence of hundreds of thousands of slaves in its West Indian and North American colonies in the eighteenth century, they found the belief in an 'empire of liberty' more difficult to maintain in the nineteenth. To be sure, the British government took steps to curb the East India Company's mercenary excesses, and the abolition of the slave trade in 1807 and slavery in 1834 went some way towards preserving Britain's self-belief in its 'empire of liberty'. But at the same time, the empire shifted away from a model based on the replication of the style of administration that had been employed in North America, with its promise of eventual self-government (even if it lay in the distant future), and towards the administration of Asian realms with large non-white populations.[15] The British found it extremely difficult to rule Indians and other non-white peoples with 'liberty' as their priority. To deal with this problem in practical terms, a view evolved in political and colonial circles that non-white peoples required different, more authoritarian, forms of imperial administration because they were innately different from people in Britain and the white dominions.[16] But many British people were not entirely comfortable with this explanation, because they could never ignore completely the contradiction between the ideal of an empire of liberty and the reality of an empire of conquest.[17]

That contradiction was responsible for the prominence of heroic failure in British culture. As the empire grew in territorial expanse and economic importance from the Seven Years War onwards, it became increasingly important to Britain's sense of itself as a nation. This meant that at the points where the empire failed to live up to its ideals, it challenged not only the efficacy of colonial administration, but also national values and self-conceptions. This generated a need back home in Britain for narratives of empire that provided moral reassurance.[18] But those heroic adventurers did not always have to succeed: as the British sought to create a vision of themselves as an imperial nation that could fulfil its idealized vision of itself as a benevolent and just ruler rather than a tyrannical conqueror, failure could be a very a useful thing to highlight.

This is where imperial heroes came in.[19] In the nineteenth century, British heroism was measured less in terms of the hero's acts and more in terms of his character.[20] This was the product of a long and complex process of defining British national identity that had taken shape over the course of the second half of the eighteenth century.[21] A key component of this identity was a commitment to sportsmanship and fair play, with good manners and magnanimity transcending the mere achievement of victory; playing the game graciously and well came to be seen as more important than winning.[22] This embrace of fair play was associated with upper-class notions of chivalry and gentlemanly conduct, but it was not limited to them.[23] Instead, it was assumed that 'the rules of honour had the assent of all classes'.[24]

In the nineteenth century, this growing emphasis on character over achievement helped to engender a definition of heroism in which failure was often a more suitable milieu than success. In Victorian Britain, as in all cultural contexts, character was determined by the specific values of the era, not by universal and timeless elements.[25] In 1871, Samuel Smiles, the pre-eminent contemporary assessor (and at times arbiter) of these values, defined character as 'that which dignifies [man], which elevates him in the scale of manhood, which forms the conscience of society, and creates and forms its best motive powers'. He went on to say that the demonstration of character demanded 'many supreme qualities', including 'truthfulness, chasteness, mercifulness; and with these integrity, courage, virtue and goodness'.[26] None of these 'supreme qualities', it should be noted, was contingent on the outcome of a person's actions; instead, they were all things that could be demonstrated whether or not those actions succeeded, and in some ways they were more easily demonstrated against a backdrop of adversity and futility.

At times, to be sure, heroes emerged in straightforward fashion from imperial victories: Havelock in the Indian Rebellion, Kitchener at Omdurman, Roberts during the Boer War. But often the soldiers who fought and perished in battles that were lost, and the explorers who died in the jungles of Africa or the frozen wastes of the Arctic and Antarctic, became bigger heroes than their victorious counterparts. If we accept, as Max Jones has asserted, that heroes are 'sites within which we can find evidence of cultural beliefs, social practices, political structures and economic systems of the past', then these failed heroes must also reflect the values and ideals of the nation that produced them.[27] Heroic failures were helpful because the British were not comfortable seeing themselves as conquerors. By presenting alternative visions of empire via heroic failure, they maintained the pretence that the British Empire was about things other than power, force and domination. An explorer who failed to complete his quest was useful for suggesting that Britain's geographical reach was not unlimited; a soldier who died in a defeat was useful for suggesting that Britain's military might was not omnipotent.

Those same explorers and soldiers were also useful for concealing the violence that often accompanied the imposition and maintenance of British imperial authority. A growing number of historians in recent years have reminded us of the true nature of the forces that built, sustained and ultimately dismantled the empire. Richard Gott writes that 'the British Empire was established, and maintained for more than two centuries, through bloodshed, violence, brutality, conquest and war'. This was not, however, the prevailing view in the nineteenth century, and in some ways it is not the prevailing view today. It was – and is – important for the British to see themselves not as aggressive, authoritarian and violent imperial conquerors, but as benevolent administrators who acquired much of their colonial territory by accident, who ruled it with a velvet glove rather than an iron fist, and who often sacrificed their own lives in order to benefit the places over which they ruled.[28]

Heroic failure, then, neither reflected nor engendered decline; on the contrary, it arose from British power and dominance, and from the need to provide alternative narratives of empire that distracted from its real-life exploitative and violent aspects by emphasizing an idealized version of the nation's character.[29] Its celebration was in many ways, however, a reflection of Britain's true might, for it was an indulgence that only the world's dominant military, naval and imperial power could afford. It generally occurred in geographical locales – such as Africa or the polar regions – that were less vital to Britain's imperial enterprise; it was thus rarely celebrated in India, which was regarded throughout the nineteenth century as Britain's most important colony.[30] Heroic failure, moreover, was military rather than naval; its heroes could be naval officers, as were Sir John Franklin and Scott of the Antarctic, but their deaths took place while they were on land, or at least on ice. This was because, even though the demands of empire required strength on land as well as at sea, the British consistently viewed the Royal Navy as the primary bulwark of empire. The army's losses, meanwhile, were seen as unfortunate but not fundamentally damaging to the nation's identity and prestige, at least not until the Boer and Great Wars.

The argument of this book focuses on the relationship between Britain and its empire, and the cultural values that were engendered by that relationship. I treat both as entities that have meaning beyond mere terminology, but that is not to suggest that either 'Britain' or the 'British Empire' were simple things. Recent scholarship has made it clear that the British Empire was not a single, hegemonic entity, but rather a complex amalgamation that operated in a variety of ways around the globe.[31] But just because it could not always rely on coercion to attain its objectives does not mean that it did not sometimes resort to coercive, and even violent, methods in an effort to do so. Those efforts, in turn, generated controversy, as they were not congruent with the vision of those Britons who saw the empire as peaceful, commercial and benevolent. The argument of this book relies on this very plurality of both the reality and the ideals of empire.

It also acknowledges the complexity of the nation that administered that empire. Throughout the period that I examine here, the Act of Union with Ireland in 1800 presented a major challenge to the cohesive existence of the 'United Kingdom' as a non-contiguous geographical entity consisting of four nations that were separated by political, economic, cultural, religious and linguistic differences. Nor did the Scots and Welsh march in lockstep with their English neighbours in this period; far from it. But, at the same time, empire was at key moments in the nineteenth century a force for cohesion, not least because it could engender shared values – be they mercenary or enlightening – about Britain's mission and purpose in the world.[32] *All* parts of the United Kingdom utilized the story of empire that heroic failure provided; it was not an exclusively English ideal. In recent years, historians have illuminated the ways in which the British Empire was truly British (and Irish as well). The Scots were proportionately more active as participants than the English, and the Welsh and the Irish could also be found as traders, soldiers and administrators wherever the Union Jack flew. We are accustomed to the heroic failures of these countries – William Wallace, Bonnie Prince Charlie, Owen Glendower, the leaders of the Easter Rising – occurring in the context of uprisings against English rule. But, as this book will show, there were also plenty of examples of Celtic heroic failures that occurred in the service of the British Empire. And they often did so while being fully conscious of their national identities. The Scottish explorer Hugh Clapperton, who died attempting to find the outlet of the River Niger in 1827, declared to his publisher and fellow Scotsman John Murray before setting off on his ill-fated African journey: 'God knows I have the pride of a loyal Scot and when I come back I [hope I] may deserve such a distinction . . . There's none who loves his country better – every rock, every tree I look on as my brother – and the sole ambition of my life has been and will be to have it said . . . he comes from Scotland. When I die I want no other epitaph.'[33] Clapperton shows how a clear sense of Scottish identity could easily be combined with the pursuit of British imperial objectives.

But if heroic failure was an inclusively British ideal, there were ways in which it was exclusive of certain sectors of British society. Because it occurred far from British shores, in the context of military actions in, or explorations of, the British Empire, women could take part in only very circumscribed ways.[34] In cultural renderings of heroic failure, women could appear only at the margins, by remaining faithfully behind as their fathers, sons, husbands and brothers left Britain to fight in dangerous wars or embark upon dangerous expeditions. A typical example is Philip Hermogenes Calderon's painting *Lord, Thy Will Be Done* (1855). (See Figure 2.) In it, a young woman sits in a modestly decorated room holding an infant, while a picture of her absent husband, who has gone to fight in the Crimean War, stands on the mantel. First exhibited the year after Balaclava, the painting would for its contemporary audience have called to mind the needless sacrifice of soldiers' lives in the Charge of the Light Brigade. When the survivors returned, women could serve as an audience eager to hear tales of their bravery and heroism. This was illustrated by Rebecca Solomon's painting *The Story of Balaclava: Wherein he Spoke of the Most Disastrous Chances* (1855), which showed a survivor of the Light Brigade relating the story of his exploits to two enraptured female listeners. (See Figure 3.) And, finally, a third role for women in heroic failure was as defenders of their male relatives' reputations and legacies. This part was played to perfection by Lady Franklin, the widow of the lost Arctic explorer Sir John Franklin, in the 1850s, and later by Kathleen Scott, who as a professional artist would herself design a number of memorials to her husband, the Antarctic explorer Robert Falcon Scott. (See Figures 4 and 5.)

Though exclusively male as an active ideal, heroic failure was not exclusively British; many other countries have produced exemplars.[35] America, for example, has the Alamo and Little Big Horn. These heroic failures, like their British counterparts, took place in the context of imperial expansion – in their cases, the westward extension of the United States – and the repression and violence that indigenous resistance engendered. That process, too, required narratives that provided alternatives to power and aggression.[36] For them to function in this way, imperial expansion had to be depicted as something other than the violent and brutal conquest that it was. The Alamo and Little Big Horn were extremely useful for that purpose, since they reversed the historical balance of power and elevated the conquered over the conqueror. Today, they are far better known than the Battle of San Jacinto, a twenty-minute rout that took place a month after the Alamo in 1836, in which 630 Mexicans were killed and another 730 taken prisoner, in comparison with thirty-nine Texan casualties. Or than the Washita Massacre of 1868, eight years before Little Big Horn, when Custer's 7th Cavalry charged into a village of sleeping Cheyenne, killing 103 people, many of them women and children.

The British, however, produced *more* celebrations of heroic failures than the Americans, who have sometimes been mystified by Britain's enthusiasm for them. *Scott of the Antarctic*, the 1948 film that left such a vivid impression on the young John Cleese, was a huge hit in Britain, becoming the third most successful release at the box office that year. It was not a success in America, however, prompting the film's producer, Michael Balcon, to remark that 'the American public has no interest in failure, even if it is heroic failure'.[37] This, as the Alamo and Custer attest, was not entirely true. But the British did have a longer and greater need for heroic failure than Americans: the conquest of the west was a relatively brief period of American history encompassing less than a century, whereas the empire was a vital part of British history for 350 years. Moreover, it was easy to view the westward expansion of the United States as inevitable and natural, as it related to a contiguous geographical landmass. The British Empire, on the other hand, involved an island nation conquering territory far beyond its shores; there was nothing inevitable or natural about it, and it could only have happened as a result of deliberate and aggressive intent. It was the need to disguise this that led J.R. Seeley to pen his famous dictum that the British had 'conquered and peopled half the world in a fit of absence of mind'. Seeley was a staunch advocate of the idea that the British were non-aggressive imperial rulers; they were unique, he believed, in lacking a 'violent military character' as colonial masters.[38] For him, it was impossible for Britain (or at least for England) to be a despotic conqueror of other peoples, because that was fundamentally incompatible with the nation's ideals and political traditions. Seeley thus crafted a counternarrative – based on absent-mindedness – to the uncomfortable realities of empire; heroic failure served as another. They were both responding to the same national needs.

This book is divided into seven chapters, arranged roughly in chronological order. The first chapter introduces the three main contexts for heroic failure in the nineteenth century: military conflicts in Asia and Africa; the exploration of Africa; and the search for the Northwest Passage in the Arctic. The second chapter focuses on Sir John Franklin, protagonist of the greatest exploration disaster in British history. Together, these two chapters show how ideals of heroism emerged in the first half of the nineteenth century that focused less on the achievements of their protagonists and more on the nobility of their characters. Chapter 3 looks at the prominent place of the charge in military heroic failure, focusing in particular on the cavalry charge of the 16th Lancers at the Battle of Aliwal in 1846, the infantry charge of the 24th Foot at the Battle of Chillianwallah in 1849 and the cavalry charge of the Light Brigade at the Battle of Balaclava in 1854. The fourth chapter looks at David Livingstone, the most famous Victorian explorer of Africa, and quite possibly the least successful. The fifth chapter examines the 'last stand' in late nineteenth-century British military history, focusing on three examples: the 24th Foot at Isandlwana in 1879, the 66th Foot at Maiwand in 1880 and the Shangani Patrol during the First Matabele War in 1893. Finally, Chapters 6 and 7 look at the two biggest stars in the late Victorian and Edwardian firmament of heroic failure: General Charles George Gordon and Captain Robert Falcon Scott. Along the way, we will see much blundering and stupidity, but also genuine nobility in the face of calamity and death. We will also see heroic failure being used to conceal poor decisions by both the heroes themselves and the political and military leaders who dispatched them to various corners of the globe. But, above all, we will see it being used to create alternate narratives to direct attention away from the uncomfortable realities of empire.

Before setting off, it is important to establish a precise definition of heroic failure. Though magnanimity, chivalry and a sense of fair play are key components of it, they and heroic failure are not one and the same thing. Nor is heroic failure the same as heroic death or heroic martyrdom. As John Cleese has already told us, the deaths of General James Wolfe at the Battle of Quebec in 1759 and of Admiral Horatio Nelson at Trafalgar in 1805 elevated them to the status of great heroes in British culture, but both died in a moment of victory, not failure. Heroic failure required a conscious sense of celebration of the striving for an object that was not attained: either a geographical goal, such as the source of an African river, the Northwest Passage or the South Pole, or a military victory. It usually entailed death, but it did not strictly speaking have to. What made the conduct of the figure in question heroic was that he had displayed physical courage and mental fortitude in the face of defeat. 'We took risks, we knew we took them,' wrote Captain Scott. 'Things have come out against us, and therefore we have no cause for complaint, but bow to the will of Providence, determined still to do our best to the last.' Scott became one of Britain's greatest heroes of the early twentieth century, not because of his deeds – no one cared that he actually made it to the South Pole – but because of the nobility with which he endured hardship and, ultimately, death. Born in 1868, Scott had come of age in an era in which heroic failure was a prominent ideal in British culture. As he lay dying, he could therefore readily imagine his own fate, and his posthumous reputation, in those terms.

CHAPTER ONE

HEROIC FAILURE IN BRITAIN PRIOR TO 1850

I N NINETEENTH-CENTURY BRITAIN, there were two primary contexts for heroic failure: warfare and exploration. These two arenas offered the obvious advantage of travel to distant corners of the world, where there were hostile enemies and dangerous, disease-ridden climates, making a tragic and heroic death extremely likely. By 1850, then, it is not surprising that a standard narrative of heroic failure in these contexts had begun to take shape. This narrative was set somewhere far from Britain.[1] It featured a lone hero, isolated from friends, family and countrymen, going out to surmount obstacles both natural and human, obstacles that cumulatively meant that he faced overwhelmingly difficult odds. He struggled mightily against them, nonetheless, never flinching or whining, until succumbing to defeat and, in many cases, death.

Military Heroic Failure

The ability of death in warfare to create a hero from even the most unpromising circumstances was demonstrated by the examples of

Major Generals Sir Edward Pakenham and Samuel Gibbs, who died in 1815 at New Orleans in the final battle of the War of 1812. A memorial statue in St Paul's Cathedral by Richard Westmacott shows the two men standing side by side, with Gibbs leaning on Pakenham's shoulder in a display of fraternity and calm resignation in the face of adversity. The inscription records that they 'fell gloriously on the eve of January 1815 while leading the troops in an attack of the enemy's works in front of New Orleans'. (See Figure 6.)

In reality, there was little that was glorious about the deaths of Pakenham and Gibbs. Pakenham had previously fought brilliantly in the Peninsular War – Wellington credited his daring flanking manoeuvre as being responsible for his victory at Salamanca – but he had not wanted to go to America to fight in a conflict that few Britons understood or cared about, while Napoleon was still on the loose in Europe. His misgivings were not assuaged by his initial assessment of the situation at New Orleans, as the swampy landscape made the swift and unified movement of troops all but impossible.[2] But knowing how difficult it would be to move the army to another position, Pakenham reluctantly agreed to go ahead with the plan of attack drawn up by Vice Admiral Alexander Cochrane, the commander of the British naval forces. On the morning of 8 January 1814, the British troops were forced to cross a mile of flat, open, marshy ground as the Americans fired at them from behind a mud-and-log rampart. Their discipline and courage might still have secured victory, but a misunderstood order meant that they had not brought the ladders required to scale the rampart. As the carnage mounted, some men refused to advance, and Pakenham galloped to the head of his lines to try and rally them. Lieutenant George Robert Gleig described what happened next:

Poor Pakenham saw how things were going, and did all that a General could do to rally his broken troops. Riding towards the 44th which had returned to the ground, but in great disorder, he called out for Colonel Mullens to advance; but that officer had disappeared, and was not to be found. He, therefore, prepared to lead them on himself, and had put himself at their head for that purpose, when he received a slight wound in the knee from a musket ball, which killed his horse. Mounting another, he again headed the 44th, when a second ball took effect more fatally, and he dropped lifeless into the arms of his aide-de-camp.[3]

This was not quite accurate: Pakenham was carried from the field still alive, but barely. He died under a tree a few minutes later, only thirty-six years old.

Pakenham's death left his second-in-command, Gibbs, in charge of the battle. He, too, made a desperate attempt to rally the troops, charging to within 20 yards (18 m) of the American front line. There, he too was shot, and he died the next day. The third-in-command, Lieutenant General John Keane, was severely wounded but survived. For the British, the Battle of New Orleans was a debacle: 291 men were killed, 484 taken prisoner and 1,262 wounded, adding up to 2,037 total casualties; three generals and eight colonels and lieutenant colonels died. A mere thirteen Americans were killed.[4] Gleig was stunned when he rode over the battlefield after a temporary truce had been declared a few days later:

Of all the sights that I ever witnessed, that which met me there was beyond comparison the most shocking, and the most humiliating. Within the small compass of a few hundred yards, were gathered together nearly a thousand bodies, all of them arrayed in British uniforms. Not a single American was among them; all were English; and they were thrown by dozens into shallow holes, scarcely deep enough to furnish them with a slight covering of earth. Nor was this all. An American officer stood by smoking a segar [*sic*], and apparently counting the slain with a look of savage exultation; and repeating over and over again to each individual that approached him, that their loss amounted only to eight men killed, and fourteen wounded. I confess, that when I beheld the scene, I hung down my head half in sorrow, and half in anger.[5]

To make matters worse for the British, the Treaty of Ghent ending the War of 1812 had been signed on 24 December, two weeks before the battle.[6]

New Orleans was a shocking defeat. A month before the battle, Colonel Frederick Stovin, assistant adjutant general to the British army, had been breezily confident. Writing to his mother from aboard HMS *Tonnant*, Admiral Cochrane's flagship, he bragged: 'I have no doubt of our success, for although the Americans are quite aware of our intentions I do not believe they can collect above 3 or 4000 men to oppose us and we have 6000 – theirs inexperienced and undisciplined; ours perfect soldiers and in the habits of victory.'[7] Afterwards, his attitude was very different. He had been wounded in the neck, but was most devastated by the loss of his 'inestimable friend' Edward Pakenham: 'It has almost unhinged me and given me a distaste [for] the service on which we are employed.' His disparagement of the Americans had vanished; he now found it to be 'truly repugnant to fight against people who speak the same language, many of whom are really your countrymen and ... claim their origins so immediately from your own soil'.[8]

Why, then, instead of quickly burying their embarrassing defeat at New Orleans, did the British choose to grant Pakenham and Gibbs the very visible honour of a memorial statue in St Paul's? To answer this question, we first need to take into account that military martyrdom held a powerful cultural appeal in the early nineteenth century. From a British perspective, martyrdom was particularly powerful when it involved men of elevated social status like Pakenham and Gibbs. This period saw the emergence of a new emphasis on duty as a social and cultural ideal among the British elite, as the upper classes responded to pressure for parliamentary reform and increased democracy by promoting a new image of themselves as a 'service elite' dedicated to supporting the national interest.[9] This fresh dedication to duty often manifested itself in the form of military and naval contributions, thereby providing a justification for continued upper-class domination of wealth, status and power in Britain.[10] In assessing the heroism of elite officers like Pakenham and Gibbs, it was of little significance that they had lost the Battle of New Orleans, especially since the defeat had occurred in a war that had minimal consequences for British power or prestige. What mattered was their willingness to serve and the fact that they had laid down their lives for their country. The fact that their deaths occurred as they tried to rally their troops from a catastrophic defeat only threw the heroism of their actions into higher relief.

To comprehend fully the heroism of Pakenham and Gibbs as it was culturally defined in the early nineteenth century, however, we need to take into account the broader context of the relationship between Britain's military forces and civil society in the first half of the nineteenth century. In this era, though many Britons took pride in the army when it won important victories, they also feared it as a potential source of repression and tyranny and believed that, in peacetime, it should be kept as small as possible. They also had little regard for common soldiers; Wellington's description of them as the 'scum of the earth' encapsulated the predominant popular perception.[11] For much of the nineteenth century, the army was an object of both suspicion and contempt.[12]

Both the elite who filled the officer ranks and the government who relied on the army to win the war against Napoleon had a strong interest in overcoming this distrust of a strong military. One strategy they used was to elevate martyrs who died in battle, who acted as reminders of the patriotic and benevolent nature of the armed forces.[13] At the same time, the nobility of death in battle helped to conceal the deficiencies of specific campaigns. During the Peninsular War in late 1808 and early 1809, Lieutenant General Sir John Moore led the 35,000 troops under his command on a rapid retreat across northern Spain in midwinter as he attempted to reach the coast and evacuate his forces by sea. He managed to get most of his men to the port of Corunna, but the arrival of the ships that were supposed to take them to England was delayed by contrary winds. As he waited, Moore was forced to hold off the French in order to buy time for the evacuation. He succeeded, but was killed when a cannonball struck him in the chest. When the news of his death reached Britain, he became an heroic martyr who was given, like Pakenham and Gibbs, a monument in St Paul's Cathedral. (See Figure 7.)

Moore's memorial, by John Bacon, provided another example of a contemporary mode of representing military leaders who had fallen in the moment of victory. This mode had evolved from Benjamin West's painting *The Death of General Wolfe* (1770), which depicted the death of General James Wolfe at the Battle of Quebec in 1759. West's painting was immensely popular: King George III commissioned a copy, and an engraved print was a tremendous popular success.[14] (See Figure 8.) *The Death of General Wolfe* influenced British martial art for decades afterwards: many subsequent depictions of death in battle featured a prostrate hero at the centre of the composition, with the action raging around him and with his most prominent officers looking on mournfully as he expired. These paintings were rarely historically accurate, but they were not supposed to be. Instead, they were intended to convey the sorrow occasioned by the death of a great hero, as well as to ensure that his demise was surrounded by appropriate ceremony and recognition of its significance.

The embedding of West's vision of Wolfe's death as the standard for heroic martyrdom in British martial culture was confirmed by the account of Corunna written by Lieutenant General John Hope, who had fought alongside Moore, two days after the battle:

> I need not expatiate on the loss the army and his country have sustained by his death ... It will be the consolation of every one who loved or respected his manly character, that, after conducting the army through an arduous retreat with consummate firmness, he has terminated a career of distinguished honour by a death that has given the enemy every reason to respect the name of a British soldier. Like the immortal Wolfe, he is snatched from his country at an early period of his life spent in her service! Like Wolfe, his last moments were gilded by the prospect of success, and cheered by the acclimation of

victory! Like Wolfe, also, his memory will for ever remain sacred in that country which he sincerely loved, and which he had so faithfully served![15]

It is thus not surprising that visual representations of Moore's death echoed West's painting. An engraving published by Thomas Kelly showed a collapsed Moore lying before the walls of Corunna. He is supported by one of his officers, while two others look on gravely.[16] (See Figure 9.) Similarly, an image in a collection of lithographs entitled *Incidents of British Bravery during the Late Campaigns on the Continent* (1817) shows Moore being carried from the battlefield.[17] Other visual representations of Moore's death, like Bacon's memorial in St Paul's, replaced the mourning officers with angels and cherubs, but still followed West in presenting a triangular block of figures at the centre, with the dying hero at the bottom. A commemorative medal, for example, featured a classicized bust of Moore on the front, while on the obverse angels crowned him with a laurel wreath and blew trumpets to welcome his ascension to heaven.[18] On the right, Britannia points towards the battlefield, which can be faintly seen in the background, to indicate the British victory.

In the years that followed, Moore was commemorated by a number of poems, including Charles Wolfe's extremely popular 'The Burial of Sir John Moore at Corunna' (1817), as well as by a statue by John Flaxman (1819) in George Square in his native Glasgow. The nobility with which Moore's death was imbued, however, could not entirely disguise the controversy surrounding the retreat to Corunna, which had been characterized by drunkenness, looting and other breakdowns in discipline. Moore lost eight thousand of his 35,000 men, and the survivors arrived back in Britain in a tattered state. His actions were fiercely debated in Britain, and one of his own officers complained that it was his own 'ill-advised measures' that had placed his soldiers in peril, while his lack of 'decision and firmness' caused him to 'commit the most glaring errors'.[19] In truth, Moore had made the best of a bad situation. He had landed in Spain with only a small force, and when support from Britain's Spanish and Portuguese allies failed to materialize he had had little choice but to extricate his men.

But even if Corunna was a victory in the sense that it delayed the French long enough to allow the British forces to be evacuated from Spain, it was the culmination of a desperate retreat. The need to conceal the latter fact led to its being celebrated, much like Dunkirk would be in the early days of the Second World War, as a rallying point for patriotic sentiment.[20] This was clear in the depiction of the retreat to Corunna in a collection of fifty-three aquatints of scenes from the Napoleonic Wars published in 1815. The accompanying text concealed the chaos of the retreat and presented the British as plucky underdogs against their numerically superior French foes: 'Though often engaged, even their rear guard was never beaten, nor thrown into confusion, but was victorious in every encounter.' At Corunna, their position was 'extremely bad', so much so that even 'some experienced general officers, of excellent judgment and distinguished valour, were so impressed with the melancholy aspect of affairs, as to consider the state of the army almost desperate'. But thanks to Moore's calm and skilful leadership, the British prevailed. Moore's death was given its own section in the collection; only General Sir Ralph Abercromby's death in Egypt in 1806 merited similar treatment elsewhere in the volume. The accompanying illustration depicted the moment at which Moore had received his mortal wound, while the text focused on the pathos of his death, as he supposedly asked each officer who came in from the field to the lodgings where he had been carried: 'Are the French beaten?'[21]

Moore's death was not the last time that heroic failure would be used to conceal a military debacle. In 1814, Major General Robert Rollo Gillespie died in the Battle of Kalunga in the Anglo-Nepalese War. From the mid-eighteenth century onwards, the Kingdom of Nepal had become increasingly expansionist, as its powerful military forces pressed westwards into the Punjab and eastwards into Tibet. The Gurkha army, though not large, combined European-style discipline with a toughness bred from living in some of the world's most rugged terrain. By the early nineteenth century, a collision between Nepal and an equally expansionist East India Company was inevitable. The flashpoint came at Oudh (or Awadh, today in the Indian state of Uttar Pradesh), one of India's wealthiest and most fertile provinces, which shared its northern border with Nepal and which the Nepalese had long coveted. The British had controlled half of Oudh since 1801, while the other half remained under the nominal control of the nawab, in reality a British puppet. Tension mounted over the control of disputed villages along the border, and in 1814 war broke out.

The British had 21,000 men available to send north, twice the number that military experts estimated were necessary to defeat the Gurkhas. The campaign, however, presented unique challenges due to the terrain and weather. The British advanced in four columns, a strategy that was intended to achieve a swift victory by cutting off the Gurkha army from Kathmandu. Led by Gillespie, the easternmost column had as its first objective the hill fort at Kalunga (called Nalapani by the Gurkhas), which protected the route west across the Dehra Dun from Srinigar. Garrisoned by six hundred Gurkhas, Kalunga was a formidable obstacle, but Gillespie was confident in the ability of his artillery to blast a breach in the walls and of his numerically superior force to take the fort quickly. He divided his force of 4,500 into four columns, which were to attack simultaneously two hours after hearing a prearranged signal. Gillespie's final order stressed the importance of 'cool and deliberate valour' over 'wild and precipitate courage', though he was to ignore his own advice, with fatal consequences.[22] On the morning of 31 October, the artillery opened up at daybreak, but the guns were too far away to inflict significant damage. The main attack was not supposed to occur until noon, but just before nine, a party of Gurkhas attempted to take some of the British guns. They were quickly repulsed, but when Gillespie saw them heading back towards the fort, he sent messages to the commanders of the other columns, ordering them to attack immediately. The columns were impossible to locate quickly in the rugged terrain, however, and none of the messages reached its destination in time. Gillespie's own column charged forward nonetheless, and were met by Gurkhas who swarmed over the walls of the fort to meet them. The attack rapidly lost momentum as the Gurkhas wielded their kukris, or curved knives, with devastating effectiveness in hand-to-hand combat. Fifty-eight dragoons were slaughtered within minutes.[23]

Frustrated and unable to countenance even a temporary defeat, Gillespie declared his intention to take the fort there and then or to be killed trying. One of his officers had spotted a small gateway in the side, and he now focused his attention upon it, despite the fact that it was heavily defended. After a six-pound gun was brought up but failed to clear the gate, Gillespie tried to convince his men to attack it from the flanks. Recognizing that this was suicidal, they refused to follow him. Gillespie charged forward anyway and was shot in the chest. He died almost immediately. The attack collapsed, and it would take another month for the British to capture the fort. It was not until the garrison was almost completely out of food, water and ammunition that it slipped away under cover of darkness. When the British entered the fort, they discovered that 520 of the six hundred Gurkha defenders had been killed, or were so badly wounded or weak from starvation that they could not escape with the survivors.

Gillespie's actions had been foolhardy, as the governor general of India, Lord Hastings, recognized. On 10 November, he wrote to Lord Bathurst, secretary of state for war and the colonies, that

> the good fortune which had attended him in former desperate enterprises induced him to believe, I fear, that the storm of the fortress of Kalanga might be achieved by the same daring valour and readiness of resource whereby he had on other occasions triumphed over obstacles apparently insuperable. The assault in which he was killed at the foot of the rampart, involved, as I conceive, no possibility of success; otherwise the courage of the soldiers would have carried the plan notwithstanding the determined resistance of the garrison.[24]

As more details became known, however, it emerged that the soldiers from the 53rd Regiment had refused to follow Gillespie in his attack on the gateway. Feeling guilty about maligning the conduct of a brave officer who had died in battle, Hastings now began to sing Gillespie's praises. The prevailing view of his actions shifted accordingly: Charles Metcalfe, British resident in Delhi, wrote in 1815 that 'the gallant Gillespie would, I am sure, have carried everything, had he not been deserted by a set of cowardly wretches'.[25]

Back in Britain, where Gillespie was regarded as a colourful and popular soldier, the news of his death occasioned an outpouring of grief. He was the subject of a fulsome memoir which held him up as an example to future generations: 'So long ... as military virtue shall be held in esteem, and so long as our national history shall be read with pride and emulation, so long will the name of this heroic character be mentioned with enthusiasm, and his exploits pointed out as examples of imitation.'[26] Instead of leading an ill-advised attack, he was pictured as having made a gallant attempt to pull victory from the jaws of defeat:

> The general considered it to be his duty to expose himself in the most conspicuous manner, that, if possible, his example might inspire and rouse the emulation of his troops into another vigorous and effectual attack upon the place. The heroic sentiment which occasioned this sacrifice has carried the renown of the British arms to a height of splendour, that, in point of radical virtue, and permanent utility, has far exceeded the Grecian and Roman glory. That daring spirit of bold enter-prize, which in Europe has stamped with immortality so many illustrious names, will be found particularly needful in the vast and complicated regions of the East, where, from the character of the people, and the tenure of our possessions, we shall be continually obliged to maintain a high military attitude.[27]

The author also included a hagiographic poem about Gillespie by 'an amiable and accomplished lady in this country' that sought to inspire Britons to follow his example:

These tender tears, to cherish'd virtue due,
This unavailing flood of genuine grief,
Gillespie! Shall thy sacred name bedew,
And give fresh verdure to each laurel leaf.
But ye who mourn the honor'd hero's death,
Arouse from woe, and lead the life he led;
Practise his virtues till your latest breath,
To be like him illustrious when ye're dead.[28]

An impressive column was erected over Gillespie's grave in Meerut, and in 1820 a statue was installed in St Paul's Cathedral. (See Figure 10.) Though it took three decades, a group of local grandees in his native town of Comber in County Down collected funds for a memorial in the form of a 55-foot-high (17 m) column topped by a statue of the dead hero. It was unveiled in 1845 before a crowd of 25,000 people.[29] (See Figure 11.)

Gillespie's actions at Kalunga were undeniably foolhardy. Even so, he became a hero. Why? There were a number of reasons. First, he was already a famous soldier who had fought in the West Indies, India and Java, playing key roles in the suppression of the mutiny at Vellore in southern India in 1806 and the conquest of the Dutch city of Batavia in 1811. A diminutive man with an outsize personality, he was known among his acquaintances for his drinking, gambling and debauchery, but at a distance he seemed a merely colourful and courageous figure. The most important reason for Gillespie's posthumous fame, however, was provided by the context in which his death took place. In the first decade of the nineteenth century, Governor General Richard Wellesley had launched an aggressive campaign to eliminate threats to British rule in India, a policy that entailed a significant expansion of the East India

Company's territorial reach. This was a moment when the ideal of the 'empire of liberty' came starkly into conflict with Britain's desire to assume a vice-like grip hold over India. It was also a moment when the British were forced to confront what it meant to rule over large numbers of non-white peoples. The indigenous populations had been small enough to allow North America and Australia to be envisioned as 'empty' lands, a pretence that the British helped to make a reality by killing off large numbers of American Indians and aborigines with violence and disease. The void was then filled with white settlers who could gradually be granted increased self-government as they travelled the road to full independence as the offspring, and political replicas, of the mother country. (Even the American Revolution was assessed retrospectively from this perspective.) But it was impossible to pretend that India was an empty zone ripe for white colonization. Indians fiercely resisted British expansion: in a process that began with the subjugation of Bengal during the Seven Years War in the 1750s and lasted for a century, it took four wars to defeat the Kingdom of Mysore, three to conquer the Marathas and two to subdue the Sikhs of the Punjab. The war against the Gurkhas in which Gillespie died was another bloody and hard-fought struggle. On the one hand, his death reassured the British that, led by such brave commanders, their military forces would ultimately prevail, even if it took longer and cost more soldiers' lives than they initially expected. And, on the other, it reassured them that their efforts to bring more of India under the authority of the East India Company – an entity that could be seen as profitable far more readily than it could be seen as benevolent – represented a fair fight rather than a one-sided affair in which a despotic power was crushing anything and anyone that dared stand in its way.

The Exploration of Africa

Explorers were some of the biggest heroes in nineteenth-century popular culture.[30] Their prominence was due in part to a sensation-seeking press, but also to key changes in the nature of exploration. Discovery, rather than curiosity, became exploration's primary motivating force, compelling explorers to push towards ever more difficult and distant goals. Exploration thus became increasingly focused on easily definable but not so easily reached objectives: first the search for the sources of the Nile and the Niger Rivers in Africa and the Northwest Passage in the Arctic, and later the quest for the North and South Poles. This brought explorers into ever more dangerous situations: between 1816 and 1841, two-thirds of Britons who ventured into the interior of Africa died.[31] But death often turned explorers into heroes, and many of them felt that surrendering their lives in the quest for geographical discovery was a worthy sacrifice.[32] In 1833, the Irish geographer William Desborough Cooley complained of the 'rage for martyrdom which seems to actuate European and particularly English travellers in tropical climates'.[33]

Exploration, then, was a realm ready-made for heroic failure. In his recent work on the exploration of Africa and Australia in the nineteenth century, Dane Kennedy cites Mungo Park, who twice journeyed into the interior of Africa between 1795 and 1805 but re-emerged only once, as a prime example of an explorer who lacked experience, expertise and even common sense. But even though Kennedy describes his story as 'tragicomic', Park nonetheless became a hero.[34] At first glance, his failure might be seen as representing a moment when exploration did not fulfil what Kennedy identifies as 'imperial society's panoply of purposes – political, economic, ideological and more'.[35] It did, however, fulfil Britain's vision of itself as an imperial nation as much as, and perhaps even more so than, did exploration's successes. The stories of failure were included for the same reason as those of success: because they promoted a view of what the public thought the British Empire should be. Generations of British schoolchildren learned that the empire was built by high-minded men who brought morality and civilization to the dark corners of the world. When they died while doing so, as Park did, they imbued, as Kennedy writes, 'the sufferings they endured with a spiritual significance, a sacrifice for some greater good that transcended the self'.[36]

Park thus blazed a trail for heroic failure in exploration in the nineteenth century. Born in 1771 into a farming family in Foulshiels near Selkirk in the Scottish Borders, he studied medicine in Edinburgh, where he developed a keen interest in botany and natural science. After moving to London in 1793, he met Sir Joseph Banks, who had achieved fame as Captain Cook's botanist on his first expedition. Banks took a liking to the earnest young Scotsman, and secured for him a place as a surgeon's mate on a voyage to Sumatra, where Park collected botanical and zoological specimens. Impressed by Park's work, Banks next suggested that he embark upon an expedition into the interior of Africa that was being sponsored by the African Association, a scientific and geographical body of which Banks was a leading member.

Though Europeans had for centuries visited the African coast to trade in slaves and goods, prior to 1800 they had made few attempts to travel inland. By the late eighteenth century, however, intellectual curiosity and economic motivations were increasing European desires to see what lay beyond Africa's edges. A particular goal was the legendary city of Timbuktu, which had emerged as a centre of the trade in gold, ivory and slaves in the Middle Ages but had thereafter dissolved into much-embellished myth.[37] The African Association felt that the best way of exploring the interior of Africa was not via large, lavishly equipped expeditions, but by means of a man travelling alone who could move quickly and inconspicuously. They had already tried such an approach with the expedition of Major Daniel Houghton from 1790 to 1791, but he had disappeared without a trace.[38]

As he prepared to set sail, Park wrote to his brother Alexander: 'I hope that He who has blessed me with tranquillity of mind will likewise smooth my way, will give me philosophy enough to overcome every obstacle and strength sufficient to surmount every danger.'[39] On this first journey, his wishes were largely fulfilled: starting from Barra, in present-day Gambia, he followed the River Niger inland for over 1,000 miles (1,600 km), mostly alone and on foot. Although he did not find the source of the Niger, he confirmed that it flowed from west to east. But it was his survival that, on this occasion at least, was the greatest cause for celebration. (See Figure 12.) In a biographical sketch of Park published in 1815, John Wishaw wrote that 'the nature and objects of his mission, his long absence and his unexpected return, excited a very general interest; which was afterwards kept up by the reports which prevailed respecting the discoveries he had made'.[40] Banks eagerly trotted the young Scotsman out before his rich and powerful friends, while the duchess of Devonshire commissioned a song about him from the Italian composer Giacomo Gotifredo Ferrari. Park's narrative of his journey, published as *Travels in the Interior Districts of Africa* in 1799, became an instant bestseller and was reprinted in multiple editions.[41] The *Gentleman's Magazine* declared that 'few books of Voyages and Travels have been more favourably received'.[42]

After the glitter of his triumphal journey faded, Park returned to Scotland and opened a surgery in Peebles, but he found it difficult to reconcile himself to the life of a rural doctor. In 1801, he wrote to Banks that 'a country surgeon is at best but a laborious employment and I will gladly hang up the lancet and plaister whenever I can obtain a more eligible situation'.[43] Two years later, that hoped-for situation arose: Park was enlisted by Lord Hobart, secretary of state for war and the colonies, to attempt once again to trace the course of the Niger. In other respects, this was a very different expedition from his first. Whereas previously Park had travelled solo, he was now given a temporary commission as a captain in the British army and accompanied by a contingent of forty-five Europeans, including thirty-five men from the Royal Africa Corps under the command of Lieutenant John Martyn.[44]

After setting forth in the spring of 1805, Park raced to make significant progress before the rainy season began in June. The expedition had barely started when the rains came, however, and the men quickly began falling ill from diseases brought by the swarms of mosquitoes that accompanied them. Park should have turned back, but by this point his confidence in his abilities as an explorer was blinding him to the realities of African travel. 'I find,' he wrote to Banks, 'that my former journeys on foot were underrated. Some of them surprise myself when I trace the same road on horseback.'[45] By the time they reached the Niger on 19 August, thirty-one men – more than two-thirds of the original contingent – had died. Nonetheless, Park pressed on to the city of Sansanding (now in south-central Mali). The following month, he dispatched letters reporting that he was preparing to depart.

And then . . . nothing further was heard from or of him, except for the occasional rumour that trickled out of the jungle. In

December 1806, Alexander Court, a British resident of Mogador (now Essaouira) in Morocco, claimed to have heard from 'a Moor arrived a few days since from Soudan' that a party of Europeans led by 'a tall, thin young man' had 'built a boat' at Sheego and 'proceeded up' the Niger: 'In their passage and near Tombuctoo they were attacked by the Tuenes (a wild race of people, of the colour of the Moors inhabiting the country round Tombuctoo).' Four of the Europeans were killed.[46] This would turn out to be a reasonably accurate account of Park's fate, though he had not managed to get nearly as close to Timbuktu as Court reported.

It would be four more years before more definitive information emerged. A British officer stationed in the Senegambia, Major Charles Maxwell, dispatched a Serahuli trader named Isaaco, who had served as a guide for Park before being sent back with his journal and final letters, to determine his fate. Isaaco located his successor as the expedition's guide, a trader named Amadi Fatouma. Fatouma reported that, in early 1806, Park had reached Yelwa in modern-day Nigeria, 1,500 miles (2,400 km) from Sansanding. But a few miles further on, at a place called Bussa (now Boussa), he and his men were attacked from the banks of the Niger, resulting in the deaths by drowning of Park and the other members of the party when they attempted to escape by jumping in the river.

Fatouma's account contained a number of disturbing revelations concerning the violence that had surrounded Park's expedition after it left Sansanding. Two days later, Park and his followers had been pursued by three canoes whose occupants were 'armed with pikes, lances, bows and arrows'. Fatouma recalled that 'we ordered them to go back but to no effect and were obliged to repulse them by force'. As they pressed on past Rabbara, three more canoes 'came up to stop our passage, which we repelled by force. On passing Timbucktoo we were again attacked by three canoes, which we beat off always killing many of the natives. On passing Gourouma seven canoes came after us and which we likewise beat off ... We were reduced to eight hands having each of us fifteen muskets always in order and ready for action.' These violent confrontations continued as they sailed down the river. After passing a village, they were chased by more canoes, upon which they again fired, killing 'a great number of men'. By now, Fatouma was becoming disturbed by the carnage: 'Seeing so many men killed and our superiority over them, I took hold of [Martyn's] hand, saying "Martin [*sic*], let us cease firing for we have killed too many already."' Martyn, however, clearly felt differently: Fatouma reported that he 'wanted to kill me had not Mr Park interfered'.[47] The expedition then enjoyed a few relatively peaceful days, but when they stopped at a small island in the river and Fatouma was dispatched to purchase provisions, he was taken prisoner by one of the natives. Park informed the local populace that if he were not released promptly 'he would kill them all and carry their canoes along with him'. This did the trick, but as they rowed away they were challenged by a large number of men on the bank who were only persuaded to 'run off to the interior' after the Europeans 'presented our muskets to them'.[48]

By November 1805, the outlook for the expedition was bleak. Martyn wrote that only seven men survived, 'out of which Dr Anderson and two of the soldiers are quite useless. The former from one disease or other has been for four months disabled; we every day suppose he'll kick it.'[49] Fatouma had promised to guide Park only as far as the Kingdom of Haroussa, and when they reached the village of Yaoure, he was discharged. The local chief, however, took him prisoner in revenge for Park's failure to pay him the tribute that was required to enter his territory. This explains why Fatouma was still present to see what happened next. The chief who was holding him hostage sent some of his men to Bussa, where a large rock entirely blocked the river apart from a small opening 'in the form of a door which is the only passage for the water to get through'. The men waited for Park's canoe to arrive and then attacked the occupants with 'lances, pikes, arrows and stones':

> Mr Park defended himself for a long time [but] two of his slaves at the stern of the canoe were killed. They threw everything they had in the canoe into the river and kept firing, but being overpowered by numbers and fatigue and unable to keep up the canoe against the current and [with] no probability of escaping Mr Park took hold of one of the white men and jumped into the water. Martyn did the same and they were drowned in the stream in attempting to escape.[50]

The near-constant violence of the final stage of Park's second expedition was almost entirely eliminated from posthumous accounts of his African career.[51] Instead, these focused on Park's personal qualities: Wishaw, for example, praised his 'enterprising spirit, his indefatigable vigilance and activity, his calm fortitude and unshaken perseverance'.[52] An anonymously penned 1838 'biography' (in reality a reprint of Park's *Travels* with the addition of a small amount of original material) described him as 'a rare example to his kind'.[53] In William Bayle Bernard's play *Mungo Park; or, The Arab of the Niger* (1841), the British governor of an African coastal factory declares as he awaits Park's arrival: 'Few I believe have failed to read the thrilling story of his adventures – of his courage and endurance ... His name is now identified in Europe with all that's honourable in enterprize or ardor.'[54] Though as in Rollo Gillespie's case it took some time, Park was given a public memorial in his native town: a statue, sculpted by Andrew Currie, was unveiled in Selkirk in 1860 (See Figures 13 and 14.)

Mungo Park served as a prototype for British heroic failure in Africa: the lone explorer bravely daring the unmapped territory of the interior and ultimately losing his life in the attempt. Others followed in his footsteps, in some cases literally. Born in 1788 in Annan in Dumfriesshire, Hugh Clapperton was one of many naval officers who, after the end of the Napoleonic Wars, found himself in need of employment and adventure. In 1820, he met Walter Oudney, a naval surgeon and fellow Scotsman who had been selected by the Colonial Office to lead an expedition into central Africa to explore the course of the Niger, following the trail blazed by Park. Oudney needed a companion, and the ebullient, physically imposing Clapperton was an ideal candidate. He happily accepted Oudney's invitation, though the salary was only £150.[55]

The expedition's prospects of success were badly compromised, however, when an army officer named Dixon Denham used his social connections to supplant Oudney as its leader. Many African explorers came to loathe each other by the end of their expeditions, but Oudney and Clapperton were barely on speaking terms with Denham by the time they left England. This was a particular problem because they disagreed about the likely location of the mouth of the Niger, the discovery of which was the primary object of the expedition. The two Scotsmen thought – rightly, as it turned out – that it would be found in the Bight of Benin, but Denham thought it flowed north to Egypt. After departing from Tripoli in

March 1822, the expedition struggled southwards, its progress hampered by constant squabbling, repeated outbreaks of malaria and the whims of the local Ottoman pashas. The fractious Britons eventually decided to split up, with Denham continuing to explore the southern and eastern shores of Lake Chad while Oudney and Clapperton joined a merchant caravan that was heading west towards Kano in modern-day Nigeria. Oudney died in January 1824; Clapperton made it as far as Sokoto before reversing course and making a miserable return journey in the rainy season.

Though it had failed even to reach the Niger, the expedition was deemed a success. Clapperton was credited by Earl Bathurst, secretary of state for war and the colonies, with having 'evinced during the whole period of his employment . . . a degree of intelligence and perseverance which do him the highest credit and have mainly contributed to the accomplishment of most important discoveries'.[56] John Murray paid £1,200 to publish the narrative of the journey, the same amount he had paid for the journal of Park's second expedition, showing that he was confident of the public's continued interest in African exploration.[57] The volume appeared in 1826 as *A Narrative of Travels and Discoveries in Northern and Central Africa*. Clapperton received £400 – more than his annual officer's pay – for his contribution.[58] It was received enthusiastically: the *Edinburgh Review* declared that 'we scarcely know, since the time of Marco Polo . . . any instance in which so much new ground has been gone over by a single mission'.[59]

Though his health had nearly been destroyed by his first journey, Clapperton was eager to go back to Africa. Only three weeks after his return to England in June 1825, Bathurst dispatched him on a second expedition, 'with the view of completing such discoveries as remain to be made in that country, as well as to accomplish

other essential objects connected with the political and commercial interests of Great Britain'.[60] In particular, Clapperton was to
map the territory between Sokoto and the Niger, thus filling in the
gap between the work done by his first expedition and Mungo
Park's second. Bathurst's correspondence relating to the expedition
provides a glimpse of how the threat of violence constantly lurked
beneath the surface of African exploration in the nineteenth
century. Much of it was taken up with the issue of the weaponry
that was to be issued to Clapperton, which included 'mountain
guns adapted for conveyance on the backs of mules', along with
'fifty rounds and fifty [cases of] shot'.[61] The expedition's ordnance
also comprised 'two light field pieces', 'two barrels of gunpowder',
'twenty-four muskets', 'two hundred rounds of ammunition', 'four
fowling pieces', 'two pairs of pistols single-barrelled', 'two rifles',
'two double-barrelled guns' and 'two pair of pistols'.[62]

The Admiralty had assigned Clapperton three companions:
the physician Thomas Dickson, the naval captain Robert Pearce
and the naval surgeon Robert Morrison. Clapperton also brought
along a Cornish servant named Richard Lander. Once they were
in Africa, however, he decided that this was an insufficient number
of Europeans with which to tackle his mission, so he engaged a
merchant named James Houtson and a sailor named James as
well, the former at a salary of £600 and the latter at £400.[63] It
proved a bad bargain, as all of the Europeans save Clapperton and
Lander died within a few weeks of their departure from the west
coast of Nigeria in December 1825. Clapperton pressed on nonetheless, and at Bussa he was shown the spot where Park had died.
But although he finally reached the Niger, he was frustrated by
the long delays caused first by it being Ramadan and then by the
onset of the rainy season. When he reached Kano in July 1826,

the local sultan refused to let him through. Hoping that he would change his mind, Clapperton returned to Sokoto, where he collapsed from fever and dysentery, lingering for a month before dying in April 1827. Of the Europeans who had started the journey now only Lander remained. He made a hazardous return to the coast – surviving trial by poison along the way – and in August 1828 he delivered Clapperton's papers to the Colonial Office. The press quickly promoted a view of Clapperton as a brave and determined explorer who had met his death in a distant and dangerous land. It was the story of Mungo Park all over again, right down to having an intrepid Scotsman in the starring role.

In 1830, Lander returned to Africa. He had orders from the new secretary of state for war and the colonies, Sir George Murray, to determine the course of the Niger once and for all.[64] After arriving at Badagry in March 1830, Lander marched inland, entered the Niger at Bussa and floated downstream to its delta in the Gulf of Guinea. He had reached the river's long-sought mouth, but no one much cared. Lander received a mere £200 for his trouble; his journal was published and sold well, but it did not turn its author into a hero.[65] In 1832, still seeking fame and fortune, Lander went back to Africa and was wounded in a clash with the locals and died at Fernando Po several weeks later. The exploration of central Africa demonstrated that achievement did not really matter: failure was far more compelling than success.

The Quest for the Northwest Passage

At the same time as British explorers were attempting to solve the great geographical puzzles of the interior of Africa, they were also looking north, towards the Northwest Passage, the fabled route through the Arctic archipelago that would provide a short cut to the riches of the East.[66] In the 1820s, the Royal Navy, confident that its doughty bluecoats and noble officers could achieve a centuries-old dream, renewed the quest for the Passage. As a result, the frozen wastes of the northern extremities of the globe became a fertile breeding ground for heroic failure. In his popular history of the search for the Northwest Passage, originally published in 1852 and reissued many times thereafter, the journalist Peter Simmonds looked back over the previous three decades of Arctic exploration:

> Our successive polar voyages have, without exception, given occupation to the energies and gallantry of British seamen, and have extended the realms of magnetic and general science, at an expense of lives and money quite insignificant, compared with the ordinary dangers and casualties of such expeditions, and that it must be a very narrow spirit and view of the subject which can raise the cry of '*Cui bono*', and counsel us to relinquish the honour and peril of such enterprises to Russia and the United States of America![67]

Simmonds's spirited defence of Britain's massive expenditure of money and manpower on a futile effort suggests that, by the mid-nineteenth century, the potential utility of the Northwest Passage was no longer the point. Indeed, Britons had long been aware that, even if it were discovered, the route was unlikely to produce any practical benefits. In the early 1790s, George Vancouver had surveyed the northern Pacific coast of North America and established that, if such a passage existed, it was not located in a latitude sufficiently temperate for it to be useful to merchant shipping.[68]

What really mattered, however, was not finding the Northwest Passage, but that the search itself should provide an opportunity to test, and prove, British mettle. In February 1850, Charles Richard Weld, assistant secretary to the Royal Society, delivered a lecture at the Russell Institution in London in which he declared: 'there is probably no portion of the history of this country which so forcibly illustrates the calm and enduring heroism of our countrymen, as that relating to the voyages of discovery in the Arctic seas. It is impossible to contemplate the terrible catalogue of suffering which the history of those voyages presents, without feelings of the highest admiration.'[69] Weld said this at a time when, despite a massive effort to find the Northwest Passage, the British had failed to do so. But this did not matter. Instead, it was 'the calm and enduring heroism' of the questers, and 'the terrible catalogue of suffering' they had endured, that were of greatest significance.

Failure was thus written into the story of British Arctic exploration from the outset. And with failure came heroism, in the form of much suffering and the sacrifice of many lives for a useless goal.[70] But, despite its dangers, naval officers and men continued to be willing to undertake the quest for the Northwest Passage because they had few other opportunities for promotion and glory after the end of the Napoleonic Wars. The £20,000 reward offered by Parliament to the Passage's discoverer further sweetened the pot for officers, while for ordinary seamen the double pay that they received for 'discovery' duty attracted plenty of volunteers for Arctic service. The public, meanwhile, generally shared the attitude of the Scottish mathematician and physicist John Leslie, who argued that, even though the Northwest Passage was likely to prove useless, a 'great maritime nation' such as Britain should look for it anyway.[71]

The Northwest Passage was a sufficiently difficult objective that success in finding it could not be the sole measure of a man's worth as a polar explorer. Instead, it was the strenuousness of the effort that mattered, and the fortitude with which the trials and terrors of polar exploration were faced. The Arctic, wrote the naval officer and polar veteran Sherard Osborn in 1860, was 'the test of British perseverance, patience and hardihood. The frozen north would only reveal its wonders slowly and unwillingly to the brave men who devoted themselves to the task. The dread realms of frost and silence were only to be penetrated by the labours of two generations of seamen and travellers. The consummation of the discovery of the North-west Passage was to be obtained but by the self-sacrifice of a hundred heroes.'[72] The British, indeed, became specialists in polar suffering, developing methods of Arctic travel that emphasized willpower and perseverance.[73] In this context, failure became proof positive of the heroism of the men who chose to subject themselves to the terrible power of the polar environment. Osborn described the Arctic as 'a region which appears only to have been intended to test man's enterprise, and to show him that, after all, he is but a poor weak creature'.[74] There was no shame in being defeated by it, only in surrendering to it or in allowing it to break one's will. As long as a man continued to strive, he possessed the stuff of which polar heroes were made.

In 1818, the Admiralty launched its first serious effort since the days of Captain Cook and Vancouver to find the Northwest Passage. The expedition's leader was an irascible Scotsman named John Ross, who, after joining the Royal Navy at age nine, had served with distinction in the Napoleonic Wars and had the scars to prove it.[75] Ross's two ships, the *Isabella* and *Alexander*, forced their way into Baffin Bay, but as they continued west into Lancaster

Sound, Ross saw high mountains looming in front of him. Deeming further progress hopeless, he turned around. After his return to England, Ross was promoted to post-captain, but some people felt that he had not tried hard enough. An indignant John Barrow, second secretary to the Admiralty and the driving force behind much British exploration in both Africa and the Arctic in the first half of the nineteenth century, wrote in the *Quarterly Review* that polar duty was 'a service for which all officers may not be equally qualified; it requires a peculiar tact, an inquisitive and persevering pursuit after details of fact not always interesting, a contempt of danger and an enthusiasm not to be damped by ordinary difficulties'.[76]

The primary result of Ross's expedition was to reawaken the British public to the allure of the Northwest Passage. Ross's second-in-command, a handsome young lieutenant named William Edward Parry, would be the next to try. He was an inveterate optimist, telling his family that the Passage would not be 'very hard to find'.[77] His breezy confidence soon gave way to the realities of Arctic sailing, however. The first of his four voyages came closest to success. Upon reaching Lancaster Sound in the summer of 1819, Parry found it to be free of ice, a once-in-a-decade phenomenon, and he quickly proved that Ross's mountains had been nothing more than a mirage created by the reflection of sunlight off the ice in the cold, dense polar air. Parry sped west, making it as far as the southwestern tip of a landmass that he named Melville Island in honour of Viscount Melville, First Lord of the Admiralty. But then the ice closed in. Parry's became the first British expedition to endure an Arctic winter, combating the frigid temperatures and constant darkness with music, amateur theatricals and a demanding exercise regimen. Having sailed so far west, they assumed that they were on the cusp of achieving their goal, but the following summer the ice refused to break up. Parry reluctantly turned back, reaching Britain in October 1820. He believed that the ice that choked Lancaster Sound meant that the Northwest Passage could only exist further south. He was wrong: Lancaster Sound *is* the eastern entrance to the Northwest Passage. His conclusion that it was not there led to many fruitless future expeditions.

The polar historian Pierre Berton places Parry among the luckier polar explorers, as he 'sailed north at the right moment, when the Arctic channels were clearer of ice than they had been in a decade'.[78] But it was adversity rather than luck that made the greatest polar heroes, as was confirmed by a vase that was presented to Parry in 1821 by the citizens of Bath. It was inscribed:

To

William Edward Parry, Esquire

Commander in the Royal Navy,

In Commemoration of

A Voyage of Discovery, Performed in His Majesty's Ships

Hecla and

Griper, Under His Command, in the Years 1819 and 1820,

In Which He Effected a Passage through Lancaster Sound into

The Polar Sea:

And Having Discovered Many New Lands,

And Passed a Winter of Ten Months' Duration, Surrounded by Ice, in

The Harbour of Melville Island;

Returned to Great Britain with the Loss of Only One Man:

Thus Carrying the British Flag into Seas over which

No Ship Had Yet Passsed,

And Displaying, throughout the Unprecedented Undertaking,

A Degree of Nautical Science, Intrepedity [*sic*], Perseverance and
Humanity,
Which Have Reflected a Lasting Honour on Himself,
His Profession, and His Country[79]

The inscription listed the key attributes of a polar hero as 'a Degree
of Nautical Science, Intrepedity [*sic*], Perseverance and Humanity'.
It was thus more important for British polar explorers to be resolute and intrepid than it was for them to possess technical skill, of
which they needed only a 'degree'. The search for the Northwest
Passage – which was not even mentioned in the inscription – had
begun as a quest for a more efficient trade route; now it had been
redefined as an arena in which the navy's best officers could test
their mettle.[80] Having gone so far and come so close, Parry had to
try again, but his three subsequent expeditions, undertaken
between 1819 and 1827, achieved little.[81] After his first expedition, Parry had become a type of polar heroic failure: the man who
had gone further than expected and come close to achieving his
goal. But the heroic failure of his first expedition became simply
the failure of the next three.

At this point, John Ross, who was eager for redemption,
re-entered the picture with a proposal to complete the Northwest
Passage using a steam-powered vessel.[82] The Admiralty was
unwilling to entrust Ross with another Arctic command, but he
convinced the distiller Felix Booth to back the venture privately.
After departing in 1829, Ross cruised through Baffin Bay into
Lancaster Sound and then, heeding Parry's advice, turned south
into Prince Regent Inlet. This was the wrong choice, as the only
outlet from there to the west lay through an impassable strait
(later named the Bellot Strait) between Somerset Island and a

peninsula that he named Boothia Felix (now the Boothia Peninsula) in honour of his patron. The strait was so small and ice-choked that Ross did not even see it, and it would not have mattered if he had. He was now trapped in the wide body of water into which Prince Regent Inlet opened, which he named the Gulf of Boothia. Recognizing that further progress was impossible, he found a safe harbour and began preparing for winter. He was in fact preparing for *four* Arctic winters, as the ice refused to release his ships. After the third, he abandoned hope for release and formulated a plan to drag the ship's boats 300 miles (480 km) overland to Fury Beach, where he knew that they would find the largely intact stores of HMS *Fury*, which Parry had abandoned there in 1825. When the ice cleared, they would then sail the boats into Lancaster Sound, where they hoped to be picked up by a passing whaler. They managed to reach Fury Beach, but Lancaster Sound was full of ice. Leaving the boats so that they could try again in the spring, they returned to Fury Beach, where they built a makeshift winter shelter made of canvas stretched over a wooden frame and insulated with a wall of snow.

Back home, Ross had been given up for dead. In July 1832, the *Athenaeum* wrote that 'all chance of the return of the vessel or crew is ... at an end'.[83] Even so, funds were raised for a relief expedition, which was led by the naval officer and Arctic veteran George Back.[84] In the end, however, Ross rescued himself: on 25 August, his men spotted a sail on the horizon. It was, amazingly, the *Isabella*, the ship that Ross had commanded on the ill-fated voyage of 1818, now a whaler. Ross was amused when the captain 'assured me that I had been dead for two years'.[85] Now miraculously resurrected, he was lauded as a hero; the press and public were jubilant at his incredible survival. The *Gentleman's Magazine* wrote that there was 'one universal feeling of joy throughout the Empire', while Barrow wrote to Murray in December 1833 that 'a great stir is making for the discovery of Ross'.[86] He dined with King William IV and was given a £5,000 reward and a knighthood.[87] He received four thousand fan letters from an adoring British public, and was awarded gold medals, gold snuffboxes, presentation swords and other trophies by scientific societies in Britain, France, Prussia, Sweden, Russia, Belgium and Denmark.[88] A tableau in the pleasure gardens at Vauxhall in London depicted Boothia, complete with icebergs, polar bears and Inuit igloos, while in Leicester Square the painter Robert Burford exhibited a 90-foot-long (27.5 m) panorama of Ross's discovery as well. The accompanying pamphlet related how the expedition had returned to Britain in October 1833 'after having been exposed to the perils and privations of four severe polar winters, the fatigues and hardships of which were freely shared by those in command, and were endured by the crew with a degree of cheerfulness, sobriety and discipline, rarely to be met with but among British seamen'.[89]

Ross's jubilant reception confirmed that the discovery of the Northwest Passage was no longer the point of Arctic exploration, for he had advanced no further towards that goal. When asked about the prospect of finding the Passage in the future, he dismissed the project as 'utterly useless'.[90] A select committee was appointed by the House of Commons to see whether Ross was deserving of any portion of the reward for the discovery of the Northwest Passage. He was not deemed to be so, but that did not matter with regard to assessing his heroic stature: 'Independently of the demonstration that the passage which had been considered by preceding navigators to be one of the most likely to lead from the Atlantic to the Pacific Ocean, does not exist ... [the select] committee cannot overlook the public service which is rendered to a maritime country, especially in time of peace, by deeds of daring enterprise and patient endurance of hardship, which excite the public sympathy, and enlist the general feeling in favour of maritime adventures.'[91] The British government thus believed that Ross had proved that the Northwest Passage did not exist. (In fact, it does exist; just not where Ross had been looking for it.) Of far greater consequence, however, was his 'daring enterprise and patient endurance of hardship'. William Desborough Cooley wrote in the *Edinburgh Review* that his expedition had been 'so like self-immolation in its risks' that it had engendered a 'national anxiety never before extended to any scientific expedition'.[92]

Publishers rushed to take advantage of the British public's appetite for tales of Ross's adventures. (See Figure 15.) The first account of the expedition was published in 1834; in the preface, the anonymous author stated that 'public curiosity has been very strongly excited to learn the result of this expedition'.[93] Throughout, the emphasis was on hardship. Ross and his men had first endured the winter of 1830–31, which was 'unparalleled in its severity', with temperatures that reached 'the lowest degree of which we have any record'.[94] Worse was to come, however, on the journey to Fury Beach:

> They underwent very great suffering, as they had to carry their fuel, their provisions, their sick and their tents and specimens. The whole of this journey was over ice and snow, and occasionally on land covered with snow. The greatest want which they experienced in their toilsome progress, was that of water, as they had to dissolve the snow to obtain it whenever required ... Latterly their only beverage consisted of water and lime juice, and this it was necessary to give out rather sparingly.

> Their sufferings from the cold, however, exceeded every thing
> they had before undergone. From this every individual of the
> whole number composing the expedition suffered severely.[95]

Published the following year, Ross's own account also stressed
privation and hardship. Of August 1830, as they hoped in vain for
the ice to release their ship, Ross wrote: 'this was a month of daily
and hourly anxiety'.[96] As they set forth on the journey to Fury
Beach, it quickly became apparent that they could only drag one
of the ship's boats at a time, requiring them to bring one forward
and then backtrack for the other, thereby tripling the distance
they had to cover. At this point, even the indomitable Ross feared
for their survival, as he and a number of his men were showing
signs of scurvy. It was no longer a question of 'whether we should
attain our object and execute our plans, but whether we should
live or die'.[97] Temperatures were so low that they had to cut their
meat with a saw and thaw it in their warm cocoa. When they
were rescued, the men of the *Isabella* were shocked by their
ragged condition: 'Never was seen a more miserable-looking set
of wretches ... Unshaven since I know not when, dirty, dressed
in the rags of wild beasts instead of the tatters of civilization,
and starved to the very bones, our gaunt and grim looks, when
contrasted with those of the well-dressed and well-fed men around
us, made us all feel, I believe for the first time, what we really
were.'[98]

In terms of finding the Northwest Passage, Ross had achieved
even less on his second expedition than he had on his first. But
whereas he had formerly been criticized for his lack of courage, he
was now a hero in the eyes of the British public, largely because he
was deemed to have suffered so much. *The Times* lauded:

Never did we read a history of almost unexampled disappoint-ment, labour, suffering and peril, written in a tone so free from querulousness. Never perhaps did a body of even British seamen exhibit an example of so much steadiness, sobriety, patience and alacrity to undergo fatigue and endure privation, and submission to judicious restraint, as the companions of Sir John Ross. The moral effect of the narrative [is] in showing how much it is in the power of man to accomplish, in the most adverse circumstances, by patient resolution acting in subordi-nation to skill and judgment.[99]

No single episode better illustrates that the key to Arctic heroism in the first half of the nineteenth century was not accomplish-ment, but rather the amount of suffering that an explorer was deemed to have endured.

In this era, British warfare and exploration provided a context for heroism in which discovery and achievement came to be secondary to pluck, fortitude and perseverance. Why did this model emerge? This was an era in which the British were strug-gling with their role as an imperial nation and global power. In the decades prior to 1800, the American Revolution and charges of corruption regarding the East India Company's rule in South Asia had raised questions about the stability of the empire. After 1800, the empire began expanding once again, adding millions of square miles over the next half-century, but the annexation of territory by force, as occurred in India and elsewhere, occasioned considerable discomfiture. While some Britons objected to the subjugation of peoples who did not wish to be subjugated, others believed that the defence and administration of a continually expanding empire would become a costly drag on the nation's economic health.

Heroic failure helped to resolve these tensions by allowing the British to appear as altruistic and self-sacrificing soldiers and explorers. The imperial world thus became a space for the British to display their sterling qualities and noble spirit, while the more pragmatic motives of territorial expansion and economic gain were concealed. Colonial warfare, the exploration of the interior of Africa and the search for Northwest Passage proved perfect venues for this purpose, with victory and discovery taking a back seat to the heroic qualities of the men who pursued them. Striving for an impossible objective was thus transformed from folly to nobility.

CHAPTER TWO

SIR JOHN FRANKLIN

THE ARCTIC EXPLORER Sir John Franklin had been missing for a decade when, in 1854, the Admiralty officially declared him dead. The few personal effects that were in its possession were sent to his daughter, Eleanor Isabella Gell. They included his dress coat from his time as governor of Van Diemen's Land, a few paintings and portraits of relatives and naval acquaintances, and a dozen or so books. Among the latter was Hugh Clapperton's journal of his second, and fatal, expedition to Africa. If Franklin read it, one wonders if it had given him pause that his own career as an explorer might end in a similarly tragic fashion.[1] For that is what happened: by the time Eleanor Gell received her father's effects, he had in fact been dead for seven years. He and his 128 men had given their lives to the quest for the Northwest Passage, in what was by far the worst disaster in the history of British Arctic exploration. Franklin was thus a failure on a monumental scale, but he nonetheless became one of the greatest Victorian heroes.[2]

Franklin Disappears

Thirty-three when he served on his first Arctic voyage in 1818, Sir John Franklin made a late start to his polar career. But he was by that point a very experienced naval officer who during the Napoleonic Wars had fought at Copenhagen and Trafalgar and had been wounded at New Orleans in 1815. (See Figure 16.) After the war ended, he found himself stuck at the rank of lieutenant, so he saw polar service as a means to promotion. He returned from his first Arctic journey, an effort to reach the North Pole via Spitzbergen, eager for more, and the Admiralty, at the peak of its enthusiasm for discovering the Northwest Passage, was happy to oblige. In 1819, Franklin was dispatched on an expedition to complement Edward Parry's first foray. While Parry pushed by sea into Lancaster Sound, Franklin would lead an expedition by land to map the northern coast of Canada, on the premise that identifying where the Northwest Passage was required determining where the North American mainland was not. He was ordered to follow the Coppermine River downstream to its mouth and then map the coast around it.

Departing in September 1819 from York Factory on the southwest shore of Hudson Bay, Franklin's eleven-man party circled west so that they could maintain contact with the fur-trading posts strung out along the Hayes River. They wintered at Cumberland House, a Hudson's Bay Company post 100 miles (160 km) west of Lake Winnipeg, and then in March went on to Fort Chipewyan on Lake Athabasca. They had completed 1,500 miles (2,400 km) of their trek to the coast, but still had 600 miles (960 km) to go. As there was little game close to the coast, there were no more fur-trading posts further north, so they would have to build their own shelter in which to spend the winter. They also had to carry their own supplies, which required the size of the party to increase to twenty: Franklin, the doctor and naturalist John Richardson, the midshipmen George Back and Robert Hood, the seaman John Hepburn, and fifteen Métis of mixed American Indian and European ancestry, whose usual occupation was selling furs to the trading companies. (Franklin was forced to offer them twice their usual rate of pay to convince them to join the expedition.) More men meant more mouths to feed, a problem that was compounded when several of the Métis' wives and children came along as well. Even though the Métis carried nearly 100 pounds (45 kg) of supplies each, they could not bring sufficient food for the entire journey, so the party had to rely on the indigenous Yellow Knife Indians to supplement their stock. As they had little sustenance to spare, their relations with Franklin's party grew increasingly fractious.

In the spring, Franklin's party descended the Coppermine, reaching the coast on 18 July. Even though it was midsummer, the seawater was full of ice, making it difficult to carry out their surveying work by canoe. Instead of the coast leading them east towards Hudson Bay, where they hoped they might meet up with Parry, it turned south into a narrow inlet. Reaching its end, they turned around, but by now it was August, and the season for exploration was drawing to a close. They continued until the coast finally turned east, but it was too late to follow it now. In a rare outburst of humour – Arctic nomenclature was usually reserved for prominent politicians and wealthy patrons – they named the spot Point Turnagain. Then, with their food supplies dwindling, they headed south. On the return journey, their only two remaining canoes were destroyed, forcing them to proceed on foot and slowing their pace considerably. When their food ran out, they ate moss, lichens, scraps of skin and bone and, eventually, the leather from their shoes. But throughout, Franklin demonstrated the fortitude and faith expected of a British explorer. 'We were now almost exhausted by slender fare and travel, and our appetites had become ravenous,' he wrote in his journal on 15 September. 'We looked, however, with humble confidence to the Great Author and Giver of all good, for a continuance of support which had hitherto always been supplied to us at our greatest need.'[3] By the time the journey ended two months later, nine of the twenty men had died, some at the hands of the others, who were so desperate for food that they resorted to cannibalism.

By any standard, the expedition was a disaster, but the struggle and privation it had endured made for a sensational story. Franklin became 'the man who ate his boots'. The first quarto edition of his journal, published by John Murray in 1823, sold out immediately.[4] Franklin's story was so popular because it abounded in pain and suffering underlain with fortitude and resolution.[5] In his *Neptune's Heroes; or, The Sea-Kings of England* (1860), William Henry Davenport Adams described the Coppermine expedition as a 'splendid display of those noble qualities which seem particularly distinctive of the Saxon race', with 'results obtained which greatly enlarged the boundaries of geographical knowledge'.[6]

In 1825, Franklin was sent back to the Arctic to explore the Mackenzie River and the Great Bear Lake, which lay to the west of the territory he had mapped on his previous expedition. This time, he ensured that both a large supply of pemmican and a sturdy fort in which to spend the winter awaited his arrival. He also commissioned special boats designed to be able to handle the rivers of the Canadian Arctic and brought a team of British sailors, so that he did not have to depend on the Métis. His foresight made for both a safer journey – there were no fatalities this time – and a more successful one. Franklin mapped 1,600 miles (2,560 km) of coastline, an impressive geographical accomplishment, and a sharp contrast to the mere 350 miles (560 km) he had mapped on the Coppermine expedition. But this expedition did not capture the public's imagination in the way that the previous one had done, because it lacked the compelling elements of privation and desperation; Sir John Barrow, second secretary to the Admiralty, dismissed the published version of Franklin's journal as 'a very dull book'.[7]

As a reward for his Arctic exertions, Franklin was given a knighthood in 1829. He was now in his mid-forties, and it seemed likely that his career as a polar explorer was over. He was given a cushy post commanding a frigate in the Mediterranean, and he got married, for a second time, to Jane Griffin, the daughter of a London silk merchant.[8] In 1836, he became the governor of Van Diemen's Land (present-day Tasmania), a penal colony inhabited by eighteen thousand convicts and a handful of free settlers. He was not popular with the latter, who resisted his efforts to modernize the colony and to enact policies that were sympathetic to the island's aboriginal inhabitants. Their complaints led to his recall in 1843.

Although unexpected and undesired, his return to Britain proved timely, as the Admiralty had decided to dispatch an expedition to survey the small sector of the Canadian Arctic that remained unmapped, and at least to identify the Northwest Passage even if the mapping could not be completed. After other, younger Arctic explorers declined the job, it was offered to Franklin, who, eager to make up for the damage done to his reputation by his unsuccessful tenure in Tasmania, readily accepted. He was fifty-nine, but the expedition was to proceed by sea rather than land, so physical stamina was not thought to be a primary requirement.

To ensure the expedition's success, Franklin was given the *Erebus* and *Terror*, two reinforced bomb ships that were thought to be invincible.[9] They were equipped with the most up-to-date technology, including railway steam engines that drove screw propellers rather than vulnerable paddle wheels and steel rudders that could be detached in icy waters to prevent damage. A steam-heating system kept the men warm, while a desalinization system provided fresh water. Forty-five tons of canned food ensured that the men would not lack for proper sustenance.[10]

Involving 130 men, the expedition represented a massive effort, intended to overwhelm the Arctic with sheer numbers. Many experts felt that smaller expeditions were better suited to the spartan environment, but optimism abounded: only a few hundred miles separated Montreal Island, the easternmost point reached by two explorers from the Hudson's Bay Company in 1839, from the westernmost point reached by Sir John Ross in the Gulf of Boothia in 1831. Surely an expedition on the scale of Franklin's could link the two? This would at last be the moment when the Northwest Passage was discovered. 'The name of Franklin alone is … a national guarantee,' declared Sir Roderick Murchison, the president of the Royal Geographical Society.[11]

The *Erebus* and *Terror* set sail from England on 19 May 1845. On 2 July, they anchored at Disko Island off the west coast of Greenland. From there, Captain James Fitzjames, the expedition's first officer, wrote an optimistic letter to Sir John Barrow: 'We are all in good humour. In fact there is one incessant laugh from morning to night. We are most comfortable and happy – plenty to do, observing all sorts of things all day and good dinners into the bargain ... We bounded along merrily shaking hands with ourselves and making imaginary short cuts thro' America to the Pacific ... We hear that this is supposed to be a remarkably clear season.'[12] Franklin's instructions called for him to cross Baffin Bay, enter Lancaster Sound and the Barrow Strait, then sail south from there to the coast of the North American mainland, where he would turn west, eventually emerging in the Bering Strait and into the Pacific Ocean. Nothing could be simpler. But the plan ignored the fact that 500 miles (800 km) of the voyage were unmapped, meaning that the actual distance that a ship needed to travel might prove much longer as it picked its way through ice and the Arctic archipelago. This had not mattered in the imaginations of the journey's planners. But now, in the Arctic, the scale of the task that lay before the travellers became very clear. On 26 July, a whaler saw Franklin's ships moored to an iceberg in Lancaster Sound, waiting for the ice to clear. And then they vanished: they were neither seen nor heard from in 1846 or 1847. Initially, there was no particular reason for alarm, as they had sufficient food to last them three years. But, by 1848, concern was mounting. If Franklin had managed to get through, he would have been heard from by now; it was thus likely that he was trapped in the ice somewhere, with dwindling food supplies.

The Search

Back in Britain, the disappearance of 130 men reawakened the public to the alluring dangers of the Arctic. Newspapers and periodicals devoted numerous articles to speculation about Franklin's fate, while churches all over the country held special services to pray for his safe return and clairvoyants reported seeing ghostly images of ships frozen in the ice.[13] Lady Jane Franklin became the embodiment of wifely devotion as she crisscrossed the country drumming up support for a rescue expedition. In 1848, the Admiralty dispatched the first public relief effort; a reward of £20,000 was offered to entice private ventures into the field as well. (See Figure 17.) Over the next decade, a total of thirty-eight public and private expeditions from Britain, the United States and Russia would search for Franklin.[14] In 1850 alone, thirteen ships (eleven British and two American) traversed the Arctic looking for the lost expedition. They found the first clue: the remains of an encampment on Beechey Island in the Wellington Channel, along with grave markers inscribed with the names of three of Franklin's men, all dated between January and April 1846. There was no message, however, to suggest where the expedition had gone next.

By now, it was extremely unlikely that any of Franklin's men were still alive, but even so, many people continued to believe that British seamen could endure any conditions. 'There is stuff and stamina in 120 [*sic*] Englishmen,' declared Sir Edward Parry, 'that somehow or other they would have maintained themselves as well as a parcel of Esquimaux would.'[15] The British public thus would not allow the search to be abandoned. The Hudson's Bay Company fur-trader William Kennedy, who led a rescue expedition in 1851, wrote that 'nothing is more common in conversation, and in the statements of the daily press, and even in publications of higher pretensions, than to find plans and proposals brought forward for the relief of our absent countrymen'.[16]

As the search for Franklin intensified, the objective of discovering the Northwest Passage receded; as John Brown, Fellow of the Royal Geographical Society, declared in 1858, it was finding Franklin, not the Northwest Passage, that was now a matter of 'the nation's honour'.[17] (See Figure 18.) It was the degree of effort, rather than success, that served as the yardstick against which the relief efforts were measured. In 1860, James A. Browne, bandmaster of the Royal Artillery, asserted that a failure to strive to the utmost to find Franklin would suggest that the English national character had diminished over the centuries: 'Englishmen love to engage in enterprise, and, notwithstanding the many failures they have ever experienced, and the disasters they have often suffered for its sake, their efforts have generally, in the end, been crowned with success; they would, therefore, seem to lack the courage of their ancestors were they not to continue that desire for the progress of discovery which so nobly characterized their forefathers for upwards of four centuries.'[18] Those who were deemed not to have exerted sufficient effort were harshly judged. In 1851, Lieutenant Sherard Osborn led an expedition that searched for Franklin on Prince of Wales Island. As they attempted to reach Cape Walker across a frozen bay, his men were caught in a vicious storm:

Our gallant fellows ... with faces averted and bended bodies, strained every nerve to reach the land, in hopes of obtaining more shelter than the naked floe afforded from the hipping effects of the cutting-gale. Every moment some fresh case of frost-bite would occur, which the watchful care of the officers would immediately detect. The man would fall out from his sledge, restore the circulation of the affected part, generally the face, and hasten back to his post. Constant questions of 'How are your feet?' were heard on all sides, with the general response,

'Oh! I hope they are all right; but I've not felt them since I pulled my boots on.'[19]

Despite these exertions, Osborn was criticized for not trying hard enough: 'Our self-importance as Arctic heroes of the first water received a sad downfall when we were first asked by a kind friend, what the deuce we came home for? ... and why we deserted Franklin?'[20] Similar disparagement met the return of Captain Horatio Austin's expedition in 1851, as the *Nautical Magazine* attested:

> Opinions of parties who appear to be ill-informed on this subject have been freely delivered, condemning Captain Austin's proceedings, and producing an impression on the public mind highly unfavourable to that officer ... The expedition under Captain Austin has been proclaimed a failure – the fairest expedition which ever left this country has been declared ineffective, because its leader adopted a course under circumstances that he considers to be the most proper one, but which does not appear to be understood by these writers ... It is asked why did not Austin proceed up the Wellington Channel? For this plain reason we may answer, because he saw that unhappily there lay a stout barrier of ice between him and the open sea beyond it of some twenty or thirty miles extent, which not only was it impossible for his ships to penetrate, but in all probability had been equally fatal to the progress of Sir John Franklin's.[21]

Francis Leopold McClintock, one of Austin's officers, learned his lesson well: as he prepared to return to the Arctic on Sir Edward Belcher's expedition of 1852, he wrote to the famous polar explorer Sir James Clark Ross that 'we are duty bound to do more than has hitherto been done; we must work hard indeed'.[22]

One by one, however, the rescue expeditions failed to find evidence of what had befallen Franklin's men after they left Beechey Island. Ann Ross, the wife of Sir James Clark Ross, wrote to Eleanor Gell in November 1849 that 'these excited hopes and weary silences are sadly trying every way, bodily, mentally and spiritually'.[23] The Admiralty, meanwhile, met with a barrage of proposals as to how to find Franklin. (See Figures 19 and 20.) Suggestions included the use of steam-powered 'ice-hammers', 'ice-saws' and other machines 'for breaking the ice in navigating the polar regions'; the release of ten thousand pigeons carrying instructions to Franklin's men in parchment bags; the construction of a steam railway engine and carriages that were 'adapted to travelling over fields of solid ice'; the launching of balloons, rockets or 'small India-rubber balls' high in the air bearing messages to Franklin's men and directing them 'to places where they might find provisions'; the fitting of ships' boats with carriage wheels that would be propelled across the ice by small steam engines; and the blasting of the ice with explosives.[24]

None of these ideas, however, seemed to offer a serious solution to the mystery of Franklin's fate. After 1851, the Admiralty, aware that Franklin and his men were almost certainly dead, became reluctant to send out further search expeditions. The British public, however, was not yet ready to give up hope, and the Admiralty found itself besieged by petitions demanding further efforts. Some of these entreaties came from family members of the lost men, while others came from scientific and learned societies, such as the Manchester Athenaeum, or from the residents of particular cities and towns. The pleas arrived from all corners of the Britain Isles: Stromness in the Orkney Islands, which had long been connected to Arctic exploration via its whaling industry, sent one, as did Dublin, Belfast and Armagh in Ireland.[25] With pressure coming from so many directions, the Admiralty opted to fund one last search expedition, led by Edward Belcher, in 1852. It was a disaster: four of its five ships became frozen in the ice and had to be abandoned.[26] Two private expeditions funded by Lady Franklin, the previously referenced one led by William Kennedy in 1851 and another by Edward Augustus Inglefield in 1852, also found nothing.

But if the dozens of search expeditions failed to locate Franklin, they did discover something else: the Northwest Passage. In September 1850, Commander Robert McClure, whom the Admiralty had dispatched in HMS *Investigator* to sail east through the Bering Strait, found the Prince of Wales Strait, which connects to the Parry Channel and is thus one route of the Northwest Passage.[27] Two years later, Kennedy's expedition discovered a passage linking Prince Regent Inlet and the Victoria Strait. The passage, named the Bellot Strait in honour of Kennedy's second-in-command, the Frenchman Joseph-René Bellot, provides an exit out of the lower end of Prince Regent Inlet and is thus the key to the southernmost route through the Northwest Passage.[28] But geographical discovery, Kennedy conceded, was 'not our object': 'Important, as under other circumstances such would doubtless have been, *ours* was indeed a far nobler one, – to rescue, or solve the fate of our long-absent countrymen.'[29] (Italics in the original.)

Kennedy was right: the news that the last pieces of the Northwest Passage puzzle had been put into place met with a muted response in Britain, as the public was much more interested in the search for Franklin. The *Nautical Magazine* published a lengthy article in November 1853, proclaiming that 'at length the great geographical question of the North-West Passage is solved', but it admitted that it had devoted so many pages to the story because of 'the general interest which prevails respecting our absent countrymen in the Arctic Regions'.[30] In his popular history of the search for the Northwest Passage, published in 1855, the journalist Peter Simmonds wrote that McClure's achievements were 'hardly heeded in the disappointment that nothing has been effected towards settling the business on which the ship was specially despatched. The discovery of Sir John Franklin would be worth the discovery of a North-west Passage a thousand times over.'[31]

By 1854, the Admiralty had spent £600,000 looking for Franklin and his men, hundreds of millions in today's money. Some of the rescue expeditions had themselves had to be rescued. There would be no more. Then, just when everyone stopped looking, Franklin was finally found. John Rae, a surgeon for the Hudson's Bay Company, had learned to live and travel like an Inuit, allowing him to survive in conditions that would have killed other Europeans. He had previously searched for Franklin on an expedition to the coast near Victoria Island between 1848 and 1851. By 1853, he was no longer looking for the missing expedition, as he harboured no illusions about the men's ability to survive in the Arctic for eight years. He was keen, however, to fill in one of the last remaining blank spaces on the map, the Boothia Peninsula, and in particular to determine whether it was connected to King William Land. In March 1854, Rae was on the shore of Pelly Bay in the southern stretches of the Prince Regent Inlet when he encountered two Inuit. He noticed that one of them was wearing a gold cap-band that looked like it might have come from the uniform of a British naval officer. When he inquired about the band, the Inuit reported that between thirty-five and forty *kabloona*, or white men, had starved to death four years earlier, 'west of a large river a long distance off'.[32]

Rae purchased the band and asked the Inuit to bring any other relics they might have of the *kabloona* to his winter quarters at Repulse Bay. He then continued on his original mission, which proved that King William Land was in fact an island, and that one route of the Northwest Passage therefore lay between it and the Boothia Peninsula. But, as had been the case with McClure's and Kennedy's discoveries, that no longer mattered; the British public would only be interested in what he discovered about Franklin's fate. On the return journey to Repulse Bay, he met more Inuit, one of whom sold him a silver spoon that was inscribed with the initials 'F.R.M.C.' Rae was puzzled by it, and speculated that the 'R.M.C.' might stand for 'Robert McClure', the commander of the government's rescue expedition of 1850. Over the winter, however, Rae interviewed other Inuit, and gradually it began to dawn on him that they were talking about Franklin's men. He realized that 'F.R.M.C.' stood for Francis Rawdon Moira Crozier, Franklin's second-in-command. Rae learned that in the spring of 1850 some Inuit who were hunting seal on the western shore of King William Island had seen a group of several dozen emaciated white men dragging a heavy boat. The white men managed to communicate that their ships had been trapped by the ice and that they were heading south in search of food. Not long after, the Inuit found an encampment with some graves and the unburied bodies of around thirty men on the coast of the mainland south of King William Island. Five more bodies were on a nearby island. The boat had been turned upside down to provide shelter. Some of the men must have survived until at least May, because the campsite contained the bones and feathers of geese, which did not arrive in the Arctic until that time in the year. A number of the corpses had been mutilated, and there were pieces of human flesh in cooking pots. This led Rae to conclude that the men had been driven to cannibalism, or what he termed 'the last dread alternative'.[33] He purchased additional relics from the Inuit, including cutlery with the crests or initials of Franklin's officers, scientific and medical instruments, watches and coins. There were two objects that had belonged to Franklin himself: a silver plate that was inscribed on the reverse 'Sir John Franklin K.C.B.', and a bronze star that he had been given when he was made a Knight Commander of the Guelphic Order of Hanover in recognition of his diplomatic services in Greece in the early 1830s.[34] Rae decided not to try and find the spot where the bodies lay, which would have required him to wait until spring and then undertake a long and arduous journey. Instead, he sped to London with the news, assuming that others could carry out the work of confirmation later.

By the time he arrived in October 1854, the Admiralty had already received a copy of his report to the Hudson's Bay Company. As confirmation, Rae produced the relics he had obtained, fifteen of which were emblazoned with the crests or monograms of Franklin and his officers. (See Figure 21.) He also described his discovery of the strait between the Boothia Peninsula and King William Island, but the Admiralty was only minimally interested in that. The day after his meeting with Sir James Graham, the First Lord of the Admiralty, the first stories of Rae's discoveries appeared in the press. To his surprise, they not only contained the information that he had provided in a carefully worded letter to *The Times*, but also details that could only be found in his longer report to the Admiralty. These details included the allegations of cannibalism.

The British public did not care that Rae had solved a vital problem in the quest for the Northwest Passage. Instead, they were angry that he had not followed up on the information he had received by travelling to the places the Inuit had described. 'That Dr Rae should have turned his back on that locality is the more extraordinary,' cried the anonymous author of *The Great Arctic Mystery* (1856), 'as he could have visited it in three or four days, and, by personal examination, assisted by his interpreter, he might have ascertained the fate of the Franklin expedition; but it is abundantly evident that geographical discovery alone influenced him.'[35] The claim that Rae could have made it to the site in 'three or four days' was a massive exaggeration, but what is more striking about this declaration is its ready dismissal of the importance of 'geographical discovery' relating to the last pieces of the Northwest Passage puzzle. The very thing that had driven British polar exploration for decades, and had supposedly motivated Franklin to head back to the Arctic, was now a mere distraction from the more important objective of determining Franklin's fate.

But what really infuriated the British public were the allegations of cannibalism. Rae found himself at the centre of a firestorm of controversy, with a furious Lady Franklin leading the charge against him. His rapid dash to England made it appear as if he were over-eager to claim the £10,000 reward offered by the Admiralty for definitive proof of Franklin's fate. By relying on Inuit accounts and not going to see the bodies for himself, Rae had left open an easy avenue of attack. The Victorians had long struggled with what to make of Inuit information regarding Franklin's fate. In 1849, the whaling master Captain John Parker reported that an Inuit had told him of seeing Franklin's ships in Prince Regent Inlet. In a letter to Eleanor Gell, Ann Ross cast doubt on the veracity of this information: 'If the account has come in reality from Esquimaux, do you think that if, in hope of gain, they invented a falsity?' She admitted, however, that she was 'still building hope upon it'.[36] As this last comment indicates, Victorian Britons often accepted Inuit evidence at face value when it concurred with what they wanted to hear. In response to the same information, Eleanor Gell's friend Rose Beaufort, daughter of the noted hydrographer Sir Francis Beaufort, wrote: 'The natives gave the intelligence spontaneously . . . and there is no impossibility in it.'[37]

Now, however, there was reason to disbelieve the Inuit testimony: the honour of the Royal Navy was at stake. The anonymous author of *The Great Arctic Mystery* wrote that the Inuit were 'notoriously addicted to falsehood and deception'.[38] There was, of course, the matter of the relics, but some stories in the press claimed that the Inuit must have obtained them from Franklin's ships after they were beset and abandoned. In her quest to defend her husband's reputation, Lady Franklin enlisted a number of prominent allies, among them Charles Dickens, the most popular writer of the day.[39] In December 1854, he published an essay in his periodical *Household Words* that staunchly denied the possibility of cannibalism. Instead, he blamed the Inuit, speculating that the 'sad remnant of Franklin's gallant band' had been 'set upon and slain by the Esquimaux themselves': 'It is impossible to form an estimate of the character of any race of savages, from their deferential behaviour to the white man while he is strong. The mistake has been made again and again; and the moment the white man has appeared in the new aspect of being weaker than the savage, the savage has changed and sprung upon him . . . We believe every savage to be in his heart covetous, treacherous and cruel.'[40] The Inuit, according to Dickens, had invented the story they had told Rae in order to cover up their crime. Here, we have a classic statement of the imperialist view of indigenous peoples, at one moment craven and cowardly, and at the next bloodthirsty and violent. Rae swiftly composed a reply, but he lacked Dickens's sensitivity to the public mood and instead relied on truth, which depended on his ability to make people grasp the nature of an environment utterly alien and incomprehensible to them. Unsurprisingly, it was Dickens's fiery indignation, rather than Rae's sober veracity, that triumphed.

Franklin's expedition, with its reinforced, steam-driven ships and its massive contingent of the best men the Royal Navy could offer, had been a test of British strength and skill. The Victorian public could easily live with, and even embrace, defeat. What they could not accept was that British sailors had failed to withstand privation and hardship with the fortitude that Franklin had displayed on the Coppermine expedition. They had long since become inured to failure in the Arctic, but they expected their vanquished heroes to resign themselves calmly to their fate. A prize poem about Franklin from Repton School in Derby from 1860 provided a model for heroic polar death:

> The whispered text, the prayer that conquers death,
> Claimed the last accent of their trembling breath:
> Their death was calm, hushed the tumultuous roar
> On that dread night, along the lonely shore.[41]

Rae had disturbed this picture by suggesting that they had killed and eaten each other in a desperate attempt to stay alive. Someone had to restore the heroism to Franklin's failure.

Definitive Proof?

By the mid-1850s, even Lady Franklin had abandoned all hope that her husband was alive, but she continued to press for expeditions to search for definitive proof of his fate, which she insisted Rae had failed to provide. The Admiralty refused to budge, however requiring her to fund any further search expeditions herself. Her continuing ability to do so was complicated by her financial and familial situation. The Victorian public saw her as a noble, grieving widow, but some members of Franklin's family saw her devotion to her late husband in a very different light. What wealth Franklin possessed had come from his first wife, Eleanor Porden; he enjoyed only a life interest in her fortune. Upon his death, that would pass to Eleanor Gell, his daughter from his first marriage. As early as 1849, Mrs Gell began making inquiries as to the disposition of her father's estate, and even accused Lady Franklin of being 'slightly deranged'.[42] She was frustrated by her stepmother's spending of what was now her inheritance on what she saw as pointless search expeditions. Even after the Admiralty removed Franklin's name from the active list in 1854, however, Lady Franklin continued to insist that it had not been conclusively established that he was dead.[43] In 1855, the Court of Chancery was forced to resolve the matter: it determined that the Admiralty's judgement was conclusive and that his estate now belonged to Eleanor Gell.

But even after losing control of her husband's estate, Lady Franklin managed to find the funds for one last search expedition in 1857, led by Francis Leopold McClintock, a naval officer who had served on three previous efforts to find Franklin.[44] The expedition spent its first year trapped in the ice of Baffin Bay, but the following summer it passed through the Bellot Strait into Peel

Sound. From the local Inuit, McClintock learned more about what had happened to Franklin. They told him that one ship had been crushed, but the other had been pushed ashore on King William Island by pressure from the ice of the Victoria Strait.[45] They knew this because they had obtained wood from the wreckage.

The Inuit sold McClintock additional Franklin relics, including silver plates bearing Sir John's crest like the one Rae had purchased in 1854. They confirmed that the survivors had headed south towards the Great Fish River, and that many 'fell down and died as they walked along'.[46] After the spring sledging season began, McClintock found the body of a young man still wearing his naval uniform and greatcoat on the south shore of King William Island. But what he was really searching for was written evidence, which to this point had proved maddeningly elusive. Finally, at Point Victory, on the northwest coast of King William Island, a sledging party led by Lieutenant William Hobson found a note in a stone cairn. Written by Lieutenant Graham Gore, one of Franklin's officers, this reported that Franklin had come very close to achieving the Northwest Passage in a single voyage. Enjoying one of the mildest seasons in Arctic history, the *Erebus* and *Terror* had sped across Baffin Bay in less than a month and had found Lancaster Sound free of ice. After that, however, they had been blocked by ice in the Barrow Strait, and had turned north to look for a way through. With winter approaching, Franklin had anchored between Beechey and Devon Islands. On Beechey Island, the men built a storehouse, a carpenter's shop and a forge; this was the encampment that had been found in 1850, with the graves of the three men.[47]

After leaving his winter harbour, Franklin pushed through the western end of Lancaster Sound until he came to a clear channel, now known as Peel Sound, pointing south, precisely the way that he wished to go. It drew him in, allowing him to steam for nearly 250 miles (400 km) through thin surface ice. He could see King William Island directly in front of him. It was late August, but with open leads and two strong ships, Franklin decided to risk getting through before winter closed in. He could have steamed to the east of King William Island, found the narrow Simpson Strait that separated it from the mainland and from there picked his way along the coast to the Bering Strait and into the Pacific Ocean; in a warm season like the summer of 1846, it would have been just possible. But prior to Rae proving otherwise, his maps would have shown King William Island to be linked to the Boothia Peninsula, so he did not go around it to the east, but to the west. This sent his ships directly into the ice that pours down from the Beaufort Sea, the obstacle that had blocked so many previous efforts to find the Northwest Passage. The limitations of the ships' puny steam engines now became apparent. Even operating at maximum capacity, they made little headway, and they were rapidly burning through the expedition's supply of coal. The only possibility was to reach King William Island and find a safe anchorage for the winter. Even this, however, proved impossible. On 15 September, they were beset 25 miles (40 km) from shore. No effort to blast, hack or push themselves free worked. They would have to spend the winter frozen in the pack ice, hoping that it did not crush the ships.

Dated 25 April 1848 and signed by Crozier and Fitzjames, a second note scribbled around the margins of Gore's first one told of how the ships had been locked in the ice since September 1846. When they had still not been released by the spring of 1848, the men made the difficult decision to abandon them. Nine officers and fifteen men had already died. The former included Gore and Franklin, who had expired from undisclosed causes on 11 June 1847. As Hobson read the second note, he would have understood that for Crozier, now in command, there were two options, both equally daunting. They could head east towards Baffin Bay, a journey of 1,200 miles (1,920 km), where they might encounter a whaling ship. Or they could head south, towards the Hudson's Bay Company's post on the Great Slave Lake. That was 850 miles (1,360 km) away, but the intervening terrain offered little sustenance. It did, however, offer the possibility of finding the Great Fish River unfrozen, which meant that they could make part of the journey by boat. They might even encounter Hudson's Bay Company searchers sent to look for them along the way.

Choosing what appeared to be the best of two desperate options, Crozier decided to head south with the expedition's 105 surviving officers and men. Dragging the heavy ship's boats, they moved at a snail's pace of only a mile a day. Recognizing that their food would run out long before they reached the Great Slave Lake, Crozier split the party in two. The strongest men attempted to go ahead at a faster pace, while the others remained behind to await rescue. Crozier managed to lead the first party to the southern coast of King William Island. They had come 80 miles (128 km) from the ships, less than 10 per cent of the distance they needed to cover. There, Crozier may have realized that he was standing on an island, and that he was therefore looking at the last unmapped stretch of the Northwest Passage. If he did, it is doubtful that he much cared.

Eleven years later, Hobson found Crozier's last camp, the one that the Inuit had told Rae about in 1854. It contained one of the ship's boats mounted on a sledge with two skeletons inside;

fourteen more bodies were underneath the boat. When he got back to Britain, McClintock astutely did not mention cannibalism. Hobson had been unnerved by the mangled and incomplete condition of one of the skeletons in the boat, but in his report, which was published on 23 September 1859, McClintock described it as merely 'disturbed, probably by animals'.[48] His discretion meant that he enjoyed a very different reception from Rae's. Showered with the freedoms of cities and honorary degrees, he became a hero. He received a gold medal from the Royal Geographical Society, a knighthood from Queen Victoria, a £5,000 reward from Parliament, and a reference on Franklin's monument in Westminster Abbey as 'discoverer of the fate of Franklin in 1859'.[49] Rae had been right all along, but McClintock got the credit.

The scale of Franklin's failure had been spectacular. Between 1800 and 1845, of the 1,500 men employed by the British in exploring the Arctic, fewer than twenty had died. Franklin lost 130. Even so, he was transformed into a hero. James Parsons wrote in 1857 that Franklin's 'character stood all but alone in zeal, bold daring and in enterprise, for a man to retain at the advanced age of sixty all the boldness and energy of youth, singularly blended with the lofty qualities of religion, is a combination rarely found in one individual; with a mind that had overcome the greatest of difficulties, was a heart as generous as it was brave'.[50]

Franklin's story, to be sure, presented its celebrants with challenges. In July 1860, Owen Vidal recited a poem about the expedition in the Sheldonian Theatre at Oxford. He struggled to make a coherent and meaningful story out of what was by any realistic reckoning a debacle. The strategy that he ultimately fixed upon was to place Franklin in the long history of British greatness by reminding the audience that he had fought alongside Nelson at Trafalgar:

> He fought beside the seamen,
> The heroes of our land,
> Whose names upon the splendid page
> Of England's hist'ry stand.

He then cited the deaths of Franklin and his men as one of the periodic sacrifices that were necessary for that greatness to be maintained. At the end of the poem, the Indian Rebellion and in particular Major General Sir Henry Havelock, who had died of dysentery only days after leading the British effort to lift the siege of Lucknow, provided a parallel example of sacrifice for one's country:

> And now the sky is overcast
> With rolling clouds of war,
> And England pours her sons to fight,
> As in the days of yore.
>
> With trumpet-blast the columns march
> Adown the shouting streets,
> 'Mid boom of guns and cheers of men
> Forth sail the succouring fleets:
>
> And now the tidings of defeat
> Some homeward vessel brings,
> And now the name of Havelock
> Throughout the island rings.[51]

The same difficulties in presenting Franklin's story were apparent in the campaign to erect a public memorial. In 1861, it was decided to commemorate him with a statue in London, paid for with £2,000 of public funds. Five years later, a statue by Matthew Noble was installed at the lower end of Regent Street in what today is Waterloo Place.[52] But what exactly was Franklin being commemorated for? His greatest contribution to Arctic exploration was his mapping of the coast of North America, but that was not what had permanently enshrined him as a hero in the minds of the British public. Nor was it enough to satisfy Lady Franklin, and no one was eager to challenge her right to determine the nature of the memorial to her beloved husband. And so it was that the plaque on the base of Noble's statue proclaimed that Franklin and his companions had 'sacrificed their lives in completing the discovery of the Northwest Passage'. This claim was based on the thinnest of evidence: that in exploring King William Land in the first year of the expedition, Franklin's men must have discovered that it was an island; they would therefore have known about the Simpson Strait even if they were unable to reach or sail through it. Since their discovery had been made before McClure's, they should therefore be given pride of place as the locators of the passage. A duplicate of Noble's statue that was erected in 1870 in Hobart, the capital of Tasmania, made the same claim. So did Charles Bacon's statue of Franklin that was erected in his birthplace of Spilsby in Lincolnshire in 1861 and Noble's monument in Westminster Abbey, which was dedicated in 1875. The monument in the Painted Hall of Greenwich Hospital, erected in 1858, did not claim that Franklin had discovered the Northwest Passage, but it did refer repeatedly to the search for it in its inscription, and included a bas-relief of a naval officer intently plotting a course. (See Figure 22.) The Northwest Passage, which had been all but forgotten in the rush to rescue Franklin, was thus suddenly revived so that it could give his heroism meaning. Its original purpose as a route for maritime traffic, however, had been abandoned; it was now merely a venue for the demonstration of British heroism.

CHAPTER THREE

THE CHARGE

O N 25 October 1854, at the Battle of Balaclava, the Light Brigade of the British cavalry charged a battery of Russian artillery that was deployed at the end of a mile-long valley. The valley was flanked on both sides by additional guns that fired down from above. The action, which was in defiance of every basic principle of cavalry action in warfare, was the result of an erroneous interpretation of an ambiguous order given by Lord Raglan, the commander of the British forces in the Crimean War, to Lord Cardigan, the commander of the Light Brigade. Of the approximately 670 men who participated in the charge, almost three hundred were killed, wounded or taken prisoner.[1] Some observers were nonplussed by this horrific casualty rate. General Sir Richard Airey, second-in-command to Lord Raglan in the Crimea, merely shrugged: 'These sorts of things will happen in war. It is nothing compared to Chillianwallah.'[2] In Airey's eyes, the Charge of the Light Brigade was just another heroic failure.

Charging to Glory: Aliwal and Chillianwallah

In the nineteenth century, military charges provided abundant material for heroic failure. They were 'death or glory' actions that either overwhelmed the enemy, resulting in epic victories, or failed calamitously, resulting in massive casualties. Despite their risks, they were a common occurrence because British military tactics in this era relied heavily on the sequence of infantry volley followed by infantry charge with fixed bayonets, and then massed cavalry charge intended to cut down the enemy troops as they retreated. The idea was to overwhelm the enemy with force, spirit and courage, not to outmanoeuvre him. This lack of tactical sophistication was in part a consequence of the purchase system for officers' commissions, as the inexperienced officers that it produced were not capable of more complex manoeuvres. More attractive to men from elite backgrounds than the infantry, the cavalry contained a higher proportion of officers who had achieved their ranks through purchase, which meant that in battle it was often a blunt instrument.

The army's reliance on the cavalry charge dated from the second half of the eighteenth century. At the Battle of Emsdorf in 1760, during the Seven Years War, the 15th Light Dragoons routed the French, and the same regiment also charged successfully at Villers-en-Cauchies in 1794. By the Napoleonic era, British cavalry officers were besotted with charging. Wellington was constantly frustrated by the behaviour of his cavalry, which he complained 'would gallop, but could not preserve their order', frequently leading to heavy losses.[3] The cavalry charges of the Peninsular War often saw his worst fears realized. While charging at Talavera in 1809, the 23rd Light Dragoons and 1st Hussars

1 Waterloo Place, London, shown looking south towards the Mall from Lower Regent Street (c. 1900). The Crimean Memorial is in its original location; the statues of Lord Herbert of Lea and Florence Nightingale are not yet present. Nor is that of Captain Scott, which was positioned in the first clump of trees on the left, just behind the hansom cab, in 1919. The statue of Sir John Franklin is on the right, blocked by the Crimean Memorial.

2 Philip Hermogenes Calderon, *Lord, Thy Will Be Done* (1855). Depicting a young wife and mother awaiting the return of her husband (seen in the portrait above the mantel) from the Crimean War, Calderon's painting shows the gendered nature of heroic failure. While men go out in the world as soldiers and explorers, women remain at home as their loyal helpmates.

3 Rebecca Solomon, *The Story of Balaclava: Wherein he Spoke of the Most Disastrous Chances* (1855). Trained by her brother, the artist Abraham Solomon, Rebecca Solomon was one of the most prominent female painters of the mid-Victorian era. This work illustrates the fascination of the British public with the disastrous Charge of the Light Brigade, as well as the limited roles available to women in stories of heroic failure.

4 Cape made from the feathers of the bright red 'apapane bird (1861). The cape was given to Lady Jane Franklin by King Kamehameha IV of Hawaii during a visit she made there in 1861 while researching a book about her husband, Sir John Franklin, who had disappeared a decade earlier as he searched for the Northwest Passage. Lady Franklin had first sailed to Alaska in her quest for information about his fate and had then gone on to Hawaii, hoping to speak to Arctic whalers who were wintering there. Upon her death in 1875, Lady Jane bequeathed the cape to G.B. Austen Lefroy, who donated it to the Bishop Museum in Honolulu in 1909. The cape symbolizes her tireless quest to determine her husband's fate and to defend his reputation.

5 Statue of Captain Robert Falcon Scott by his widow, Kathleen Scott (1915). Two years after the statue was installed in Waterloo Place in London, a marble replica was erected in Christchurch, New Zealand. Kathleen Scott also sculpted the bust of her late husband over the entrance to the Scott Polar Research Institute in Cambridge and the statue of a nude youth, arms outstretched, in the Institute's garden. The base of the latter is inscribed 'lux perpetua luceat eis' ('may eternal light shine upon them').

6 Memorial to Major Generals Sir Edward Pakenham and Samuel Gibbs, St Paul's Cathedral, London (1823). The inscription on Richard Westmacott's memorial to Gibbs and Pakenham claims that they 'fell gloriously' at the Battle of New Orleans. In reality, the battle was a debacle for the British.

7 Monument to Sir John Moore, St Paul's Cathedral, London (1815). John Bacon's monument to Moore is a classicized representation of military martyrdom, showing a muscular male figure and a female angel lowering his prostrate body into a sarcophagus. In the decades surrounding 1800, visual representations of high-ranking officers' deaths in battle were prevalent in British culture. Though Corunna was a desperate battle fought at the end of a chaotic and costly retreat, Moore's death was seen as an heroic sacrifice.

8 Benjamin West, *The Death of General Wolfe* (1770). Illustrating the death of General James Wolfe at the Battle of Quebec in 1759, West's painting set the standard for visual representations of battlefield martyrdom for decades to come. Despite initial controversy over West's decision to depict his subjects in contemporary rather than classical dress, it proved wildly popular and many people purchased engravings for display in their homes.

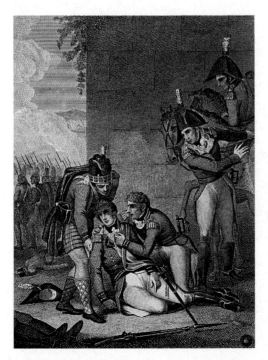

9 An engraving published by Thomas Kelly of the death of Sir John Moore (1810). Depicting Moore dying at the moment of victory, the work was clearly influenced by West's *The Death of General Wolfe* (see Figure 8). On the left, a soldier from a Highland regiment, identifiable by his kilt and tartan stockings, helps to support the prostrate Moore. In the background, other Highland soldiers march into battle; they were prominently featured in order to reassure the British public, who by the early nineteenth century had come to associate the Highland regiments with bravery and steadfastness. The 21st, 26th, 42nd, 71st, 79th and 92nd Highlanders all fought at Corunna. Highland soldiers, specifically the 78th Fraser Highlanders, also feature prominently in West's painting.

10 Monument to Rollo Gillespie in St Paul's Cathedral (1820). Designed by Francis Leggat Chantry, it was placed on the opposite side of the south door from the memorial to Pakenham and Gibbs, and its inscription included the identical phrase 'fell gloriously'.

11 Monument to Rollo Gillespie in Comber, County Down (1845). In the early 1840s, a group of local grandees organized a committee with the purpose of collecting funds for a memorial to Gillespie. Most of the support came from local gentry, soldiers who had served under him and Freemasons. (Gillespie had been a member of the order.) Designed by a local architect named Johnston, the monument took the form of a 55-foot-high (17 m) column topped by a statue of Gillespie in his uniform. Unveiled in 1845, it oddly described his thirty-year military career as 'brief but glorious'.

12 Engraving of Mungo Park by W.T. Fry (1820). Park is shown in heroic mode, surrounded by African weapons and implements. The image at the top of a naked Park in a boat alludes to the privations of his journey, and may refer to an incident described in the journal of his first expedition in which he was robbed of his clothes by an Arab slave-trader.

MONUMENT

TO THE MEMORY
OF THE CELEBRATED
AFRICAN TRAVELLER
THE LATE

MUNGO PARK.

In consequence of a numerously signed REQUISITION, addressed to me by the INHABITANTS of the BURGH of SELKIRK, I hereby call a MEETING of the INHABITANTS of this TOWN, and of all those who may feel interested in the matter, to be held within the

COURT-HOUSE OF SELKIRK,

ON MONDAY,

The 20th day of December, current,
At One o'Clock Afternoon,

For the purpose of adopting measures for the ERECTION of a MONUMENT to the MEMORY of the above CELEBRATED INDIVIDUAL, in THIS, his NATIVE COUNTY.—

Wm. MUIR,

CHIEF-MAGISTRATE.

Selkirk, 1st December, 1841.

Printed by T. Brown, Selkirk.

13 and 14 Poster and monument relating to Mungo Park. Dating from 1841, the poster (left) advertises a meeting to discuss raising funds for a monument to Park, describing him as 'the celebrated African traveller' but does not identify him with any particular achievements. Sufficient funds were collected for a statue of Park, though plans for additional figures of two Africans and two Scottish Highlanders had to be scrapped. The monument (below) in Selkirk, Scottish Borders was sculpted by Andrew Currie, a relative of Park, and dedicated in March 1860. The figure of Park holds a scroll which reads: 'Die on the Niger', a reference to a phrase from Park's last letter, in which he stated: 'If I could not succeed in the object of my journey, I would at least die on the Niger.' The specific form of commemoration thus shows that the manner of Park's death was a more important aspect of his heroism than his accomplishments as an explorer.

15 Illustration from Robert Huish, *The Last Voyage of Capt. Sir J. Ross… to the Arctic Regions in 1829–33* (1835). This image depicts the moment when Ross and his men were rescued by the *Isabella*. It was his miraculous deliverance after he was assumed to be dead that transformed Ross into a hero, not any progress he had made towards discovering the Northwest Passage.

16 Portrait of Sir John Franklin by an unknown artist (c. 1810). Franklin is depicted as a young naval officer, either during the Napoleonic Wars or at the beginning of his career as a polar explorer around 1820.

17 Stephen Pearce, *The Arctic Council Planning a Search for Sir John Franklin* (1851). The public's need to feel that serious efforts were being made to rescue Franklin was captured in Pearce's painting, which was commissioned by Sir John Barrow. It represented the 'Arctic Council' as a formal body that included ten of the most prominent Arctic explorers and government officials involved in the search. In reality, they probably never met as a group, but the painting's depiction of them with grave expressions as they pointed at maps and documents spread before them on a table helped to demonstrate that everything possible was being done. The work was made into an engraving that was dedicated to Lady Franklin and sold to the public.

MR HAMPTON'S FIRE BALLOON

PROPOSED AS AN AUXILIARY TO THE ARCTIC SEARCHING EXPEDITION.

18 and 19 Two of the numerous proposals for schemes to rescue Franklin (c. 1850). Above is 'Mr Hampton's Fire Balloon'; below is Stephen Stokes's proposal for a 'combination of kites, so as to lift a man to view the surrounding country'. Stokes claimed that his idea had the advantages of 'simplicity', 'trifling expense' and 'the distance the kites might be seen'. On the back of Stokes's letter was a scrawled note from an unidentified Admiralty official to the First Lord, Sir Francis Baring: 'Shall we ask him to fly a kite in the Admiralty's garden?' It is unclear whether this was meant seriously or sarcastically; the Admiralty was sufficiently desperate to find Franklin to try almost anything.

20 Poster relating to the search for Franklin (1848). The poster advertises the Admiralty's £20,000 reward for definitive information as to Franklin's fate.

21 Page from the *Illustrated London News* (1854). The image depicts some of the relics retrieved from the Inuit by John Rae.

22 Memorial by Sir Richard
Westmacott in the Painted Hall
of the Royal Naval College in
Greenwich (1858). The two figures
flanking a list of the names of the
dead provide a narrative of the
expedition's history. On the left, a
British naval officer studies a globe
and a map of the Arctic, planning
the expedition's route prior to
departure. On the right, a mitten-
wearing seaman hangs his head in
despair while pinnacles of ice tower
behind him. The monument thus
suggests that the harshness of the
Arctic environment had proved
insurmountable even for the
best-laid plans and most capable
explorers. This mitigated Franklin's
failure and made his men appear
all the more brave and resolute in
their willingness to take on such a
formidable challenge.

23 Monument to the 16th Lancers,
Canterbury Cathedral (1848). Edward
Richardson's monument shows a
dismounted Lancer offering water to
a wounded comrade who leans against
a palm tree. Though the inscription
records that it was in honour of all the
members of the regiment who died in
the Anglo-Sikh Wars, the name 'Aliwal'
is carved in large letters at the top. This
lithograph was printed by Leighton and
Taylor in 1850 and sold to the public.

24 and 25 The Charge of the 16th Lancers at Aliwal (1846). After Aliwal, numerous heroic images of the 16th Lancers charging into the Sikh square were sold to the public. William Spooner's depiction (above), which formed part of his series *War in the Punjab* (1846), was typical. It shows a single mounted soldier from the 16th Lancers surrounded by three Sikh warriors thrusting at him with their spears, thereby emphasizing how the British were outnumbered at Aliwal. The Sikhs are clad in colourful tunics and curly-toed shoes, marking them as exotic and alien foes. (In reality, the regular infantry of the Khalsa wore European-style red jackets and blue trousers.) Also dating from 1846, the military illustrator Henry Martens's depiction of the charge of the 16th Lancers (below) shows the British cavalry in a neat row bearing down upon the turbaned Sikh infantry. Other artists' works, including those by Charles Bilger Spalding (1849) and Michael Angelo Hayes (c. 1850), were also sold as lithographs and emphasized the heroism of the Lancers' impetuous charge.

26 and 27 The Charge of the 24th Foot at Chillianwallah (1849, 1860). Like that of the 16th Lancers at Aliwal, the 24th Foot's charge at Chillianwallah was celebrated in a number of contemporary images. Based on a drawing made during the battle by Lieutenant James Henry Archer of the 96th Regiment of Foot, a lithograph (above) issued by Rudolph Ackerman depicts the 24th Foot charging 'through jungle and water'. In 1860, an engraving by J. & F. Tallis (below) showed the colours of the 24th Foot being found on the battlefield afterwards, draped over the body of a dead soldier. The surrounding ground is littered with the remains of the battle, including dead Sikhs and horses, while the kneeling British soldier who found the colours looks up towards a mounted officer in reverence and sorrow.

28 and 29 Ensign Bethune Duncan Grant's images of Aliwal (1850). In the first watercolour (above), three men from the 16th Lancers spear a Sikh artilleryman with their lances, while another Sikh lies dead beneath the hooves of one of their horses. A third, apparently wounded Sikh cowers beneath a gun carriage as two of the Lancers prod him with their weapons. In the second image (below), Grant drew a Gurkha soldier from the Indian Army grasping a wounded Sikh by the hair and cutting his throat with his kukri, while a compatriot loots the corpse of a dead Punjabi soldier. Grant's depictions of the brutality perpetrated by the British and their Gurkha allies in the Anglo-Sikh War provide a stark contrast to the heroic images of Aliwal and Chillianwallah that were created by military artists and sold as engravings and lithographs to the British public.

galloped straight into a dry creek bed, which destroyed the order of their line. They then continued past the French infantry square and attacked the French cavalry with no infantry support. The 23rd lost almost half its strength.[4] Two years later, General William Carr Beresford sent his cavalry after the withdrawing French garrison at Campo Mayor. The 13th Light Dragoons initially captured sixteen guns, but were forced to abandon them when the French infantry arrived on the scene. The 13th lost around a quarter of its men. At Maguilla in 1812, the cavalry once again charged forward recklessly, pursuing the French for 8 miles (12.8 km) before encountering their reserve, by which point they were too exhausted to fight and retreated in a panic instead. The British commander, General John Slade, desperately resorted to offering any man who would stand with him £50. Slade later reported: 'Our misfortunes arose from too great eagerness and zeal in the pursuit, after having broke [*sic*] the enemy's first line, each regiment vying with each other who should most distinguish itself.'[5]

Things did not improve at Waterloo. After the initial infantry actions, the earl of Uxbridge ordered the Household and Union Brigades of heavy cavalry to charge in order to relieve the pressure on the British infantry. The Household Brigade crashed into the French cavalry, dispersing them and driving them into the British infantry, while the Union Brigade slammed into the French infantry, crushing them beneath the hooves of their horses and slashing them with their swords. Then the old bugbear of the cavalry – a loss of control and discipline – reappeared. They galloped after the fleeing French infantry, with their eyes on the main enemy battery of seventy guns, which stood on a ridge ahead of them. They managed to put over half the guns out of action, but then were met by counterattacking French cavalry. Uxbridge desperately sounded the retreat, but they had to fight their way through fresh infantry and cavalry to get back to the British lines. Exhausted and isolated, they were cut down in droves: the Union Brigade suffered 525 casualties out of 1,181 men, the Household Brigade 533 out of 1,226.[6]

Thanks to these escapades, cavalry soldiers in the first half of the nineteenth century were regarded as impetuous, foolhardy and unreliable. Moreover, by midcentury, the replacement of the musket by the rifle had made cavalry charges riskier and less effective. It is conventionally assumed that it was the introduction of the breech-loading repeating rifle and more powerful and accurate artillery that decreased the effectiveness of the cavalry charge by the end of the nineteenth century. Even so, the charge still had numerous proponents in the British military establishment, who developed new tactics that took into account the increased firepower of the infantry and artillery. In an age before mechanization, the cavalry served the vital purpose of making rapid movement possible.[7] It was not until the First World War that the age of the cavalry charge truly came to an end. One of the last charges in Western military history took place during the retreat from Mons in August 1914, when the 2nd Cavalry Brigade advanced against the German 1st Army in an attempt to protect the British Expeditionary Force's vulnerable left flank. The result was a swift rebuff and 250 casualties.[8]

Cavalry charges could thus still achieve impressive results on the battlefield in the late nineteenth century. This was particularly true in colonial theatres, where enemy forces were usually less well armed than their British counterparts. Not surprisingly, then, it was at the height of the empire that perceptions of the cavalry began to change. Whereas previously its failures had been blamed on impetuous soldiers who refused to follow orders and exercise restraint, now the cavalry came to be celebrated for its dash. A case in point occurred during the Anglo-Sikh Wars of the 1840s. In the first half of the nineteenth century, the Sikh state encompassed over 200,000 square miles (518,000 sq km), stretching from Tibet and Kashmir to Sindh and from the Khyber Pass to Nepal.[9] Ranjit Singh, the maharajah of the Punjab, knew that it was only a matter of time before the East India Company turned its attention towards his wealthy, fertile and strategically located realm. He thus began building a powerful army that at the time of his death in 1839 numbered over seventy thousand men.

Ranjit Singh's sons, however, proved to be weak-willed and inept, and as a result the military came to dominate the Punjab's political affairs. Desperate to regain their authority, the civil authorities sought British help. Their strategy was to provoke the Sikh military command, or Khalsa, into starting a war by convincing them that a British attack was inevitable, and then to limit the army's supplies and relay its plans to the enemy. In this way, the army would be destroyed, and the civil authorities would regain control over the Punjab. For its part, the East India Company was not particularly eager to fight a costly war against such a powerful enemy, but it was not particularly eager to avoid one, either. Sir Henry Hardinge, the governor general of India, was an ex-soldier who was not afraid to use military means to expand British power, while the commander-in-chief of the British military forces in India, Sir Hugh Gough, was an equally bellicose character.

In November 1845, the Sikh army crossed the River Sutlej, which had been established by a treaty in 1809 as the border between the Sikh state and the East India Company's territory. Company forces moved to meet it, and on 28 January 1846 the two armies clashed at the village of Aliwal. The Company's troops, under the command of Sir Harry Smith, quickly captured the village, but the Sikhs made a strong cavalry counterattack. Smith ordered two cavalry squadrons from the 16th Lancers and the 3rd Bengal Light Cavalry to repulse them. The Lancers quickly chased the Sikh cavalry from the field and galloped into an artillery battery, putting it out of action, but then failed to halt their advance and ran up against an infantry square that had formed to meet them. Knowing that to retreat at this point would expose the men to withering fire from the rear, the officers urged the cavalry onwards. Their horses leapt over the crouching men into the centre of the square, where they engaged in a fierce fight. Out of 598 casualties from the Company's forces at Aliwal, 245 were cavalry and 142 from the 16th Lancers. Fifty-nine of the 151 Company troops who were killed in the battle were from the regiment.[10]

In military terms, the charge of the 16th Lancers at Aliwal marked a return to the Napoleonic era's rash conduct of the cavalry. What had changed in the intervening decades, however, was the military and public perception of their actions, which were now viewed as heroic rather than impetuous. Hardinge's official dispatch to the British government in London stated: 'Her Majesty's 16th Lancers, on this occasion, have added to their former reputation acquired in various fields of battle in Asia, by routing the enemy's cavalry in every direction, and by resolute charges of two of its squadrons . . . penetrating the enemy's square of infantry.' Smith's dispatch, meanwhile, referred to the 16th's 'gallant and determined style'.[11] The charge at Aliwal came to be regarded as the most significant moment in the history of the 16th Lancers. (See Figure 23.) To this day, the regiment (now the Queen's Royal Lancers) crimps its lance pennons sixteen times to represent the way they became soaked with blood at Aliwal and then dried stiffly in the hot Indian sun. (See Figures 24 and 25.)

Two weeks after Aliwal, the East India Company won a victory at Sobraon that brought the First Sikh War to an end. Instead of annexing the Punjab, however, Hardinge opted to install a puppet government, under the nominal leadership of Duleep Singh, one of Ranjit Singh's sons, who was only eight years old at the time. But, in 1847, a rebellion broke out, and Company troops once again marched north. On 13 January 1849, Gough's army of twelve thousand men confronted thirty thousand Sikhs at the village of Chillianwallah. Although it was late in the day and his men were tired from a long march, Gough ordered an advance. For reasons that remain unclear, Brigadier General Colin Campbell ordered the 24th Foot, who were on the right side of the line, to use only their bayonets and not to fire as they moved forward.[12] To make matters worse, their supporting artillery battery had been moved to relieve pressure elsewhere in the line. The results were predictable. Private Henry Plumb later wrote to his siblings: 'when we first took up the charge they were pouring long shot and shell into our line, and as we neared this awful battery they poured grape into us . . . It was then that our fellows got mowed down in sections. Still gallantly on did the Brigade advance, closing as the poor fellows fell.'[13] Some men managed to reach the battery and begin spiking the guns, but they faced a barrage of musket fire from a Sikh infantry regiment that had been concealed by thick vegetation. The remnants of the 24th Foot 'retired in disorder', according to Private Plumb, and 'awful indeed was the slaughter'. The regiment lost over half its 1,050 men, with thirteen officers and 271 men killed and ten officers and 280 men wounded.[14]

The decimation of the 24th had been utterly unnecessary, the result of a misguided order rather than any military imperative. Lieutenant R. B. Smith described to a fellow officer of the Bengal Engineers, William Wilberforce Harris Greathed, the chaos that had ensued from Gough's tendency to improvise on the spot and his 'childish excitement' at the prospect of a battle:

> Experience caused me to 'hae ma doots' of the Chief's adhering to any plan when he was ... in action and I said the night before the battle that I was well satisfied that matters would be carried on, on the ordinary Goughian system. Accordingly we had not advanced above a few miles when our line of march was charged. We edged more to our left where the jungle was known to be dense, the attack on Rupool was abandoned and we arrived at Chillianwallah without any plan of action at all.

The guns in the centre of the line had been firing for only about 'half an hour' and those on the flanks had not yet 'fired a shot' when

> Campbell was ordered to advance his division direct upon the enemy's guns in his front and to take them. This he did, advancing with the smallest possible aid from the artillery with him as this had not had time to come into action and after the clearing the jungle he came upon the enemy line. When he did so, he was so roughly handled that his right brigade, consisting of H.M.'s 24 and 25th ... turned their backs and fled, pursued

by the Sikhs for a long distance, suffering frightfully and not rallying till they were behind Chillianwallah.

At the end of the battle:

> All the troops were ... withdrawn, our wounded were left on the field, more disabled guns (our own among the number) left on the ground than we could bring away in the dark, the prestige of victory (such as it was) lost ... Our total loss has been very heavy – 50 officers and 2400 men killed and wounded. ... In the 24th above 21 officers and about 500 men are killed and wounded. 13 officers of the regiment were buried the night before last in the same grave.[15]

For obvious reasons, Gough took a different line in his official dispatch to the government of India reporting on the battle at Chillianwallah and justifying the heavy casualties it had produced. He attributed the losses to an 'unhappy mistake' that had occurred when the men of the 24th had moved forward too quickly, causing them to leave behind their sepoy support and to arrive at the guns 'completely blown'. But he emphasized their heroism in withstanding heavy fire: 'In justice to this brigade, I must be allowed to state that they behaved heroically; and but for their too hasty, and consequently disorderly advance, would have emulated the conduct of the left brigade, which, left unsupported for a time, had to charge to their front and right, wherever an enemy appeared.'[16] Campbell, who found himself on the receiving end of criticism after Chillianwallah for his inexplicable order not to fire, took a similar view.[17] He blamed the 24th's heavy casualties on the fact that it had made 'an isolated attack, its flanks being unsupported', but praised the 'gallantry displayed in the assault'.[18] This became the standard line, and the 24th Foot's action at Chillianwallah was enshrined in British memory as an heroic failure. As had occurred with Aliwal, numerous visual representations were issued as engravings or lithographs. (See Figures 26 and 27.) And as had also occurred with Aliwal, the episode became enshrined in regimental memory. In 1853, a memorial, in the form of a stone obelisk inscribed with the names of the dead, was erected by the regiment in the garden of the Chelsea Royal Hospital in London.[19]

The two wars in the Punjab were brief but brutal affairs, with the bloodshed far greater on the Sikh side: the East India Company lost a total of 6,500 men, while the Sikhs lost nineteen thousand. At Aliwal alone, three thousand Sikhs died, twenty times the number of Company soldiers who perished. Aliwal and Chillianwallah were, in other words, not noble struggles between well-matched opponents but crushing defeats for the Sikhs and major steps towards the Company's annexation of the Punjab. This underlying reality was conveyed by Bethune Donald Grant, a nineteen-year-old ensign in the Bengal Army, who drew or painted in watercolour several scenes from Aliwal that depict bloody scenes of both British and Gurkha soldiers brutally slaughtering their Sikh foes.[20] In this context, the celebration of the heroic failure of the charges at Aliwal and Chillianwallah helped to conceal the reality of the military power that the East India Company had been able to wield over the Punjab. (See Figures 28 and 29.)

The Charge of the Light Brigade

Captain Soame Gambier Jenyns survived the Charge of the Light Brigade, the most famous heroic failure in British military history.

(See Figure 30.) Two years later, in 1856, he returned to his familial home, Bottisham Hall in Cambridgeshire. A large crowd cheered him as he rode into the village on his horse, Ben, another survivor of the charge. The parish priest observed: 'it must have been gratifying to our gallant friend to see the welcome accorded, while there was not a man, woman or child, but what turned out to do him honour'. In 1873, two years after he retired from the army, Jenyns died suddenly while out shooting on his father-in-law's estate in Shropshire. His funeral cortege in Bottisham featured a military band and a column of Hussars; Ben, now twenty-five years old, was led behind the coffin. Hundreds of people packed the church and the surrounding streets; after the coffin was placed in the family vault, three volleys were fired by a rifle team, followed by a trumpet flourish.[21] A memorial was later installed in the chancel of Bottisham church that referred to Jenyns as a survivor of the Charge of the Light Brigade.

Jenyns's example illustrates how the Charge of the Light Brigade was enshrined as an heroic failure. The survivors became celebrities who were fêted at annual banquets and, as the decades passed, were given lavish public funerals. This was despite the fact that the charge was a disaster that had resulted from a string of errors and misunderstandings in the British chain of command.[22] It had occurred during the Crimean War, which resulted from conflicts among the European powers as they grappled with the long, slow decline of the Ottoman Empire. For their part, the British saw the war as necessary to ensure that Russian expansionism did not threaten the route to India. In the autumn of 1854, 27,000 British, thirty thousand French and seven thousand Turkish troops invaded the Crimean Peninsula, with their primary target the Russian naval base at Sebastopol. British forces included a division of cavalry, split into a Heavy and a Light Brigade. Traditionally, light cavalry (smaller men and horses) had been used to carry out reconnaissance work, while heavy cavalry (bigger men and horses) were used to overwhelm the enemy in battle. But in the decades after Waterloo, the army had shrunk from 250,000 men to 110,000, and such specialization was no longer possible. The two types of cavalry were thus now used almost interchangeably.

In the 1850s, cavalry officers continued to be predominantly men from elite backgrounds who had purchased their commissions and promotions. Lord Lucan, who commanded the cavalry at Balaclava, had joined the army the year after Waterloo and had spent much of his career on half-pay, as many wealthy officers did to avoid being sent to colonial theatres. Through purchase he had risen from being a sixteen-year-old ensign in 1816 to the rank of lieutenant colonel only ten years later. He had been promoted to major general in 1851, even though he had not been on active service for fourteen years.[23] In command of the Light Brigade, meanwhile, was the 7th earl of Cardigan, who, like Lucan, had had no battlefield experience. He, too, had been promoted through purchase, rising from cornet to the lieutenant colonelcy of the 15th Hussars in only eight years between 1824 and 1832. Four years later, he paid £40,000 for the more prestigious lieutenant colonelcy of the 11th Hussars.

Cardigan was Lucan's brother-in-law – Lucan was married to his sister Ann – but in this case the familial connection bred enmity rather than accord. Lady Lucan had complained to her brother that her husband mistreated her, which chilled relations between the two men. Just prior to their departure for the Crimea, Lady Lucan had left her husband, increasing the animosity between them even further. 'They do not speak,' wrote Lieutenant Colonel Edward Hodge of the Heavy Brigade. 'How this will answer on service I do not know.'[24] Such squabbles among the British commanders were deemed unimportant, however, as the army expected to take Sebastopol in a matter of weeks. Confidence was further boosted by the first confrontation with the Russians, at the Battle of Alma, which resulted in an emphatic British and French victory.

Next, the British turned their attention to Balaclava, a fishing village 6 miles (9.6 km) from Sebastopol that possessed a deep, sheltered harbour in which the fleet could land the army's supplies prior to the attack on the Russian base itself. The British seized the village without opposition, but the Russians soon mounted a counterattack. On 25 October, the Russian commander, Prince Alexander Menshikov, ordered an infantry advance of thirty thousand men. The six hundred Turkish militia who manned the poorly constructed redoubts that defended the British position were quickly overwhelmed. All that now stood between the Russians and Balaclava was a 'thin red line' of 93rd Highlanders, who withstood the Russian charge, thereby passing into British military legend, though their victory did not become nearly as famous as the Light Brigade's defeat shortly afterwards. The Heavy Brigade then charged the Russian cavalry, pushing them back despite the fact that they were outnumbered nearly three to one and were fighting uphill.

With the initial Russian attack blunted, Lord Raglan endeavoured to retake the redoubts before the Russians could regroup. He wanted to use General Sir George Cathcart's infantry division for this purpose, but they had not yet arrived on the battlefield. He thus opted to send the Light Brigade forward without infantry support. This was in direct contradiction of standard military practice, but he assumed that the Russians were in such disarray that the redoubts could be occupied quickly. Lucan, however, interpreted Raglan's order as meaning he should advance only after the infantry arrived, so he kept the Light Brigade waiting at the entrance to the northernmost of the two valleys that formed the battlefield's terrain. Viewing the scene from the heights above the battlefield, Raglan could not understand why Lucan was not advancing as ordered. When he heard a report that the Russians were dragging away the British guns from the redoubts, his impatience boiled over. (Losing a gun was considered a severe embarrassment for a British general; Wellington was famous for never having done so.) At 10:45 a.m., Raglan issued what became the most infamous order in British military history: 'Lord Raglan wishes the Cavalry to advance rapidly to the front – follow the Enemy and try to prevent the Enemy carrying away the guns.'

Fifteen minutes later, the order was pressed into Lucan's hands by Captain Louis Nolan, aide-de-camp to General Richard Airey, Raglan's second-in-command. Lucan was unclear what it meant. Most military historians believe that the Russians were not attempting to take away the guns from the redoubts, and in any event Lucan would not have been able to see them from his position even if they had been. Nor could he see any enemy retreating that he could 'follow'. He asked Nolan for clarification. Nolan told him that he should 'attack immediately'. When Lucan asked what precisely he should attack, several witnesses later claimed that Nolan gestured with his arm towards the end of the valley. Lucan was astonished that Raglan would issue such an order. To launch a cavalry charge of well over a mile without infantry support down a valley that was defended to the front and on both sides by artillery was suicidal. But instead of sending Nolan back to Raglan for further clarification, Lucan rode over to Cardigan and ordered him to attack the battery at the far end of the valley. The astounded Cardigan protested on the grounds that 'there is a battery in front, a battery on each flank, and the ground is covered in Russian riflemen'.[25] Lucan acknowledged this, but confirmed that the order had come directly from Raglan.

When the trumpet call for the advance came, even the lowest-ranking private could see that a mistake had been made somewhere in the chain of command. They had proceeded between 100 and 200 yards (90–180 m) when the Russian guns on the sides of the valley opened up and shells began tearing gaps in the line. Some of the men tried to quicken the pace, but Cardigan kept them steady. Because the distance that had to be covered was so great, the Light Brigade had to move forward slowly, at a rate of about 4 miles (6.4 km) an hour, down most of the length of the valley, only increasing the pace to a full gallop for the last 250 yards (228 m).[26] This meant that it took about seven minutes to reach the Russian battery. Fewer than half of the British troops who had started in the front line made it to the battery, while the second line no longer existed in any meaningful form.

The Charge of the Light Brigade had taken barely twenty minutes from start to finish. The participants were unaware that they had just been part of what would become one of the most famous military events in British history. Many of them did feel, however, that something extraordinary had occurred. Captain Jenyns declared: 'never was such murder ordered'.[27]

George Goad, a cornet in the 13th Light Dragoons, described the charge as 'the most terrible thing you can conceive'.[28] Lieutenant Fiennes Wykeham Martin of the 4th Dragoons wrote to his brother:

> My Regiment is cut up and the rest of the Light Brigade are completely annihilated owing to a mistake in the orders. We charged for about a mile and a quarter down a valley flanked on both sides with artillery and infantry and with a tremendous force of cavalry at the bottom. They bowled us over right and left with grape shot, balls and round shot. Of 700 men who went into action only 190 came out and all for no good as we were not backed up. We have twice heard from a Russian officer who was taken prisoner, that our little Brigade charged 20,000 – rather long odds![29]

Captain Arthur Tremayne of the 13th Light Dragoons, whose horse had been shot from under him as he reached the Russian guns, wrote to his family that the charge had been 'the most tremendous cavalry action ever recorded'. Tremayne was well aware that the order had been a blunder: 'It was seen by all to be madness, unsupported by guns, or infantry ... I am sincerely grateful to God for my preservation ... and though one is always more or less in a dangerous position in war, no danger can be greater than that I have escaped.'[30] A week later, on 3 November, he added: 'All agree in saying that there must have been some mistake in the order, as no such cavalry attack is on record.'[31] The men recognized the significance of what had occurred as much as did the officers. 'Thank God I escaped that dreadful massacre ...,' wrote Henry Gregory of the 13th Light Dragoons to his sister.

'A more dreadful sight I never saw, for our poor men was [*sic*] actually mowed down by dozens … The ground was actually strewed with dead men and horses, and men and horses running about in all directions, it was a horrible sight for any human being to witness.'[32]

There have been plenty of battles in which generals have sacrificed large numbers of men to achieve victory. In these cases, the heavy losses are accepted as the cost of war. The Light Brigade's casualty rate of around 40 per cent was certainly high, but it was lower than that of other famous charges, including Pickett's Charge at the Battle of Gettysburg during the American Civil War in 1863, in which over half the participants on the Confederate side were killed or wounded. In fact, given the foolhardiness of the advance of unsupported cavalry against well-placed artillery, the casualties at Balaclava were remarkably *low*.[33] But it was the utter futility of the charge that made it so famous. If it had succeeded, or had it even been possible for it succeed, it would not occupy the prominent place in British memory that it quickly came to take up. Alone among the examples of charges cited in this chapter, it had no military purpose whatsoever. It was caused by a series of blunders, mistakes and misunderstandings so numerous that historians still fiercely debate which one was the most significant.

The futility of the Charge of the Light Brigade was comprehended immediately, and was highlighted by the two most widely read accounts. The first was provided by William Howard Russell, the war correspondent of *The Times*, who watched the charge alongside Lord Raglan.[34] Russell's first report of Balaclava reached Britain on 14 November 1854, less than three weeks after the battle. It emphasized the pointlessness of the charge:

As they passed towards the front, the Russians opened on them from the guns in the redoubt on the right, with volleys of musketry and rifles. They swept proudly past, glittering in the morning sun in all the pride and splendour of war. We could scarcely believe the evidence of our senses! Surely that handful of men are not going to charge an army in position? Alas! it was but too true – their desperate valour knew no bounds, and far indeed was it removed from its so-called better part – discretion.[35]

The second account was Alfred Tennyson's 'The Charge of the Light Brigade', one of the best-known poems in the English language, which was based on Russell's account. Tennyson later claimed to have been so inspired after reading it that he wrote the poem in a few minutes. It was first published in the *Examiner* on 9 December. Tennyson attributed the blame for the charge to an anonymous 'someone' who had 'blundered', while the men of the Light Brigade were identified only as 'the six hundred':

> Theirs not to make reply,
> Theirs not to reason why,
> Theirs but to do and die.[36]

The way of presenting the charge espoused by Russell and Tennyson soon became the prevailing mode, shifting it from a military disaster to an episode whose very pointlessness made it something uniquely noble. In 1855, an anonymous publication satirized Russell's role through a series of cartoon-like depictions of the activities of 'our own correspondent' in the Crimea. In one scene, the correspondent 'becomes frantic with enthusiasm at beholding the splendid charge of cavalry at Balaclava', thereby simultaneously poking fun at and acknowledging the public's near-reverential view of the charge.[37]

Visual as well as verbal representations played a key role in enshrining the Charge of the Light Brigade in heroic myth. Though he did not arrive in the Crimea until mid-November, three weeks after the event, the Scottish artist William Simpson included a watercolour of it among the dozens of paintings he sent back to be made into engravings by the London art dealers Colnaghi. (See Figure 31.) The engravings were first exhibited at the Graphic Society in 1855, and eighty of them were published in a volume entitled *The Seat of War in the East* later that year. Their popularity was such that a selection was issued in a smaller octavo volume, with an introduction by the military historian George Brackenbury. Brackenbury demonstrated that Tennyson's version of the Charge of the Light Brigade had by this point taken firm hold: 'The Light Cavalry was ordered to advance, without supports, over a plain of nearly a mile and a half in length, and exposed to a crushing fire of artillery and musketry in front and on both flanks. Without a murmur or a moment's hesitation these lion-hearts rushed on to the discharge of the fearful duty assigned to them; resolved, since the ordinary alternative of death *or* glory was denied, to do *and* die.' (Italics in original.) He concluded: 'The Light Cavalry charge was over; a glorious and ineffaceable page has been added to the records of chivalry, and to the annals of England.'[38]

The ensuing decades would see the appearance of a multitude of visual depictions of the charge. In general, the visual representation of warfare during the Crimean War moved away from the traditional emphasis on the heroism of elite officers and towards scenes featuring the common soldier. A particular focus was camp life during the devastating winter of 1854–55.[39] As the *Athenaeum* declared in its review of Simpson's paintings:

> All looked with painful interest at views of the spots . . . where the flower of England, unscathed by fire, unsmitten and unhurt, rotted away, with their faces turned towards England. For them, there will be no victory, no rejoicing – for them, no open arms and happy faces, no flags waving or jubilee of bells – but in their stead, cold, narrow graves, in an enemy's country, on a spot perhaps to be blasted by a great nation's greatest and most terrible disgrace.[40]

In this context, the Charge of the Light Brigade was useful for confirming this perception of the inept commanders who had needlessly squandered the lives of their men, while at the same time emphasizing the heroism of the common soldiers.

The Crimean War did not, however, lead to the complete eradication of conventional forms for depicting heroism in battle. Instead, the older and newer visions of military heroism existed side by side. To be sure, there was much criticism of the elite commanders whose errors had led to the Charge of the Light Brigade. The war is often given credit for engendering the drive for military reform that culminated in the Cardwell reforms of the early 1870s, which abolished the sale of commissions and made promotion contingent on merit and experience rather than birth and wealth. But those reforms were not enacted for another fifteen years; in the intervening period, a fierce debate raged both within the political and military establishment and among the public at large as to whether the old, aristocratically based system was really so terrible. In a speech to the House of Lords in 1856, for example, the prime minister, Lord Palmerston, interpreted the Charge of the Light Brigade as confirming, rather than undermining, the value of aristocratic leadership on the battlefield:

> Talk to me of the aristocracy of England! Why, look to that glorious charge of the cavalry at Balaclava – look to that charge, where the noblest and wealthiest of the land rode foremost, followed by heroic men from the lowest classes of the community, each rivalling the other in bravery, neither the peer who led nor the trooper who followed being distinguished the one from the other. In that glorious band there were sons of the gentry of England; leading were the noblest in the land, and following were the representatives of the people of this country.[41]

Contemporary accounts of the Charge of the Light Brigade reflected this tension as to whether oligarchy or meritocracy represented the best path forward for the British Army. Certainly, there was ample criticism of some aristocratic commanders: there was no danger that either Raglan or Lucan would emerge from the Crimea as a hero. But Lord Cardigan was a different matter: he was seen not only as blameless – he had questioned Raglan's order appropriately and then followed it when Lucan insisted that he must – but also as heroic. (See Figure 32.) When asked how Cardigan had behaved in the charge, Captain William Morris of the 17th Hussars, another hero of the charge who will be discussed below, replied: 'He led like a gentleman.'[42] Stories flew around the British camp that Cardigan's horse had leapt over the Russian guns at the end of the valley as if he were fox-hunting. Even his bitter enemy Lucan had to concede that Cardigan 'led this attack in the most gallant and intrepid manner'.[43]

Deteriorating health led to Cardigan's departure from the Crimea in December 1854. When he landed at Folkestone on 13 January 1855, he was greeted by a cheering crowd and a brass band playing Handel's 'See, the Conquering Hero Comes!' All along the route of his train journey to London, people gathered to watch him pass, despite bitterly cold winter temperatures, and every station was bedecked with bunting. His portrait and prints of his horse leaping over the Russian guns were sold all over the country. He was, as a popular music-hall song extolled him, 'Cardigan the Brave'; even *Punch* temporarily abandoned satire to show him charging at the Russian cannon. The 'Cardigan jacket', patterned after the woollen garment he had worn during the Crimean winter, became a popular fashion.[44] Both Houses of Parliament offered their official gratitude, and he was invited to dine with Queen Victoria at Windsor, where the next morning he regaled the royal children with the story of the Charge of the Light Brigade. In February, a banquet was given in his honour at Mansion House by the Lord Mayor of London. He paraded to the event through the capital's streets in his full-dress uniform, riding Ronald, the horse that had carried him during the charge – the crowds were so eager to obtain a souvenir that they plucked hairs from the latter's tail and mane.[45] In the pamphlet *Our Heroes of the Crimea* (1855), the journalist George Ryan wrote: 'It may be said without fear of contradiction, that the Earl of Cardigan is now the most popular soldier in England. As a gallant chevalier he won his golden spurs in a tilt with giants. All salute him as the lion of the British Army; and a clasp to the Crimean medal will tell how he led heroes to fight on that bloody field, which gives to the world an example of devoted valour unequalled in warfare.'[46]

Another hero to emerge from the Charge of the Light Brigade was Captain Louis Nolan, who prior to the Crimean War had a reputation as a skilled trainer of cavalry soldiers and horses and had authored two books on cavalry tactics. Although his regiment, the 13th Light Dragoons, was not sent to the Crimea, he was detached from it and placed on the staff of Brigadier General Airey so that he could help with the acquisition, transport and management of the horses for the cavalry division. After delivering the fateful order to Lucan, Nolan decided to ride forward in the Charge of the Light Brigade. It proved a fatal choice: most eyewitness accounts cite him as the first man killed, after a shell fragment struck him with full force in the chest.[47] Once the recriminations began, Nolan was an obvious potential scapegoat, as he had not only delivered the infamous order to Lucan but had also possibly conveyed to him an erroneous sense of its meaning. Lucan, certainly, found it expedient to blame Nolan. In a letter published in *The Times* in March 1855, he claimed:

> After carefully reading this order I hesitated, and urged the uselessness of such an attack and the dangers surrounding it. The aide-de-camp, in a most authoritative tone, stated that they were Lord Raglan's orders that the cavalry should attack immediately. I asked him, 'Where, and what to do?' as neither enemy nor guns were within sight. He replied, in a most disrespectful but significant manner, pointing to the further end of the valley, 'There, my Lord, is your enemy; there are your guns'.[48]

But although Lucan hinted that Nolan's conduct had bordered on insubordination, he could not assign him all of the blame for the debacle, for by doing so it would have appeared that he had been unwilling to stand up to a junior officer. Indeed, the *Morning Chronicle* wondered how such a relatively low-ranking officer could have been responsible for such a massive disaster: 'What baffles the understanding is, in what respect Captain Nolan, whose position was merely that of an aide-de-camp, should thus have proved the unwitting instrument of the Light Brigade's destruction.'[49]

For that reason, few people saw Nolan as the primary culprit for the fiasco. Instead, he was often depicted as a martyred hero. (See Figure 33.) His friends and admirers collected funds for a memorial, which was installed on the wall of Holy Trinity Church in Maidstone in Kent, where the depot for cavalry regiments serving in India was located. Each year, the Balaclava Commemoration Society held an annual dinner for veterans of the battle. In 1875, it was accompanied by a 'Balaclava Festival' in the central hall of Alexandra Palace. The centrepiece of the exhibition was an obelisk topped by a figure representing Honour and surrounded at the base by 'relics of the engagement'. The obelisk listed the names of the seven officers who had been killed, with Nolan's centrally positioned and in larger lettering.[50]

A third individual who emerged from the Charge of the Light Brigade as a hero was Captain William Morris of the 17th Lancers. In March 1854, Morris was made deputy assistant quartermaster general of the forces that were being assembled for the upcoming Crimean campaign. This meant that, like Nolan, he served under General Airey, the quartermaster general. Still recovering from a serious bout of cholera, Morris arrived at Balaclava only days before the debacle. The senior officer of the 17th Lancers, Colonel John Lawrenson, was on leave, and his second-in-command, Major Augustus Willett, had died of cholera on 22 October.

Despite his weakened state, Morris stepped in and took command of his old regiment on the day of the battle. When the Heavy Brigade charged in support of the 93rd Highlanders, Morris tried to lead the 17th forward to take advantage of the disarray of the Russians, but he was sharply rebuked by Cardigan. Several witnesses reported that Morris was furious at not being allowed to advance and, slapping his leg with his sword, said as he rode away from Cardigan: 'My God, my God, what a chance we are losing.'[51] His wish for action was shortly to be granted. The Light Brigade was waiting at the entrance to the valley when Nolan, who knew Morris from Airey's staff, galloped up carrying Raglan's order. Nolan asked Morris where he could find Lucan. Morris pointed him out, then asked: 'What is it to be, Nolan? Are we going to charge?' As he spurred his horse towards Lucan, Nolan shouted back over his shoulder: 'You will see. You will see.'[52]

After relaying the order to Lucan, Nolan rode back to Morris and asked him permission to ride with his regiment, which Morris readily granted. Unlike Nolan, Morris survived the long ride down the valley. When he reached the Russian battery, he was accompanied by about twenty men, who charged the enemy cavalry positioned behind the guns. Seeing a high-ranking officer, Morris thrust his sword into the man's body up to the hilt. He was then unable to extricate his blade, however, and as the man fell from his horse Morris was dismounted as well. He was still struggling to reclaim his sword when he received a severe blow to the head from a Russian sabre. He blacked out for a moment; when he recovered, he found that his sword had somehow come free, but he was now surrounded by Cossacks, one of whom delivered another head wound courtesy of his lance. The episode was witnessed by Sergeant Major Abraham Ransom:

Then I saw an act of heroism; [Captain] Morris was on foot, his head streaming with blood, engaging five or six Cossacks ... Morris sought to defend himself by the almost ceaseless 'moulinet' or circling whirl of his sword and from time to time he found means to deliver some sabre cuts upon the thighs of his Cossack assailants. Soon, however, he was pierced in the temple by a lance-point, which splintered up a piece of bone and forced it under the scalp.[53]

Morris was saved by the arrival of a Russian officer, who intervened to prevent the Cossacks from finishing him off. He surrendered his sword, but as more British troops arrived behind the guns the Russians found themselves with more pressing business. His head bleeding profusely, Morris tried to mount a riderless horse, but could only manage to grab the saddle. He was dragged along until his dwindling strength caused him to lose his grip. As a Cossack approached, he desperately lunged for a second horse and struggled into the saddle. The horse was shot from under him as he attempted to ride back to the British lines; pinned beneath on the ground, he lost consciousness temporarily. After he awoke, he began limping down the valley on foot. He was almost back to the British lines when he saw the body of his friend Nolan and collapsed beside it. He was found there by Captain John Ewart, who sent word back that an officer required aid, and shortly thereafter Surgeon James Mouat and Sergeant Charles Wooden arrived on the scene. Both would later be awarded the Victoria Cross for saving Morris, as they were forced to fight off several Cossacks when carrying him to safety.

Morris's injuries included two severe cuts to the head, a broken right arm from a sabre blow and a broken rib on his lower left side.

After two months in the military hospital at Scutari, he returned home to convalesce in January 1855 and was invited to dinner by Queen Victoria. By June, however, he was back in the Crimea, where he was a figure of renown. Captain Henry Clifford of the Rifle Brigade reported to his family:

> I saw a Capt. Morris yesterday, you have perhaps seen his name in the papers. He behaved most splendidly in the unfortunate charge at Balaclava, and was badly wounded in the head with a sabre cut, had three ribs broken and side very much torn, with a thrust from a lance and his right arm cut to the bone by a sword. No one thought he would live, but he is well enough to walk about now, tho' looking very ill and after spending a few months in England has come out here again.[54]

That same year, he was promoted to major and made a Knight Commander of the Order of the Bath. He was also made a Chevalier of the Légion d'Honneur by the French. In his native Devon, Morris became a local hero. In 1856, he was honoured by a banquet at the Globe Hotel in Great Torrington, near his birthplace of Hatherleigh. The ceremony was presided over by Sir Trevor Wheler, a veteran of Waterloo, who declared that they were gathered

> to congratulate that gallant officer on his safe return to his native shores and are desirous of placing on record the deep sense we entertain of the zeal and gallantry he has shown on all occasions when his services have been required by the country . . . I do sincerely believe that if the British cavalry had to give this sword to one of their officers more deserving than another,

though there might be great difficulty in making their selection, their unanimous verdict would be 'Give it to Colonel Morris, the bravest of the brave.'[55]

The local poet Edward Capern composed fulsome verses in his honour:

Hail to thee! Hail to thee! Champion of Liberty!
Fresh from the field of his struggle and pain,
Hail to thee, hail to thee, bold son of chivalry,
Hail to the land of the Hero again.

Capern's poem displayed the key component of heroic failure in the mid-Victorian era: the link between 'chivalry' and 'struggle and pain'. Suffering was heroic and noble, even, or perhaps especially, if it occurred in a context of futility. Morris's response to the adulation, meanwhile, embodied perfectly the ideal of the self-sacrificing hero who accepted his suffering as being all in a day's work: 'I have been promoted and rewarded by Her Majesty for my services, while other men more deserving than myself have either lost their lives or owing to unfortunate circumstances have gained nothing.'[56]

After the Crimea, Morris returned to his regiment and was sent to India in 1857 to help quell the rebellion that had broken out earlier that year. The following year, while stationed at Poona in the Bombay Presidency, he died of dysentery. His fellow officers collected funds for a memorial tablet, which was installed in the church at Poona. It referred to the Charge of the Light Brigade only obliquely by listing the battles in which Morris had fought, including Balaclava. Back home, however, his role in the charge was the focal point of memorial efforts. In 1860, a 60-foot-high (18 m) granite obelisk was erected on Hatherleigh Moor. A bas-relief on the base by E. B. Stephens showed his limp body being carried from the battlefield, with the single word 'Balaclava' inscribed beneath. It was an odd depiction of a soldier: Morris was wounded to the point of helplessness in what was presented as the most noteworthy moment of his career. But it was in keeping with contemporary notions of heroic failure, in which heroism was defined more by suffering in defeat than by any action undertaken in victory.

CHAPTER FOUR

DAVID LIVINGSTONE

B ETWEEN 1870 AND 1900, the British Empire added over 5 million square miles (13 million sq km) of territory, a faster rate of expansion than in any other period. For most Britons, assumptions of the essentialness of the empire to the nation's economic health, coupled with fears that territory would be claimed by a rival if it was not claimed by them first, ensured strong support for imperial expansion. At the same time, however, voices of dissent expressed discomfort with the idea of Britain as such an aggressively imperialist nation. A small but influential cadre of staunch anti-imperialists stood against the prevailing tide and offered a variety of arguments, both moral and pragmatic, against the expansionist imperative.[1] More mainstream 'liberal imperialists', meanwhile, wished for expansion to continue, but for it to be instilled with a moral purpose that would overlie sheer military might. In this context, it was imperative to create narratives of empire that highlighted the moments in which the British could be viewed as nobly sacrificing themselves as part of their broader effort to bring morality, justice and spiritual enlightenment to the 'dark places' of the world.

It was the expansion of the empire in Africa that created the greatest need for these narratives, as it entailed the conquest and domination of large non-white populations. There was no way, in other words, to pretend that Africa was an empty land awaiting European exploitation. Driven by two motives that were not particularly attractive – profit and international competition – the colonization of Africa represented imperialism in its most naked form. In consequence, it required elaborate justifications to transform it from something blatantly mercenary and nationally self-aggrandizing into something noble and heroic. This is where imperial heroes came in.[2] They helped Britons to minimize in their conceptions of empire the brutality, violence and coercion that the colonization of Africa entailed and in their place to emphasize idealism, morality, piety and duty. Victorian Britain's greatest African hero, David Livingstone, was a failed missionary turned explorer who died while looking for the source of the Nile in the wrong place. It was his very lack of readily definable accomplishments, however, that made it possible to transform him into the personification of the ideals of the empire, rather than of its harsh realities.

The Ideal Explorer-Hero

In 1865, during his last trip to Britain, David Livingstone met Lady Jane Franklin. At the time, he was Britain's most famous explorer, and was about to embark upon a search for the source of the River Nile that would consume the final seven years of his life. (Sir Roderick Murchison, who as president of the Royal Geographical Society in the early 1850s had led the calls for search expeditions to rescue Franklin, would soon be calling for expeditions to rescue Livingstone.) Later, Livingstone made a connection between his own and Franklin's enterprises. Writing from Ujiji on the eastern shore of Lake Tanganyika in November 1868, he observed: 'The discovery of the sources of the Nile is somewhat akin in importance to the discovery of the Northwest Passage, which called forth ... the energy, perseverance and the pluck of the Englishman. And anything that does that is beneficial to the nation and its posterity.'[3] Here, Livingstone acknowledged that his work, like Franklin's, was defined as an heroic endeavour less for its practical utility and more for the fortitude and determination that it demanded. Like Franklin, Livingstone failed in his most important objectives, which in his case were to spread Christianity in Africa and to locate the source of the Nile.[4] But that did not matter. For, also like Franklin, he came to be more important for the values that he represented than the things that he accomplished.[5]

In Livingstone's case, those values were embodied not only by his career as an explorer but also by his life story, which featured numerous elements that were easily mythologized. Born in impoverished circumstances in 1813 in Blantyre in Lanarkshire, he went to work in a cotton mill at age ten. (See Figure 34.) After a twelve-hour day spent in sweltering heat crawling around dangerous machinery, he attended school for two hours each evening. Then, back home in the single-room tenement that he shared with his parents and four siblings, he read until his mother forced him to blow out the candle. He struggled to reconcile his love of science and his father's strict Presbyterian religious beliefs until, at the age of nineteen, he read Thomas Dick's *The Philosophy of a Future State* (1829), which convinced him that there was no contradiction between science and Christianity. This reconciliation of his intellectual interests and religious beliefs helped Livingstone to conceive the idea of becoming a medical missionary. At age nineteen, he was promoted to spinner, and he began saving his increased wages to pay the fees for the medical school at Andersonian University in Glasgow, where he enrolled in 1836. Two years later, he was accepted for training as a missionary to China by the London Missionary Society, but when the Opium War broke out, Livingstone was forced to come up with a new plan and determined to go to Africa instead.

After taking his medical degree in November 1840 and being ordained as a Nonconformist minister, Livingstone arrived in Cape Town in March 1841. Having married the daughter of his fellow missionary Robert Moffat, he established a mission station, first at Chonwane, which he had to abandon due to a lack of water, and then further north at Kolobeng. There he converted Sechele, chief of the local Kwena, but the latter's new-found faith lasted only six months. Sechele was the first and last convert he ever made. Sechele's lapse gave Livingstone serious doubts about the efficacy of the preaching of the gospel as a missionary strategy. Instead, he began travelling into the interior of Africa with the goal of opening it up to European traders and missionaries, in whose wake he believed Christianity would inevitably follow. In 1852, he set out to cross the African continent from west to east, in search of a malaria-free zone that could serve as a site for a missionary station. Beginning in Linyanti in what is now Zambia, he travelled 1,200 miles (1,920 km) west to Luanda (today the capital of Angola) on the Atlantic coast, reaching it in April 1854. Severely debilitated after suffering over two dozen bouts of fever, he was too weak even to write his own letters for two months. After recovering, he returned to Linyanti in order to continue his journey eastwards to the Indian Ocean. Setting off in November

1855, he soon discovered what the local peoples called Mosioatunya ('the smoke that thunders'), an immense waterfall that he renamed Victoria Falls in honour of his sovereign. To the east lay the elevated, cool, fertile Batoka Plateau, which he thought would make an excellent location for a missionary station.

In May 1856, Livingstone arrived at Quelimane in what is today Mozambique. From his starting point in Cape Town, he had travelled 5,000 miles (8,000 km) and had accomplished the first crossing of sub-Saharan Africa by a European. In Britain, he was lionized as a hero, and crowds mobbed him in the street. He received a gold medal from the Royal Geographical Society, an honorary doctorate from Oxford and a private audience with Queen Victoria. To commemorate his being given the freedom of the City of London, the Lord Mayor, Sir Robert Carden, presented him with a wooden casket decorated with silver embellishments. (See Figure 35.) On the top, a three-dimensional figure of Livingstone shakes hands with an African chief under a palm tree. More palm trees decorate the corners, while silver panels on the sides depict a globe, navigational instruments and African scenes. A spectacular and expensive object, it shows the level of fame and heroism to which Livingstone had ascended.

But what exactly had he done? The globe and navigational instruments hinted at some sort of geographical accomplishment, but the main scene showed Livingstone greeting an African by shaking hands, an indication of equality between the white man and his black counterpart. For many Britons, it would have recalled the famous 'Am I Not a Man and a Brother?' medallion created by Josiah Wedgwood during the campaign for the abolition of the slave trade in the late eighteenth century. It thus alluded to Livingstone's efforts to end the ongoing slave trade in Africa, and cast him in a moral light. In any practical sense, however, Livingstone's journey had been a failure. He had set off to prove that the Zambesi could be used as a highway for commerce and missionary activity into the interior of Africa. It was, in fact, useless for this purpose. In order for a mission station or trading post on the Batoka Plateau to be viable, it had to be reachable via the Zambesi from the east coast, but the Kebrabasa Rapids, which would be discovered two years later, made such a voyage impossible.[6] The precise details or achievements of his transcontinental trek were unimportant, however; instead, it was Livingstone's determination and diligence that registered most with his contemporaries in Britain. The Lord Mayor of London praised his 'zealous and persevering exertions', while the Glasgow Town Council expressed their regard for his 'undaunted intrepidity and fortitude, amid difficulties, privations and dangers'. The United Presbyterian Church of Glasgow declared that Livingstone had exhibited 'an amount of energy and intrepidity' that placed him in 'the very van of bold and enterprising spirits'; nothing had 'daunted' him, 'not forest nor swamps, not flooded plains nor rapid rivers, not burning fevers nor savage man'.[7]

Livingstone's account of his journey, entitled *Missionary Travels and Researches in South Africa* (1857), sold an astonishing seventy thousand copies. It not only defined Livingstone in the eyes of the Victorian public, but also southern Africa.[8] The interior of Africa had already been reshaped in the British imagination by Mungo Park, Hugh Clapperton and others from a site of curiosity to one of geographical discovery and scientific research, but Livingstone now refashioned it into a place that Britons were duty-bound to improve and transform.[9] Now, any attempt to assist Africa and its peoples was inherently heroic, even if it failed, since it was inherently a selfless effort to benefit humanity.

Livingstone became a hero in Britain in 1857, the same year in which a bloody and violent rebellion erupted against British rule in India. His missionary activities in Africa provided a counterweight to what had occurred in the subcontinent, which some Britons saw as divine retribution for an empire that had come to be based on commercial profit rather than on the religious salvation of its subjects. Livingstone sympathized with this view. When he spoke in Cambridge University's Senate House, he declared: 'I consider we made a great mistake when we carried commerce into India, in being ashamed of our Christianity ... Those two pioneers of civilisation – Christianity and commerce – should ever be inseparable; and Englishmen should be warned by the fruits of neglecting that principle as exemplified in the management of Indian affairs.'[10] At a time when the Indian population had made it clear that they did not view the British as their benefactors, and when many Britons had been deeply shaken by the force and scale of the rebellion, Livingstone provided reassurance that the empire could still be a morally and spiritually uplifting enterprise.

He knew better, of course: he had seen first-hand what Europeans had done to Africa with their insatiable desire for gold, ivory and slaves. But he was able to convince himself, and his fellow Britons, that somehow it would be different in the future. His grand schemes for the colonization and development of central Africa, however, were beyond the limited capacities of missionary societies; they required the backing of the British government. He thus left the employ of the London Missionary Society and became British consul of an ill-defined region encompassing Mozambique and the area to the west, with the goal of carrying out further explorations along the Zambesi and ultimately of establishing a

British colony in the region. (He ignored the fact that much of this territory had already been claimed by the Portuguese, and that, even if it had not been, the British government had no interest in colonizing it.)

In 1858, his discovery of the Kebrabasa Rapids shattered his dream of reaching the Batoka Plateau by river, but, ever the optimist, he turned towards a new objective, the River Shire, which flowed into the Zambesi about 100 miles (160 km) from the coast.[11] Following it north, he traced its origin to Lake Nyasa (now Lake Malawi), but there he discovered that Arab slave-traders were already well established in the region, leading to violent conflict among the local tribes. Moreover, the Portuguese were determined to protect their claim to the region, by military means if necessary. These factors meant that no English merchants were likely to set foot in what Livingstone had named the 'Shire Highlands', but he was running out of options for a place to establish a permanent British commercial and missionary presence in the interior of Africa.

Livingstone's efforts to convince the British government to begin the process of formal colonization bore little fruit. 'I am very unwilling to embark on new schemes of British possessions,' wrote the prime minister, Lord Palmerston, in response to his repeated entreaties.[12] His pleas for humanitarian intervention in Africa produced more tangible results, however. Livingstone's lectures inspired four universities – Oxford, Cambridge, Durham and Trinity College Dublin – to dispatch a combined mission to central Africa. Livingstone recommended that it establish a station in the Shire Highlands, even though he was well aware of the difficulties it was likely to encounter. The outcome was more disastrous than even he could have predicted. The mission's leader,

Charles Mackenzie, the first Anglican bishop to go to central Africa, was determined to intervene immediately to curb the slave trade, which embroiled the mission in tribal warfare even before it had reached its destination in Magomero in present-day Zambia. When the party was challenged by a group of Ajawa warriors, Livingstone ordered his men to open fire. At least six Africans were killed; to reinforce the point, Livingstone marched to their village and burned it to the ground. At few other points in his career was the contrast between his ideals and his conduct so starkly set in relief.

Over the ensuing months, Mackenzie continued to launch attacks on the Ajawa in a misguided attempt to impose order on the chaotic region. The situation worsened when he died of fever in early 1861, thus depriving the mission of its leader. In 1863, Livingstone's supporting expedition was recalled by the British government, and the universities' mission was withdrawn soon thereafter. The Shire Highlands experiment had been an ignominious failure: twelve of the missionaries had died, and everything that Livingstone had promised – the navigability of the Zambesi and the Shire, the healthy climate, the fertility of the Shire Highlands, the peaceful local population – had turned out to be false. *The Times* was blunt in its assessment:

> We were promised cotton, sugar and indigo, commodities which savages never produced; and of course we got none. We were promised trade, and of course there is no trade, although we have a Consul at 500*l.* a year. We were promised converts to the Gospel, and not one has been made. We were told that the climate was salubrious, and a Bishop and some of the best missionaries of the temperate region of South Africa, with

their wives and children, have perished in the malarial swamps of the Zambesi. In a word, the thousands subscribed by the Universities, and the thousands contributed by the Government, have been productive only of the most fatal results.[13]

After the failure of the Shire Highlands mission, Livingstone faced an uncertain future. He had spent over a decade trying to establish a permanent British mission and settlement in the upper Zambesi region; it was now clear that this was impossible. To continue working in Africa, he would have to complete the transition from missionary to explorer. He therefore immersed himself in answering the greatest African geographical question of the age: finding the source of the River Nile. In the late 1850s, Richard Burton and John Hanning Speke had become the first Europeans to reach Lake Tanganyika, and the latter, while Burton lay prostrate with illness, had discovered a second lake, which he named Lake Victoria, from which he claimed the Nile flowed. In 1862, Speke had returned to Lake Victoria and found an outlet, Ripon Falls, on its northern side that he argued confirmed his claim. Two years later, however, Samuel Baker found another possible source, a body of water that he named Lake Albert, which lay 150 miles (240 km) northwest of Lake Victoria. Denying both Speke's and Baker's claims, Livingstone believed that the source of the Nile lay even further south than Lake Tanganyika.

In 1866, Livingstone disappeared into the interior of Africa; nothing would be heard from him for over five years. As time passed, the mounting concerns for his welfare and inevitable rumours of his death did much to repair the damage done to his reputation by the Shire Highlands debacle. His fellow missionary Horace Waller wrote to him in 1869 that he was now surrounded 'with a halo of romance such as you can't imagine'.[14] Two more years would pass, however, before the journalist Henry Morton Stanley 'found' Livingstone in Ujiji on the shores of Lake Tanganyika.[15] Stanley had been dispatched by the scoop-seeking editor of the *New York Herald*, James Gordon Bennett, who believed that news should be created, not merely reported. Like Livingstone's, Stanley's life was a rags-to-riches tale. Born into illegitimacy and poverty in North Wales, he grew up in a work-house before emigrating to America in 1859, when he was eight-een. He fought on both sides of the Civil War and then evolved from soldier to war correspondent, eventually wangling a job at the *Herald*. The moment in which he met Livingstone in Ujiji enshrined both of them in legend; the mere 'mention of your name', wrote Waller to Livingstone after the story reached Britain, 'makes the rafters shake!'[16]

The greeting that Stanley purportedly uttered to Livingstone – 'Dr Livingstone, I presume?' – became one of the most famous phrases of the Victorian age, not least because it was made comical by its obsequious politeness and its absurdity: the question was uttered, after all, by one of the only two white men for thousands of miles to the other, and the answer was hardly in doubt.[17] Britons readily saw it as proof of the gaucherie of Americans, among whom they counted Stanley, because they were unaware of his Welsh birth. In fact, he may never have actually said those words: he later destroyed the relevant pages of his diary, and Livingstone did not mention them in the version of the meeting that he recorded. They did not appear in the *Herald* until August 1872, three months after the story that Stanley had found Livingstone had broken. But despite the fact that he was much ridiculed for the phrase, Stanley never denied having said it.

Posthumous Glory

Resisting Stanley's entreaties to abandon his expedition and return home, Livingstone continued to search for the source of the Nile. Now sixty years old, he was suffering from a variety of ailments, and in the spring of 1873 he became so weak that his men had to carry him on a litter. They decided to return to Ujiji so that he could recover, but along the way Livingstone collapsed completely. In the village of a chief named Chitambo, his followers built him a hut in which he could rest. After lingering for two weeks, he was found dead one morning – probably on 1 May. According to legend, he was discovered kneeling by his bed in prayer, but in reality pain from a large blood clot that had formed in his intestine had probably caused him to hunch into a fetal position.

Two of Livingstone's companions, Abdullah Susi and James Chuma, were determined to return Livingstone's body to his own people. This was a highly dangerous undertaking, as many of the tribes along the route back to the coast forbade the carrying or moving of corpses. Nonetheless, Susi and Chuma built a special enclosure so that they could secretly embalm the body by salting it and drying it in the sun. After removing the internal organs and burying the heart in a tin flour-box under a tree, they wrapped the rest of the body in bark, sailcloth and a sheath of calico in order to disguise it as a bundle of cloth. They then carried it 1,500 miles (2,400 km) to Zanzibar; ten men died along the way.

A European received the first definitive news of Livingstone's death in October 1873. In Unyanyembe in what is now Tanzania, Chuma, who had gone ahead of the main caravan in order to obtain supplies, met Lieutenant Verney Lovett Cameron of the Royal Navy, who was leading an expedition sent by the Royal

Geographical Society to relieve Livingstone.[18] Upon learning that he was too late, he tried to convince Chuma and the others to bury the body, but they would not be dissuaded from completing their mission. Cameron himself continued on to Ujiji in order to retrieve Livingstone's books and papers, but he sent his companions William Edward Dillon and Cecil Murphy to accompany the body to Zanzibar.[19] The journey was so arduous that along the way Dillon 'shot himself in a fit of delirium'.[20]

The news of Livingstone's death reached Zanzibar in January 1874. From there, the information was relayed to the Foreign Office by the acting British consul, Captain William Prideaux, who reported that

> as a mark of respect to the memory of Dr Livingstone, the flag-staff of this Agency was kept at half-mast from sunrise to sunset on the 5th of January. This example was followed by His Highness the Sultan, by Her Majesty's ships of war then in harbour ... and by the Consular representatives of the other Foreign Powers in Zanzibar, from all of whom I received letters of condolence on the death of this eminent explorer and distinguished servant of the Queen.[21]

Once the news reached Britain, Livingstone ascended to the greatest heights of heroism. A large crowd met his coffin at Southampton on 15 April 1874. A special train carried the body to London, where it lay in state in the Royal Geographical Society for two days prior to the funeral in Westminster Abbey. (See Figure 36.) Agnes Cotton Oswell, the wife of Livingstone's friend and fellow African explorer William Cotton Oswell, recorded in her diary that as the coffin was carried through the streets of

London the crowd that gathered to see it included 'every grade of life, from the Queen to the humblest crossing-sweeper'.[22]

In the months and years that followed, Livingstone was transformed into an object of quasi-religious veneration. (See Figure 37.) Suspending its rule that a person had to have been dead for ten years prior to having his portrait put on display, the National Portrait Gallery immediately acquired a small pencil sketch of Livingstone by Joseph Bonomi.[23] Soon, plans were under way for dozens of memorials, scattered throughout Britain, Africa and the rest of the empire. Over a hundred biographies would be published, and Livingstone became the subject of countless songs, poems, plays, novels and other works of fiction and non-fiction. Although his birthplace in Blantyre did not officially open as a museum until the 1920s, the then-current occupant began admitting visitors in 1882; a visitors' book in the collection of the David Livingstone Centre records the names of 9,943 visitors up to 1913. Most were local or from other parts of Scotland, but visitors also came from all over England, Wales and Ireland, as well as the United States, Jerusalem, Germany, Switzerland, Paraguay, Italy, China, Canada, southern and central Africa, Syria, Australia, New Zealand, Japan, Ceylon, India and the Straits Settlements.[24] In 1899, the mvule tree under which Livingstone's heart had been buried became diseased and had to be cut down. Pieces of the tree were treated as sacred relics, and items made from it were sold as souvenirs.[25] (See Figure 38.)

Amidst this flood of adulation, however, there was still only a vague understanding of what precisely Livingstone had accomplished. His work as a missionary had produced no converts, and his geographical achievements had been feats of endurance rather than discovery. It was that very endurance, however, that had transformed him into the greatest explorer-hero of the Victorian age. From his childhood, when he refused to accept the life of poverty and ignorance that lay before him, to the end of his life, when he continued his explorations despite his rapidly declining health, Livingstone was defined not by what he accomplished but by his refusal to submit or surrender.[26] Driven by willpower rather than ambition, Livingstone was perceived as free from venal motives. The periodical *John Bull* posthumously described him as 'self-yielding in these all too selfish days' and as a man whose 'heroic sacrifice has led the van'.[27]

In the final decades of the nineteenth century, however, it was Henry Morton Stanley's mode of exploration – marching behind the barrel of a gun – that prevailed in Africa, while Livingstone's philanthropic vision crumbled in the face of international competition, ambition and (often illusory) economic profit. Stanley may not deserve the amount of blame that he has been apportioned for what occurred in the 'scramble for Africa', and especially in the Belgian Congo, where he served as King Leopold II's chief agent in the 1880s.[28] But if Livingstone had blurred the distinction between mission work and exploration, Stanley, as Felix Driver has written, blurred that between 'exploration and warfare so profoundly that it becomes almost unrecognisable'.[29] In the 1890s, Stanley acknowledged his role as Livingstone's mirror image: 'My methods ... will not be Livingstone's. Each man has his own way ... The selfish and wooden-headed world requires mastering, as well as loving charity.'[30] Livingstone, naively, believed that the British could bring commerce and Christianity to Africans while avoiding colonialism's most destructive effects. Stanley, realistically, knew that African imperialism was really about money and power; unlike other explorers, he did not remove the episodes in which he beat and whipped his porters from the published version of his journal. His attitude to Africa was unabashedly proprietary: as he neared the famous rendezvous with Livingstone, he wrote of feeling 'proud that I owned such a vast domain'.[31] But in their contrasting personalities, Livingstone and Stanley allowed the British to have their African cake and eat it too. (See Figures 39 and 40.) Revering Livingstone allowed them to believe that commerce and national self-aggrandizement were genuinely compatible with Christianity and cultural enlightenment in Africa. Stanley, meanwhile, carried on with the business of acquiring territory and extracting profit from it. His honest brutality made it all the more imperative for Britons to be able to point to a hero who was not associated with aggression, violence and bloody conquest. Livingstone's failure to achieve more in Africa thus became the source of his heroism. He was, in the end, a poor imperialist, but he was a great imperial hero in the eyes of a Victorian public who desperately wanted to see Britain's endeavours in Africa as noble and benevolent. In Livingstone's hands, wrote Sir John Scott Keltie, assistant secretary of the Royal Geographical Society, in 1893, the scramble for Africa became 'a kind of holy crusade'.[32] It was, of course, nothing of the sort, but Livingstone made it possible to maintain the illusion.[33]

But that was the mythic version of Livingstone. The real man had been more like Stanley than either he or his subsequent mythologizers would have admitted, for he was not above the use of violence when other methods failed. He beat and threatened to shoot his African followers when they did not obey, and once told one of his European companions when he was having difficulty with his African servants 'to break their heads if they did not do' as he commanded.[34] We have already seen how he shot at Africans while defending the Shire Highlands mission in 1861, and he did so again when attempting to sail a steamer up the Rovuma in 1862. Over the course of his career, he was responsible for the deaths of at least eight Africans. An episode that occurred on his final journey is revealing. After parting from Stanley in August 1872, Livingstone had headed south to Lake Bemba in northern Zambia, but his explorations were hindered by the refusal of the local peoples to let him use their canoes to cross the lake. He 'therefore seized seven canoes by force and when the natives made a show of resistance he fired his pistol over their heads, after which they ceased to obstruct him'.[35]

Livingstone was not, then, the saint of posthumous mythology. But the unsaintly Livingstone died in 1873, while the saintly one lived on. In 1896, the National Portrait Gallery acquired a portrait of him by Frederick Havill. The original accompanying label read: 'David Livingstone, 1813–1873. African traveller and missionary. Explored the interior of Africa and published various accounts of his travels, during which he shewed great courage and self-sacrifice, both as explorer and missionary.'[36] Here, we see many of the complexities of Livingstone's African career encapsulated in barely thirty words. There is the confusion as to whether he was explorer or missionary, and no clear statement of what precisely he accomplished in either arena. What is emphasized above all, however, is his 'great courage and self-sacrifice', demonstrating that achievement mattered less than character when the Victorians assessed their explorers.

CHAPTER FIVE

THE 'LAST STAND'

IN THE EARLY 1890s, looking for more rich deposits of gold to match those of the Witwatersrand, Cecil Rhodes's newly char-tered British South Africa Company (BSAC) expanded north-wards into Mashonaland, or modern-day Zimbabwe. This brought the BSAC into conflict with the Ndebele people (called by the British the 'Matabele') who inhabited the region.[1] Though they were not as formidable in battle as the neighbouring Zulus, the Ndebele were a similarly militaristic society and in the late nine-teenth century could put an army of fifteen thousand men in the field. Rather than resisting, however, they initially attempted to accommodate the BSAC's interest in their territory. In 1888, their leader, Lobengula, agreed to the Rudd Concession, which granted him a subsidy of £100 a month, a thousand Martini-Henry rifles and an armed steamer in return for 'charge over all the metals and minerals' in his kingdom, as well as 'full power to do all things that they may deem necessary to win and procure the same'.[2] Lobengula believed that the BSAC's interest was exclusively in the eastern part of his kingdom, where relatively few Ndebele lived. He was also given verbal assurances by Rhodes's agent Charles Rudd, for whom the agreement was named, that the BSAC would send no more than ten men into his territory to pursue mining activities.

As so often proved to be the case in southern Africa, however, an initial European promise of only limited territorial ambitions soon evolved into more expansionist activities. In 1888, the government of the Cape Colony declared that all the land south of the Zambesi, including Mashonaland, was within Britain's sphere of influence. British colonial administrators saw the BSAC as a handy instrument for extending their colonial domain on the cheap, as the bulk of the cost would be underwritten by Rhodes. And certainly Rhodes, with his growing thirst for territorial domination as well as gold, was happy to oblige. As hundreds of men representing the 'Pioneer Column' of the BSAC began to arrive, Lobengula quickly recognized his error and tried to stop them, but it was too late. As the BSAC's presence continued to expand, a clash became inevitable, and in the summer of 1893, the British got an excuse to start a war. The Ndebele began carrying out a series of increasingly aggressive cattle raids against the Mashona people who also inhabited the region. Despite the fact that Lobengula had ordered his men not to harm Europeans or their property, the white population sought the safety of the larger settlements. This disrupted both mining and agriculture, and the BSAC determined that it could not be tolerated. In 1893, it declared war on the Ndebele, citing as justification their 'insolence and aggressive acts'.[3]

It was not, in the end, much of a war. In the initial encounter, the Battle of Shangani, 3,500 Ndebele surrounded an encampment of seven hundred BSAC volunteers that was well defended with Maxim guns and artillery. Repeated charges produced horrific bloodshed, and by the end of the fight over five hundred Ndebele lay dead. A week later, six thousand Ndebele attacked the same column at Bembezi, with even more catastrophic results: almost half of the Ndebele were killed or wounded. BSAC forces then marched on to Lobengula's capital at Bulawayo and began making plans to dismember the Ndebele kingdom, but they were premature in assuming that the war was over. A column of four hundred men was dispatched to round up Lobengula, who had gone into hiding. There were still plenty of Ndebele warriors looking for a chance to attack, however, and on the night of 3 December, a patrol of thirty-three men, under the command of Major Allan Wilson, was surrounded and killed, with no survivors. Ndebele observers claimed that they had fought until they ran out of ammunition; by the time the last man, reportedly Wilson himself, had been killed, the patrol had slaughtered five hundred Ndebele.

Back in Britain, Wilson's men, who came to be known as 'the Shangani Patrol' were widely celebrated. (See Figure 41.) Augustus Harris's patriotic play *Cheer Boys Cheer!*, which premiered at the Theatre Royal Drury Lane in 1895, concluded with Wilson's men singing 'God Save the Queen' after their ammunition had run out and they stood waiting for death. Four years later, the scene was duplicated in the spectacle *Savage South Africa* in the Greater Britain Exhibition at Earl's Court in London. It starred an African who called himself Peter Lobengula and who claimed to be Lobengula's son, as well as a number of other African performers. A film of the show by the Warwick Trading Company was exhibited to the public in 1899. The story of the Shangani Patrol came to be well known throughout the empire; in 1904, in a piece about the unveiling of a memorial to Wilson and his men in Rhodesia (the name given to Mashonaland after 1895), the Toronto-based

Canadian Magazine declared: 'There is no more tragic incident, no record of greater bravery, in the annals of the Empire than the story of the Shangani Patrol. The calm courage, the unflinching facing of certain death on the part of this little body of men, made a great impression upon the natives, and did much to inculcate a respectful admiration for the race which these men so nobly and so magnificently represented.'[4]

For the Ndebele, however, the defeat of the Shangani Patrol was a minor victory in a disastrous war in which they suffered over ten thousand casualties. (The British lost only a hundred men.) In 1896, they rebelled against British rule again; this time, there were fifty thousand African casualties, as opposed to a mere four hundred British. By the end of the Second Matabele War, the Ndebele's power, and indeed existence as an independent society, had been permanently destroyed. An anonymous British soldier made a series of sketches of the conflict that are now in the collection of the National Army Museum. (See Figures 42 and 43.) One caption reads: 'Gallant defence of the guns by Blue Jackets and 50 CMP [Company Mounted Police]. The Maxim did terrible execution'; another, 'The 7th Hussars and CMP are sent in chase and do good work. Thus ended the fight for the hills in which we lost 25 killed and 147 wounded. Enemy lost about 3000 killed and wounded.'[5] These drawings provide a vivid contrast to the emphasis on the fate of the Shangani Patrol, and are a much more realistic depiction of the wars against the Ndebele, which were among the most lopsided conflicts in British history. But even this anonymous soldier was not immune to the need to conceal the uncomfortable reality. On the last page of his sketches, he drew a 'Private Youngman' of the 7th Hussars executing a 'desperate leap' as he was 'chased by about 100 blacks'.[6] Even someone who knew the reality of the wars against the Ndebele could not entirely resist the urge to reposition the British as embattled underdogs.

The Matabele Wars were a prime example of how the army and its auxiliary colonial forces served as the primary instruments of Britain's rapid imperial expansion in the late nineteenth century. The soldiers regarded by Wellington and the public as the 'scum of the earth' now became imperial heroes.[7] But at the same time, the army struggled to cope with the new demands imposed upon it by such rapid territorial expansion, and with the need to adapt to new weapons that drastically changed battlefield tactics. The hidebound military of the Crimean War grudgingly gave way to the impetus of reform, but this was a long, slow process that was not yet complete when the Boer War broke out in 1899. Along the way, there were a number of defeats and debacles – but these proved useful, in a nation that had long resisted embracing a militaristic culture, for both garnering support for the continued use of the army as a tool of imperial expansion and for attracting the necessary resources for reform.[8]

The positioning of imperial conquest and the military action it entailed within late Victorian culture was thus a complex issue. It required the use of symbolic imagery that could mitigate the discomfiture occasioned by the rapid growth of the empire, the bloodshed it produced and the powerful military apparatus it required. The 'last stand', such as that of the Shangani Patrol, was ideal for this purpose, and it recurred in late-nineteenth-century visual representations of warfare. These included Richard Caton Woodville's *Jameson's Last Stand* (*c.*1896), which depicted the end of Leander Starr Jameson's abortive attempt to instigate a rebellion in the Transvaal in 1896; William Barns Wollen's *The Last Stand at Gundermuck, 1842* (1898), which depicted the desperate stand by the rear guard of the British garrison as it attempted to retreat from Kabul during the First Anglo-Afghan War; and Woodville's *All That Was Left of Them* (1902), which depicted C Squadron of the 17th Lancers standing against an attack by Boer commandoes in the Battle of Elands River during the Boer War in 1901. There were three last stands, however, that the late Victorians found particularly compelling. One was that of the aforementioned Shangani Patrol; the others were that of the 24th Foot at the Battle of Isandlwana during the Anglo-Zulu War in 1879 and that of the 66th Foot at the Battle of Maiwand during the Second Anglo-Afghan War in 1880.

'Gallant Resistance': Isandlwana

In January 1879, the officers of the 1st Battalion of the 24th Regiment of Foot invited their counterparts in the 2nd Battalion to a celebratory mess in their camp at Helpmekaar in Natal. By this point, the former had been stationed at the Cape for several years, while the latter had only recently arrived. The battalions would now be fighting alongside each other for the first time in the war that had just been declared against the Zulus. They were not only celebrating the upcoming campaign, however, but also the anniversary of the most famous moment in the regiment's history. Thirty years earlier, on 13 January 1849, the 24th Foot had made the disastrous charge at Chillianwallah that had resulted in the loss of over three hundred men. Two officers from the 1st Battalion, Captain William Degacher and Lieutenant Francis Porteous, offered a toast, expressing the hope 'that we may not get into such a bloody mess, and have better luck this time!'[9] Three weeks later, Degacher and Porteous, along with twelve other officers from the 1st Battalion and four from the 2nd Battalion, lay dead on the battlefield at Isandlwana. Instead of having 'better luck' this time around, their regiment had for the second time been at the epicentre of one of the greatest heroic failures in British military history.

After the great warrior and chieftain Shaka assumed its leadership in 1816, the Zulu kingdom rose from a tiny, insignificant tribal group to a powerful political and military entity that controlled territory stretching from what are today the borders of Swaziland and Mozambique in the north to Natal in the south. Shaka built what by African standards was a massive army of 25,000 men and used it to overturn the traditional system of ritualized warfare by fighting wars of annihilation, in which the losers were either killed or assimilated into his forces. Within a few years, he controlled over 11,000 square miles (28,500 sq km) of territory, inhabited by 250,000 people.[10]

In 1828, however, Shaka was murdered in a coup engineered by two of his half-brothers. If he had lived a hundred years earlier, he would have left the Zulu kingdom all but invulnerable. But the kingdom's emergence had occurred simultaneously with the fundamental alteration of southern African politics caused by the British acquisition of the Cape Colony from the Dutch in 1806. The British initially saw the Cape purely as a strategic stopping-off point for their naval and merchant shipping, and were content to leave the Zulus and the other tribal groups who occupied the interior of southern Africa largely to their own devices. Complicating matters, however, were the Boers, the descendants of the colony's original Dutch settlers. Between 1834 and 1840, fifteen thousand Boer *Voortrekkers* headed north from the Cape into Natal as they sought freedom from British control. The British wanted neither to see a rival European colony established nor to have to cope with the instability resulting from the warfare that would almost certainly break out between the Boers and Africans as they competed for land and resources.[11] In 1843, they therefore annexed Natal as a province of the Cape Colony. At the same time, they signed a treaty with the Zulus that established the border between Natal and Zululand as lying along the Thukela and Mzinyathi Rivers, with the intention of preventing further Boer incursions into Zulu territory.[12]

If the British and the Zulus were reasonably satisfied with this arrangement, however, the Boers were not. Determined to get out from under British authority once again, they headed further north, into the territories that would later become the Transvaal and the Orange Free State. There, they again encroached on Zulu land, a problem that became more acute as more settlers arrived. The situation was further complicated by the discovery of large deposits of diamonds along the Orange River in the late 1860s, creating a powerful economic incentive for the British to reassert their claim to the region.

These pressures for the expansion of British authority in the interior, however, went against the wishes of the Liberal government that came to power in 1868, which favoured a 'static' imperial policy and instead sought to grant the Cape Colony increased self-government, as had already occurred in Australia, New Zealand and Canada.[13] Those places, however, differed from the Cape Colony in two very significant ways. First, there was no equivalent of the Boers, or European settlers who sought to establish independent republics outside British authority. (Canada, to be sure, had the Québécois, but their cultural and religious differences had been accommodated through a series of concessions dating back to the Seven Years War.) The second factor was the presence of a large number of indigenous people. By 1900, the aboriginal populations of Australia and New Zealand had declined from a pre-contact peak of a million each to under 100,000, while that of Canada had declined from two million to under 150,000. In South Africa, in contrast, a million whites and 3.5 million indigenous Africans competed for the same territory.

The already complex political dynamic in the Cape Colony was further complicated in 1874, when a Conservative government under Benjamin Disraeli replaced Gladstone's Liberals, bringing a more forthright imperial policy to Westminster with it. The colonial authorities at the Cape convinced the new colonial secretary, the earl of Carnarvon, to countenance a scheme of confederation for South Africa as the best means of protecting Britain's interests in southern Africa. Confederation entailed the annexation of not only the Boer republics but also Zululand; in this new British vision of a united South Africa, an independent Zulu kingdom could no more continue to exist than an independent Boer republic. The lieutenant governor of Natal, the distinguished general Sir Garnet Wolseley, believed that in military terms the annexation of Zululand would be a simple task, as he had been convinced by Britain's experts on indigenous affairs that the Zulus regarded their leader, Cetshwayo, as a tyrant and were eager to depose him. Wolseley was also convinced that the new Martini-Henry rifle would give the British near-omnipotency on the battlefield.

The annexation of Zululand, however, required a better justification than British convenience. The British got one in 1876, when a conflict broke out between the Boers and the Zulus. Though the Boers quickly gained the upper hand, the war crippled the Transvaal's treasury, giving the British a pretext to declare that annexation was the only thing that could save the Boer state. Though the Boers were far from eager for a British takeover, in their impoverished and demoralized state they made little protest. The annexation of the Transvaal in turn provided an excuse for carrying out the annexation of Zululand, which could now be presented as necessary to protect the Boers in their new role as British colonial citizens. The British, who had previously sought to balance Boer and Zulu interests, thus shifted towards a more pro-Boer policy. In November 1878, Sir Bartle Frere, the governor of the Cape Colony, issued an ultimatum in which he demanded that the Zulus remake their entire society by dismantling their army and placing themselves under the direction of a resident British official. This was, of course, impossible for the shocked Zulus to comply with, and they now conceded that a war with the British, which they had long sought to avoid and feared they could not win, was unavoidable. They were given only thirty days to submit to the ultimatum, and when the deadline expired on 31 December, the British invaded Zululand.

The British believed that they would easily crush the opposition. 'If we are to have a fight with the Zulus,' declared Lieutenant General Lord Chelmsford, commander-in-chief of the British forces in South Africa, 'I am anxious that our arrangements should be as complete as it is possible to make them. Half measures do not answer with the natives. They must be thoroughly crushed to make them believe in our superiority, and if I am called upon to conduct operations against them, I shall strive to be in a position to show them how hopelessly inferior they are to us in fighting power, altho' numerically stronger.'[14] Here, Chelmsford illustrates the complexities of Britain's sense of itself as an imperial power in the late nineteenth century. On the one hand, he positions the British as underdogs who must find ways to overcome the numerical superiority of indigenous peoples. But, on the other, he is full of confidence that Britain's technological advantages in weaponry will prove decisive. His wish to 'crush' the Zulus fulfilled British desires for power and dominance, but sat uneasily with more benevolent conceptions of the purpose of empire. These contradictory sentiments engendered competing desires for the outcome of the war: the British of course wanted to win, but they also wanted to see themselves as noble and benevolent rather than bloodthirsty and rapacious. There was thus a clear need for heroism of a non-aggressive sort. That need would be fulfilled, albeit at a high cost of British lives.

Chelmsford assumed that the Zulus, aware of Britain's superiority in weaponry, would seek to avoid a pitched battle. Instead of concentrating his forces, he thus divided his sixteen thousand men into five columns, which permitted more rapid movement. He took charge of the third, or central, column himself. The plan was for them to converge on Cetshwayo's capital at Ondini. He underestimated, however, the Zulus' confidence in their military prowess, and their faith in their preferred strategy, known as 'the horns of the buffalo', in which the flanks of their attack enveloped the enemy while the centre engaged the bulk of the opposing forces.

After crossing the border into Zululand, Chelmsford decided to establish a forward camp in the shadow of a sphinx-like hill called Isandlwana. He assumed that, as he moved north, the Zulus would retreat towards Ondini and harass the British with small-scale attacks. The poor site chosen for the camp reflected Chelmsford's complacency. Rather than lying on open ground that would allow a large Zulu force to be spotted from some distance away, it was overlooked by the rocky promontory of Isandlwana and the rising ground that led up to it, which would allow a Zulu army to approach virtually unseen. Chelmsford did not think that this would matter, as he did not expect a full-scale Zulu attack and was confident of his ability to repel one even if it came. He made no attempt to post sentries behind the hill, where they could see an oncoming Zulu force, or *laager* (i.e., entrench) his army by using his supply wagons as a defensive barrier. Cetshwayo, however, had formulated a strategy that directly contradicted British expectations. Aware that his best chance of dissuading the British from bringing the full brunt of their military resources to bear was to inflict an early defeat upon them, he sent twenty thousand troops to confront the invading army. He hoped that once they were made aware of how difficult it would be to conquer the Zulus, they would be convinced to reconsider their planned annexation of Zululand.

Early on the morning of 22 January 1879, Chelmsford rode out at the head of a column in order to carry out reconnaissance in the hills surrounding Isandlwana. This left Lieutenant Colonel Henry Pulleine of the 24th Foot in charge of the camp, but, at around 10 a.m., Lieutenant Colonel Anthony Durnford arrived from Helpmekaar with a contingent of Natal volunteers; he outranked Pulleine and thus assumed command. Durnford encapsulated all of the complexities of the Anglo-Zulu War. On the one hand, he was brave and eager for action, but, on the other, he recognized that the war against the Zulus was unjust. 'As a soldier I should delight in the war,' he wrote, 'but as a man I utterly condemn it.'[15]

Whatever his personal opinion, however, once the war started, Durnford's duty was to fight. Upon hearing reports of increasing Zulu movements, he decided to take aggressive action. Pulleine protested that his orders were to defend the camp rather than to go on the offensive, but Durnford countered that Chelmsford had ordered him to attack if a suitable opportunity arose. He set off with a detachment of mounted troops to chase down the Zulus. He had only gone about 4 miles (6.4 km), however, when two scouts informed him that a huge Zulu army lay directly ahead. Durnford ordered a retreat, but it was too late. His advance guard had spotted a few Zulus running away and had chased them up a ridge. What they saw upon reaching the top was a shock: a massive Zulu army of around twenty thousand men. It is still debated whether the Zulus intended to attack that day, or whether they did so only after the British blundered into them. Whatever the case, their presence in such large numbers took the British totally by surprise. As the Zulus swept towards them, Durnford ordered a fighting retreat to the camp. Upon reaching a deep *donga*, or dry watercourse, he commanded his small force to take up a defensive position. Their steady, accurate fire impeded the progress of the Zulu advance for perhaps half an hour, but they could not hold them indefinitely as their ammunition supply was dwindling.

Back at the main camp, one of Durnford's officers, Captain George Shepstone, galloped up to Pulleine and reported that a massive Zulu force was rapidly advancing towards them. Pulleine, however, failed to recognize the magnitude of the threat. Instead of concentrating his forces in a tight defensive formation that would have maximized their advantage in firepower and might have saved them, he deployed them along a wide front. The difficulty of holding such an extended line quickly became apparent. Lieutenant Horace Smith-Dorrien of the 95th Regiment later recalled that the Zulu advance was 'a marvellous sight, lines upon lines of men in slightly extended order, one behind the other, firing as they came along, for a few of them had firearms, and bearing all before them'.[16] The advance was temporarily halted by a barrage of British artillery and rifle fire, much of the latter coming from the 1st Battalion of the 24th Foot, whom Pulleine had deployed in a forward position in order to bolster the right side of the line. But the Zulus could only be checked, not halted. As Durnford's men ran out of ammunition and ceased firing, they left the 1/24th exposed and undermined the stability of the entire British right flank. The Zulus saw this and surged forward into the camp. 'In a moment,' wrote Captain Edward Essex, 'all was disorder.'[17] As the British frantically fled across the rugged terrain, those on foot were swiftly run down and killed; only those on horseback stood a chance. Nine hundred and twenty-two British soldiers and 840 African auxiliaries perished at Isandlwana; only fifty-five of the former and 350 of the latter survived. Some men fled almost immediately, while others doggedly resisted. In the end, it made little difference which option they chose. In the nineteenth century, only the retreat from Kabul proved a bloodier British defeat, and even then Isandlwana topped it for the number of British regulars who were killed. (710 perished at Kabul.) A staggering 75 per cent of the men who fought on the British side at Isandlwana died.[18]

Isandlwana was a traumatic defeat, made more so by the fact that it had been inflicted by a non-European foe. The British public required three things to cope with a military disaster of such epic proportions: redemption, retribution and remembrance. The first was made possible by the outcome of another battle that took place on the same day. At Rorke's Drift, a fording point of the Mzinyathi, there was a homestead owned by a Swedish missionary named Otto Witt, who, when the invasion of Zululand began, lent his property to the British army for use as a supply depot and hospital. The post was defended by a garrison of two hundred men from the 2nd Battalion of the 24th Foot, under the command of Major Henry Spalding. On the afternoon of 22 January, however, Spalding had ridden to Helpmekaar to try and speed the arrival of some promised reinforcements. This left Rorke's Drift under the command of Lieutenant John Chard of the Royal Engineers, who was there to ensure that the ponts, or floating bridges, that the army needed to cross the Mzinyathi when it was in flood remained secure. The highest-ranking remaining officer from the 24th, meanwhile, was Lieutenant Gonville Bromhead, who like Chard had no combat experience.

After the camp at Isandlwana was overrun, Rorke's Drift lay directly in the path of the Zulus.[19] Chard and Bromhead initially thought of attempting an evacuation, but realized that they could not move quickly with the thirty-five invalids who were in the hospital. They thus began preparing to defend the post with the hundred able-bodied men who were available. In a fierce fight that lasted until well after dark, they managed to hold off between three and four thousand Zulus. Only fifteen British soldiers were killed and seventeen wounded, while 350 Zulu corpses lay on the battlefield. Eleven Victoria Crosses were awarded, the highest total ever given for a single engagement.

Rorke's Drift went a long way towards counterbalancing Isandlwana, but it could not entirely mitigate the disaster. For that to occur, something positive had to be extracted from Isandlwana itself. To this end, the last stands made by some of the men as the Zulu attack swept over the British camp were ideal. (See Figure 44.) The largest group was the seventy men, mostly from the Natal Carbineers, who had remained with Durnford. They fired until they ran out of ammunition and then continued the fight hand-to-hand until they were killed to a man. The Zulu commander Mehlokazulu later recounted: 'It was a long time before they were overcome – before we finished them. When we did get to them, they all died in one place, together. They threw down their guns when their ammunition was done, and then commenced with their pistols, which they used as long as their ammunition lasted; and then they formed a line, shoulder to shoulder and back to back, and fought with their knives.'[20] The men of the 24th Foot also attempted to maintain pockets of resistance. In his dispatch after the battle, Chelmsford referred to the 24th's 'gallant resistance', and this line was quickly taken up by the press. The *Illustrated London News*, for example, described the 24th as standing 'high among the most distinguished regiments in the British Army'.[21] Soon after the battle, H. B. Worth published a poem entitled 'In Memory of the Officers, Non-Commissioned Officers and Men of the 24th Regiment':

> Great Britain mourns the valiant sons she's lost
> And bitter tears this tragedy has cost,
> They fighting died, and all the world must say
> Each nobly 'did his duty on that day.'
> Each single man, a hero in the strife,
> O'erwhelmed by numbers, dearly sold his life,
> Though great our loss, the enemy lost more –
> For every Briton slain they counted four.[22]

In 1883, a painting entitled *The Last of the 24th Isandula* [*sic*] was exhibited by the Irish artist R. T. Moynan. On his knees and about to topple from his rocky perch, the regiment's last survivor stretches out his left arm as he submits to his sacrifice in

Christ-like fashion.[23] Moynan's image bore little relation to the brutal reality of the battle, but the Victorian public had little stomach for that. A sketch made by the artist Melton Prior of the bodies that still lay on the battlefield four months later had to be pruned of its most gruesome elements before it could appear in the *Illustrated London News*.[24]

Two soldiers from the 24th Foot came to be regarded as Isandlwana's greatest heroes. After the camp was overrun, Lieutenant Teignmouth Melvill retrieved the regiment's Queen's Colour from the tent in which it had been stored and attempted to carry it to safety. Lieutenant Nevill Coghill saw him struggling to cross the Mzinyathi and came to his aid, but the current swept the colour away. Melvill and Coghill managed to reach the Natal bank of the river, but there they were both killed by the Zulus. Within days of the battle, the story of their effort to save the colour was circulating, and the men patrolling the banks of the river kept a watchful eye out for it. On 3 February, the bodies of Melvill and Coghill were discovered; the next day, the colour was found. It was carried proudly back to Rorke's Drift, where the entire garrison assembled to receive it, and was then taken to Helpmekaar.[25] In his report, issued on 21 February, Colonel Richard Glyn drew Chelmsford's attention to

the noble and heroic conduct of Lieutenant and Adjutant Melville [*sic*] who did not hesitate to encumber himself with the Colours of the Regiment in his resolve to save them, at a time when the camp was in the hands of the enemy and its gallant defenders killed to the last man in its defence, and when there appeared but little prospect that any exertions Lieutenant Melville could make would enable him to save his own life. Also later on the noble perseverance with which when struggling between life and death in the river, his chief thoughts to the last were bent on saving the colours. Similarly I draw his Excellency's attention to the equally noble and gallant conduct of Lieutenant Coghill, who did not hesitate for an instant to return unsolicited and rode again into the river under a heavy fire of the enemy to the assistance of his friend.[26]

Back in Britain, the story of Melvill and Coghill's heroic action first appeared in the press in mid-March.[27] The 'saving of the colour' quickly became the most celebrated moment of Isandlwana. In his poem 'In Memory of the Officers, Non-Commissioned Officers and Men of the 24th Regiment', H. B. Worth wrote:

> The colours true were lost, but not disgraced,
> And, now recovered, on them may be placed
> Another record that fresh lustre gives
> To the proud list of names, that yet still lives
> Emblazoned on the archives of the past
> That to the end of time will be honoured last.[28]

In his poem 'The Zulu War' (1879), George Walter Boyce described how Melvill and Coghill

> Bore the Colours safe that day;
> Using them for their funeral shroud,
> As they fell, while bearing them away,
> And every one of their deeds are proud.[29]

148

In the early 1880s, the Fine Art Society commissioned the military artist Alphonse de Neuville to depict two scenes illustrating Melvill and Coghill's exploits. In the first painting, *Saving the Queen's Colours* [*sic*], they are shown attempting to carry the Colour through a mass of Zulu warriors; in the second, *Last Sleep of the Brave*, their bodies are discovered on the riverbank.[30] De Neuville's paintings were very popular, as was indicated by their frequent reproduction as engravings and lithographs. They helped make the story familiar to Britons back home. In its review of the paintings, the *Spectator* declared:

> English gentlemen who 'sit at home at ease' could hardly help feeling sentimental, for a few minutes, over the story of how the two officers fought their way through the Zulus; how they rode away, wounded to the death, with the colours they had saved; and how they were found in the early morning lying dead, side by side, still holding the torn flag. The incident is one which requires no School-board to explain its meaning, or any philosophy to appreciate its beauty. It is just one of those sparks of derring-do, which help to make a tradition for the race, rather than obtain any very definite end.[31]

In 1907, five years after posthumous Victoria Crosses were first permitted, Melvill and Coghill were each awarded one.[32]

The second element in the effort to recoup the disaster at Isandlwana was retribution. 'Our only cry now is revenge, revenge,' declared Sergeant John Tigar of the 24th Foot in a letter to his mother.[33] This sentiment was to have bitter consequences for the Zulus. As Chelmsford's force made its way back to the battlefield at Isandlwana, it brought with it a number of prisoners they had taken during their march, and they rounded up more stragglers from Isandlwana. These Zulus were all shot. At Rorke's Drift, meanwhile, as many as five hundred wounded Zulus were massacred the next day as British troops and their African allies roamed the battlefield; Inspector George Mansel of the Natal Mounted Police later described the scene as being 'as deliberate a bit of butchery as I ever saw'.[34] For the remainder of the war, the British used Isandlwana as an excuse to massacre Zulus. Two months later, the British won a decisive victory at Khambula. In the battle itself, two thousand Zulus died, in contrast to a mere twenty-six British soldiers. The carnage continued afterwards: an enlisted man described how a patrol had discovered about five hundred wounded men the next day. Although they begged for mercy, 'they got no chance after what they had done to our comrades at Isandlwana'.[35]

At home, however, retribution was a more complicated issue. To be sure, plenty of people called for vengeance. Worth wrote:

> With British blood the plains of Afric stream
> And wholesale death and slaughter is my theme:
> War was not waged for conquest or for lust,
> Ere long the savage foe must bite the dust,
> For England promptly will avenge their fall,
> Such carnage doth for swiftest vengeance call.[36]

These demands for revenge for Isandlwana were often couched in moral terms, with the Zulus presented as uncivilized savages who were in need of correction at British hands. 'The tide of savagery has periodically been rolled back,' wrote Alexander Wilmot in his *History of the Zulu War* (1880), 'and it was either necessary that this should be done, or that white men should abandon South

Africa.'[37] Other observers pointed to Cetshwayo's tyranny and cruelty. The Reverend Holditch Mason, a former missionary in South Africa, wrote in a pamphlet that was published in 1879:

> People in England, reared up within the shelter and protection afforded by the natural barriers of our sea-girt island home, and taught to regard wanton cruelty with horror, even when practised in the vivisection of dumb animals, can scarcely realise the idea of human beings suffering torture, too terrible to mention, at the hands of the Zulus. Nor can they wonder at the consternation of the scattered British colonists of Natal on discovering, as they did, when Ketchawayo [Cetshwayo] came to the throne a few years since, that he was fully bent on a war of extermination against Europeans of all nationalities, and that he was already stirring up the natives over all South Africa, and destroying those amongst his own people known to be in favour of peace and civilisation.[38]

In February 1879, John Noble, the author of a number of books on South Africa, read a paper before the Royal Colonial Institute in which he referred to Cetshwayo as a 'ferocious savage' who was a 'constant menace' to the European settlers of the Transvaal. 'If we leave the aboriginal races,' he asserted in his conclusion, 'in ignorant barbarism, forming communities of savage tyrants and slaves, we are strengthening powers of evil which will again and again reproduce themselves.'[39]

Other Britons, however, saw the war as an unprovoked invasion of sovereign territory. John Colenso, Bishop of Natal and a vehement opponent of the war, declared that:

England's collisions with the savage races bordering upon her colonies have in all probability usually been brought about by the exigencies of the moment, by border-troubles, and acts of violence and insolence on the part of the savages, and from the absolute necessity of protecting a small and trembling white population from their assaults. No such causes as these have led up to the war of 1879. For more than twenty years the Zulus and the colonists of Natal have lived side by side in perfect peace and quietness.[40]

The solicitor and labour reformer Robert Spence Watson delivered a lecture in Newcastle in May 1879 in which he described the war as 'a stain on the honour of this nation': 'The English people are engaged in a strange enterprise in South Africa. They are deliberately and of malice aforethought compassing the subjugation and possible extermination of a gallant though savage people. They have embarked on an aggressive war which must be troublesome and costly in any event; – a war in which failure is not to be thought of, but in which, the greater the success, the greater their disgrace.' He added: 'We invaded their country, and the Zulus, in self-defence, have killed 2500 of our troops in all, while we have upheld our *prestige* by killing three times as many Zulus.' (Italics in the original.) As a concluding question, he asked: 'Will [England] not show the nations of the world that, to her, honour is dearer than revenge; and that Justice and Mercy, Honesty and Truth, are more righteous and more powerful factors in the dealings of man than all the gigantic and infernal paraphernalia of thrice-accursed War?'[41]

The one thing that both sides could agree on, however, was the heroism of the men who had fought the Zulus.[42] The journalist

James Ewing Ritchie opposed the war on the grounds that it was immoral and expensive: 'The mob and the pictorial papers will glorify the returning heroes who have crushed a savage who was mad enough to defy on his own behalf and that of his people the British power, and the British public will have to pay the bill.' He criticized the desire for revenge after Isandlwana:

> At the present moment we are witnessing a sorry spectacle for a Christian nation – that of a whole people hemmed in one corner of Eastern Africa, waiting to be swept off the face of the earth by the finest soldiers and the most scientific instruments of murder England has at her command. Their crime has been that in defending their native soil from the tread of the foe, they annihilated an English regiment, and for such an act there is no hope of pardon, in this world at least ... Already in England and in Africa the blood-stained demon of war has sown her seed and reaps her harvest; already there have been bitter tears shed over hundreds of fallen warriors in desolated homes, and women wail and children vainly cry for loved ones whose bones now bleach the distant plain of Isandula [*sic*]. And there will be sadder and darker tragedies to come if the wild instincts of the people are to be gratified and the Zulu Kaffirs are to be exterminated.

But even Ritchie admired the men who had fought and died: 'We have sacrificed valuable lives, but the men who have fallen have been embalmed in the nation's memory, and the story of their heroism will mould the character and fire the ambition and arouse the sympathies of our children's children, as they did of our fathers in days gone by.'[43]

Ritchie's reference to the men who had perished at Isandlawna being 'embalmed in the nation's memory' was accurate. Only a year after the battle, pilgrimages to the battlefield were already being undertaken by a handful of hardy tourists. The travel writer R. W. Leyland decided to visit South Africa on account of 'the prominence into which it had been brought by the late Zulu War'. At Isandlwana, 'the scene of the catastrophe', he

> walked about in the grass, picking up numbers of bullets, empty cartridges and various other articles. Among them was a small cake of paint in a little tin case, a lead pencil, several uniform buttons, a stud, tent pegs, nails, etc., etc., all lying as thrown down. But the most unpleasant sight were many bleached human bones. They had been washed by heavy rains out of the shallow graves in which they had been interred . . . We noticed some bodies partially exposed, portions of skeletons being visible. In one instance the leg bones, encased in leather gaiters, protruded at the bottom of a grave, and close by were the soldier's boots, containing what remained of his feet.[44]

Bertram Mitford, who toured South Africa in 1882, declared in the introduction to his travel narrative that he had gone there 'with the object of making the round of the battlefields'.[45] At Isandlwana, he saw the cairn marking the last stand of Durnford's men and the graves of the British dead. His experience of touring the battlefield was similar to Leyland's:

> there is no lack of traces of the melancholy struggle. In spite of a luxuriant growth of herbiage the circles where stood the rows of tents are plainly discernible, while strewn about are tent

pegs, cartridge cases, broken glass, bits of rope, meat tins and sardine boxes pierced with assegai stabs, shrivelled up pieces of shoe leather, and rubbish of every description; bones of horses and oxen gleam white and ghastly, and here and there in the grass one stumbles on a half-buried skeleton.[46]

Back in Britain, Isandlwana was commemorated via a number of memorials to the fallen. In the parish church at Bredgar in Kent, for example, a memorial was erected to Private Ashley Goatham of the 24th Foot, who had died at the age of twenty-four. The stone obelisk read:

They stood their ground cool and bold
In that disastrous day
And fought like warriors we are told
Till all were cut away.[47]

The heroism and sacrifice of the men who fought at Isandlwana thus became the source material for reshaping the battle from a disaster into a test that had proved the mettle of ordinary British soldiers.

This was not, however, what it had truly been about. Instead, its most direct consequence was the destruction of the military capacity of the Zulus and the dismemberment of their kingdom. In the Anglo-Zulu War, six thousand Zulus perished, four times as many deaths as the British suffered. In the final major confrontation, at Ulundi, 1,500 Zulus died as opposed to only thirteen British soldiers.[48] After fleeing from the battlefield, Cetshwayo was swiftly captured, deposed and imprisoned. The British divided Zululand into thirteen chiefdoms, each one under the control of a compliant leader. This 'divide and rule' strategy, however, soon collapsed into infighting and civil war. In 1882, the British attempted to restore Cetshwayo to power, but the back of the Zulu kingdom had been broken, and he could do little to diminish the chaos. After a clash with his rival Zibhebu, he was deposed for a second time, and died soon afterwards. His son Dinzulu attempted to form an alliance with the Boers against the British. He defeated Zibhebu in 1884 and briefly regained authority over a portion of Zululand, but the British had no wish to see a resurgence of Zulu power, and they annexed Zululand in 1887. Thus ended the long struggle of the Zulus to maintain their independence in the face of European colonialism.

Maiwand

Eighteen months after Isandlwana, the British Army experienced another disaster. In the late 1870s, the British faced a Russian incursion into Afghanistan, which posed a threat to the Northwest Frontier of India. This was not a new issue: Russia's efforts to infiltrate Afghanistan diplomatically dated from the 1830s and had already led to the First Anglo-Afghan War of 1839–42. That conflict had produced the disastrous retreat from Kabul, in which 16,500 British soldiers, Indian sepoys and camp followers had perished.[49] The British had recovered, however, and had ultimately emerged victorious. Two decades of uneasy peace followed.

But, in the 1860s, the Russians renewed their expansion into Central Asia, as was reflected in the establishment of the new province of Turkestan in 1867 and the annexation of Samarkand (today in Uzbekistan) in 1868. In response, the British stepped up their intelligence activities, leading to the most intense phase of the 'Great Game' of spying and covert manoeuvring in the region. With the advent of the more pro-imperial Conservative government in 1874, British policy became more aggressive, and the preservation of Afghanistan as a buffer zone, even if it entailed military action, was seen as essential.[50] The new policy was enthusiastically embraced by the new viceroy of India, Lord Lytton, who took office in 1876 and swiftly moved to strengthen Britain's position along the Northwest Frontier. This in turn led to an intensification of Russian activity in Afghanistan.

The first steps along the road to war had thus been taken, and all that was required now was an excuse for fighting actually to begin. In 1878, the Afghans refused to allow a British diplomatic mission on its way to Kabul to cross the Khyber Pass. Lytton demanded an apology from Amir Sher Ali, who suddenly found himself in the impossible position of offending either the British or the Russians no matter what he did. He thus did nothing, and in November, the British massed their forces on the Afghan border in preparation for an invasion. But, as had been the case in the late 1830s, the conquest of Afghanistan proved to be more easily imagined than accomplished. The limited resources that the British were able to deploy and the difficulties of the rugged terrain combined to make military operations extremely challenging. The Afghans could not hope to match the British in firepower, but the tribal warriors known as *ghazis* were motivated by a religious fervour that made them formidable foes. Against inexperienced troops, their screams and swinging of their *tulwars*, or curved swords, could be devastating.

From the perspective of the British commanders, however, the Afghans did not pose a serious threat. Much like their counterparts in Zululand, they went to war flush with confidence, and in the initial stages of the war combined sloppy reconnaissance with aggressive frontal attacks in a manner that courted disaster. Desiring a quick end to the war, the British were extremely ruthless towards the Afghan population, and floggings, hostage-taking and executions were common occurrences as they marched deeper into the country. As the British neared Kabul, a panicked Sher Ali fled, leaving power in the hands of his son Yakub Khan. Given little choice, the latter signed a peace treaty that granted the British considerable sway over Afghan affairs. But this apparently swift and tidy conclusion to the war proved a delusion. In July 1879, the new British permanent envoy to Kabul, Sir Louis Cavagnari, and his eighty-person retinue were murdered by Afghan soldiers who opposed the terms of the treaty. This shocking event demanded retribution, and it was not long in coming. British forces were once again sent into Afghanistan; the instructions given by Lytton to their commander, Major General Frederick Sleigh Roberts, conveyed the bloody-mindedness that now governed their actions:

> You cannot stop to pick and choose ringleaders. Every soldier of the Herati regiments is *ipso facto* guilty and so is every civilian be he priest, or layman, mullah or peasant who joined the mob of assassins. To satisfy the conventions of English sentiment it will probably be necessary to inflict death only in execution of the verdict of some sort of judicial authority. But any such authority should be of the roughest and readiest kind such as a drumhead Court Martial. It is not justice in the ordinary sense, but retribution that you have to administer on reaching Kabul ... Your object should be to strike terror, and strike it swiftly and deeply.[51]

Roberts was in full accord with this policy, telling Yakub Khan, who desperately (and probably truthfully) pleaded his innocence, that 'the great British nation would not rest satisfied unless a British army marched to Kabul and there assisted Your Highness to inflict punishment as so terrible and dastardly an act deserves'.[52]

After capturing Kabul in October 1879, Roberts immediately began rounding up dozens of suspects in the murder of the Cavagnari mission and executing them; by mid-November, nearly a hundred men had been hanged. This orgy of retribution discomfited some British observers. Colonel Sir Charles MacGregor, who was in charge of the tribunals that assessed the guilt or innocence of the suspects, complained: 'I do not think that men who merely fought against us without being concerned in Cavagnari's business should be killed but Bobs will kill them all.'[53] Outside Kabul, meanwhile, a number of surrounding villages were burned and the inhabitants forced to pay exorbitant fines. Roberts's political advisor, Sir Mortimer Durand, recorded in his diary: 'I think this sort of thing is wrong and impolitic. It causes deep and lasting resentment and it will not quiet the country.'[54] Indeed, Afghan mullahs were issuing increasingly vociferous denunciations of the 'infidels', and in December 1879 a ring of Afghan forces, comprising as many as 100,000 men, tightened around Kabul, awakening memories of the previous British occupation four decades earlier. Roberts, however, had learned the lessons of that disaster, and when the attack came on 22 December, he was able to repel it.

Now that the Afghans had made it clear that they had not been pacified by Roberts's draconian tactics, the British determined that nothing less than the complete conquest and dismemberment of the country would do. Lieutenant General Sir Donald

Stewart was dispatched to Kabul with a fresh contingent of troops from the Bengal Army to assume control of the situation. In its first action, Stewart's force won a hard-fought victory at Ahmed Khel, but the bulk of the Afghan soldiers escaped. In the south of the country, meanwhile, Afghan strength was growing under the leadership of Ayub Khan, Yakub Khan's brother and the ruler of Herat. By the summer of 1880, he had 25,000 troops under his command and had gained enough confidence to advance on the British garrison at Kandahar. In response, 2,700 men marched out under Brigadier General George Burrows to meet the threat.

Burrows understood that he was in a precarious situation. He was significantly outnumbered, and in order to meet Ayub's oncoming army, he would have to cross a barren desert that lacked supplies, forage and water. Manoeuvring to cut him off from Kandahar, Ayub crossed the Helmand River and took up a position near the village of Maiwand. Burrows now decided that the best option was to march to Maiwand and take on Ayub before his forces could fully assemble. His officers were confident in their ability to handle Ayub's army, despite its superior numbers. 'We thought that ... we should give them a good drubbing wherever we met them,' wrote Major George Crawford Hogg of the Poona Horse.[55] But what neither he nor Burrows knew was that Ayub had already amassed enough men to outnumber the British by more than ten to one.

By 27 July, the British were tired, hungry and thirsty from their long, slow trek across the desert in the blistering summer heat, which by midday reached temperatures of over 50°C. At 10 a.m., they had been marching for three-and-a-half hours when the first signs of the enemy were detected. Hogg was sent forward to conduct a reconnaissance, but due to the hilly terrain and a haze that hung over the sand that morning he saw only scattered groups of cavalry and infantry, not Ayub's full force. Burrows ordered an advance, but when the first units crossed one of several *nullahs*, or ravines, that scarred the plain, they could see around twenty thousand infantry and four thousand cavalry ranged in front of them. 'They were drawn up in thousands and thousands,' Hogg recounted, 'covering four or five miles of ground, and to be compared only to ants swarming out of their nests.' To sound the retreat now would have been disastrous; 'there was nothing for it but to fight it out in the open plain without any protection.'[56]

Seeing that he had caught the British in the open, Ayub ordered his cavalry to surround them, while his artillery began launching a devastating barrage at their exposed position. 'The enemy who had kept perfect silence for more than half an hour,' recalled Captain Mosley Mayne of the Bombay Light Cavalry, 'suddenly opened fire, battery after battery, till we could count about 30 guns ... There was not a vestige of cover.'[57] The *ghazis*, meanwhile, began creeping forward through the *nullahs*, with the intention of completing the enveloping movement that the cavalry had begun. Mayne recalled:

crowds of white-coated Ghazies ... streamed into the enclosures and village to our right. The firing then became general, the enemy gradually advancing and at this time developing flanking movements to both flanks, until we were ... in a sort of horse-shoe, and completely out-flanked on both sides. Sharp firing from the baggage in our rear told that the baggage-guard too were engaged ... The fire both from their artillery and small arms was very hot indeed. I was hit twice though only slightly wounded, and my horses kept dropping and men too.[58]

The British had nowhere to go: their superior small-arms fire-power could hold off the *ghazis* for a time, but their badly outgunned artillery – they had only twelve guns to Ayub's thirty-four – could not stop the constant rain of what Hogg described as 'round shot after round shot, shell after shell and every conceivable missile' from being 'hurled at our dazed heads hour after hour'. Hogg saw 'horses shot[,] poor brutes, with all their bowels hanging out, with broken legs and broken backs, some spinning around, some trying to gallop away from the hellish scene'. His men, too, were suffering badly, 'their legs shot off, torn by fragments of shell, struck by bullets here, there and everywhere ... wretched wounded men lying, imploring for help, unable to move, and, yet, not a man spare to carry them off'.[59]

Under such strain, the infantry could not hold out indefinitely. The British left was the weakest point in the line: its guns had been moved to the centre to bolster the defences there, and the 30th Native Infantry, known as 'Jacob's Rifles', had, after three hours of continuous firing, lost a fifth of its men, while the survivors were running low on ammunition. They were exhausted, starving and parched with thirst, and their Martini-Henry rifles were beginning to overheat and jam. At around 2 p.m., Mayne 'heard shouts and loud exclamations' from behind him and turned to see a 'confused mass of gun teams, infantry and ghazies all mixed together and our brigade in an utter rout'.[60] The 30th had broken and run, followed by the 1st Bombay Grenadiers. In their panic, they careened into the third and last infantry regiment, the 66th (Berkshire) Foot, who had been rock steady up to this point but now also broke. Although Hogg recalled that the 'European officers did all they could to rally their men', it 'was of no avail and the retrograde movement could not be stopped'. Burrows ordered

162

a cavalry charge, but it failed. As Hogg ruefully observed, 'the battle was of course then clean lost', as 'the infantry legged it as fast as they could from the ferocious ghazis'. The wounded were abandoned and 'hacked to pieces as they lay . . . on the ground'.[61]

The fleeing British were hotly pursued by Afghan cavalry. Kandahar, the nearest safe haven, was 50 miles (80 km) away, across rugged terrain inhabited by hostile villagers who were unlikely to treat the British with mercy. Many men were so exhausted that they simply lay down and waited to die. The 66th Foot, however, managed to retire in formation, which meant that they stopped periodically and fired at the Afghans as they retreated. As they fell back into the village of Khig at around 3 p.m., approximately two hundred survivors made the first of several stands in its walled gardens, in which they lost around sixty men. The 140 survivors fell back further into the village, where they made a second stand in which they lost a further eighty or so men. Now numbering only fifty-six, they retreated into another walled garden. Here, they made their last stand, lining the interior of the walls and shooting at the Afghans as they entered. But the enemy's numbers were too great, and they were overwhelmed and killed to a man. An Afghan officer later described their final moments:

> Surrounded by the whole of the Afghan army, they fought on until only eleven men were left, inflicting enormous loss on their enemy. These men charged out of the garden, and died with their faces to the foe, fighting to the death. Such was the nature of the charge, and the grandeur of their bearing, that although the whole of the ghazis were assembled around them, no one dared to approach to cut them down. Thus, standing in the open, firing steadily and truly, every shot telling, surrounded

by thousands, these officers and men died; and it was not until the last man was shot down that the ghazis dared advance upon them. The conduct of those men was the admiration of all that witnessed it.[62]

This was a bright spot in an otherwise disastrous battle. Out of Burrows's force of 2,700 men, twenty-one officers and 948 men were killed and another 169 wounded. (Only those wounded who could save themselves survived.) Out of its 516 officers and men, the 66th Foot lost 286, or 62 per cent. This was not quite as high as Isandlwana's 75 per cent death rate, but it was still horrific.[63] The response from Britain's military commanders, politicians and public echoed that to Isandlwana the previous year: redemption, retribution and remembrance. The soldiers who had fought were exonerated of blame, as it was argued that Burrows (who had survived) had been sent out with far too small a force. Once he located the enemy, he had only two choices: to turn around and go back to Kandahar, which would have rendered his expedition pointless and almost certainly engendered accusations of cowardice, or to continue forward and fight. As gunner Francis Naylor recalled: 'What was to be done? What road can you take when there is only one to use? We were like a gigantic creature which can only travel one way, and that is, ahead. There was only one thing to do, and one thing only, and that was to get the business through.'[64]

After Maiwand, full authority over military operations in Afghanistan was restored to Roberts, who immediately dispatched two divisions to relieve Kandahar, which was now under severe pressure from Ayub's forces. They reached the demoralized garrison on 31 August; the speed of their march became the most famous moment in Roberts's long career. He now had nearly fifteen thousand men (3,800 British and eleven thousand sepoys and Afghans), and with characteristic impatience decided to attack immediately. In the ensuing Battle of Kandahar, British forces routed the Afghans, losing only thirty-seven men to Ayub's 1,200. Having made their point, the British evacuated Afghanistan, leaving it in the hands of a new emir, Abdur Rahman, who would be responsible for maintaining his country as a buffer state against Russian encroachment. He was given a lavish annual subsidy to ensure that his loyalty did not waver.

As had happened with Isandlwana, efforts were made to erase the trauma of a devastating defeat by emphasizing the heroism of the men who fought. And as had occurred with the last stand of the 24th Foot, the last stand of the 66th Foot became a key moment in the battle. In 1882, the scene was painted by Frank Feller, who depicted a weary knot of men, led by a stoical officer with his arm in a sling, attempting to hold off a huge mass of Afghans.[65] Even more romanticized was Harry Payne's version of the 66th's last stand, painted in 1892, in which the soldier in the centre stands with his left leg thrust defiantly forward as he reaches in his ammunition pouch for another round; to his right, a comrade who has just been shot in the chest slumps back. But also as with Isandlwana, there existed unpleasant reminders of the reality of the battle. Shortly after Maiwand, Major Henry John Nuthall of the Bengal Staff Corps painted a watercolour of the ground on which the 66th had made its last stand, still strewn with dead horses and with a mass grave in the centre.[66] (See Figure 45.)

In July 1881, the 66th Foot was amalgamated with the 49th Princess Charlotte of Wales's (Hertfordshire) Regiment of Foot.

The 2nd Battalion of the new regiment, called the Princess Charlotte of Wales's (Berkshire) Regiment, was assigned to guard duty at Osborne House.[67] In August, Queen Victoria personally presented five men from the former 66th with the Distinguished Conduct Medals they had won at Maiwand. Afterwards, she requested to meet Bobbie, the small white dog who served as the regiment's mascot and who had been wounded in the battle.[68] Maiwand also became the focus of a large-scale war memorial that was, unusually for the time, not funded by the armed services or the government, but by the public. In 1881, the money was requested for a memorial to be erected in Reading in Berkshire, where the 66th Foot was based. It flowed in rapidly, with the officers of the 66th leading the way with a contribution of £125. The total of £1,088 was, in fact, sufficient for two memorials: a window in St Mary's Church, which was installed in 1882, and a monument in Forbury Gardens. For the latter, George Blackall Simonds, a noted artist and the son of a local brewery owner, was selected as the sculptor. Simonds proposed that the memorial take the form of a massive cast-iron lion on a plinth, on which the names of the 328 men who had died would be inscribed; in this regard the memorial was similar to the earlier monument honouring the 24th Foot's charge at Chillianwallah in the grounds of Chelsea Royal Hospital in London. The memorial was unveiled in 1886; today, it serves as the symbol of the city in which it is located, as is confirmed by its appearance on the badge of Reading Football Club.[69]

Perhaps the most prominent way in which Maiwand lived on, however, was in literature. Rudyard Kipling based a short story, 'The Drums of the Fore and Aft' (1888), and a poem, 'That Day' (1894), on the battle. William McGonagall's poem 'The Last

Berkshire Eleven' (1899) also celebrated Maiwand. The battle's most famous literary appearance, however, occurs in Arthur Conan Doyle's *A Study in Scarlet* (1881). In the opening sentences, the reader is informed that Dr Watson was seriously wounded in the 'fatal battle of Maiwand'. Later, in what is perhaps the most famous introduction in literary history, Sherlock Holmes's first utterance to Watson is: 'How are you? You have been in Afghanistan, I perceive?' Later, Holmes tells him how he knew:

> The train of reasoning ran: 'Here is a gentleman of a medical type, but with the air of a military man. Clearly an Army doctor then. He has just come from the tropics, for his face is dark, and that is not the natural tint of his skin, for his wrists are fair. He has undergone hardships and sickness, as his haggard face says clearly. His left arm has been injured. He holds it in a stiff and unnatural manner. Where in the tropics could an English Army doctor have seen much hardship and got his arm wounded? Clearly in Afghanistan.'[70]

Holmes's deduction is based on the fact that Watson has been wounded, confirming Maiwand's cultural resonance in Britain as a violent, scarring event.

The last stand was a compelling military image in late Victorian culture. Its prevalence helped to assuage some of the discomfiture occasioned by the nature of military conflict in the late Victorian British Empire. New weapons such as breech-loading repeating rifles and machine guns provided greatly improved firepower from the days of Wellington. In many imperial locales prior to the middle of the nineteenth century, the British had faced roughly equivalent armaments, and conquest was a process measured in decades. After 1870, however, the advantage shifted decisively towards Britain. The expansion of the empire in the late nineteenth century was thus not only more rapid but also more bloody, brutal and violent for those who stood in its way. The need to highlight instances that mitigated this thus became all the more pressing, but such a strategy could not completely conceal the reality of what was happening. Britain's late nineteenth-century wars in Africa and Afghanistan produced temporary setbacks in the form of the defeats at Isandlwana and Maiwand and the loss of the Shangani Patrol, but these were inaccurate reflections of the balance of power between Britain and those who resisted its efforts to expand its colonial authority. The combined British death toll in the Anglo-Zulu, Second Anglo-Afghan and First Matabele Wars was 2,600. For the Africans and Afghans, meanwhile, it was 21,000. The Afghans would soon recover much of their independence, but the power of the Zulu and Ndebele kingdoms was forever destroyed.

CHAPTER SIX

GENERAL GORDON

IN EARLY OCTOBER 1884, a relief expedition steamed up the Nile in an effort to reach Major General Charles Gordon at Khartoum in the Sudan. Gordon, along with a garrison of Egyptian troops and the civilian inhabitants of the town who had not fled, was being besieged by the forces of the Mahdi, the leader of an Islamic revolt against the authority of Britain's ally the khedive of Egypt. Gordon had been sent to evacuate the garrison, but had instead refused to abandon Khartoum, gambling that William Gladstone's Liberal government would be forced to send a relief expedition. He was right, but it had been dispatched only at the eleventh hour in response to mounting public and political pressure. General Sir Garnet Wolseley divided the force into two columns: in an effort to reach Khartoum more quickly, a small contingent struck out across the desert on camels, while the main body of the army floated up the Nile in boats. Major G. B. Martin of the Royal Artillery served on the staff of Colonel William Butler, who had been placed in charge of building the boats for the river column. Martin sent a series of letters reporting on the column's progress to Brigadier General Sir William Howley Goodenough, who was in charge of the Royal Artillery in Egypt but who had remained in Cairo. On 3 October, Martin reported to Goodenough that Butler had 'written a good boatsong' that imitated Alfred Tennyson's 'Six Hundred'. The men enjoyed singing it, as 'the air is a rolling one such as soldiers love'.[1]

Tennyson's 'Six Hundred' was, of course, a reference to 'The Charge of the Light Brigade', the famous poem about the cavalry disaster at Balaclava during the Crimean War. Martin was unaware, however, that as he steamed up the Nile he was heading towards another heroic failure that would become equally famous. For the relief expedition failed to reach Gordon in time: a small advance force arrived at Khartoum on 28 January 1885 to find it a smoking ruin. It had fallen to the Mahdi two days before.

'Knight-Errant in the Cause of Right': Gordon as Hero

Of all the late nineteenth-century imperial heroes, General Charles George Gordon is one of the most difficult to comprehend from a modern perspective. On the one hand, he was a religious zealot whose evangelical fervour filled with him a sense of righteousness and certainty that seems to represent the worst of the high Victorian determination to impose British values upon the rest of the world. Add to this the accusations of paedophilia that have surfaced in recent Gordon biographies, and a perfect picture of a moral hypocrite emerges. But, on the other hand, Gordon had a healthy respect for true believers like himself, even when they were of non-Christian faiths, and he felt a genuine connection to, and responsibility for, the people of the Sudan, even if that meant sacrificing his own life. Was his death at Khartoum in 1885 a madman's final grandiose gesture, or was it the action of a moralist who was determined to fulfil the commitment that Britain had made to the Sudan? Gordon may have been eccentric, and by the end possibly insane, but there was truth when he pointed an accusing finger at a late Victorian imperialism that wanted power and profit but quickly retreated when the situation became too complicated or the costs became too high, ignoring the consequence for the peoples left behind.

In the 1880s, Egypt was still technically part of the Ottoman Empire, but in practice the khedive was all but independent from the sultan's authority. This had permitted Isma'il Pasha (1863–79) to launch an ambitious programme of reform, including the construction of a railway network and the rebuilding of Cairo along Parisian lines. The centrepiece of his plans was the Suez Canal, which opened in 1869 and linked the Mediterranean to the Red Sea, thereby eliminating the need to make a long journey around the southern tip of Africa. None of these schemes came cheaply, and by the 1870s, Isma'il's debts had soared to over £100 million. (His lavish personal spending habits did not help.) This vast sum was owed almost entirely to European creditors, who assumed that their governments would ensure the security of their investments even if the khedive balked at paying. The situation quickly became ruinous. Isma'il was forced to sell everything of value that he owned, including his shares in the Suez Canal Company, which the British prime minister Benjamin Disraeli purchased for a bargain-basement sum of £4 million in 1875. But even that was not enough, and in 1876, he suspended repayments on his loans. With the British taking the lead, the European powers promptly deposed Isma'il in favour of his eldest son, Tewfiq Pasha.

At the same time, trouble was brewing in the Sudan, the million square miles (2.59 million sq km) of territory to Egypt's south. Inhabited by feuding tribes who spoke four hundred different languages, the Sudan possessed only one commodity that had any value: slaves. In the dreams of the khedives, it was a prosperous and modern extension of Egypt; in reality, they ruthlessly extorted taxes and winked at the slave trade so long as the traders continued to contribute to their coffers. The Sudanese, however, were too fractious to mount any unified resistance.

Increasing European control of Egypt led to one revolt; the unstable situation in the Sudan to another. In Egypt, mounting anti-foreign sentiment provoked an army colonel named Ahmad Urabi (his name was usually altered to 'Arabi' in European accounts) into leading a coup in 1879 that temporarily deposed Tewfik Pasha. Britain's Liberal government now found itself in the first of many difficult positions it would experience in Egypt. Gladstone felt genuine sympathy for the Egyptian people's right of self-determination, but his initial inclination to support Urabi's revolt evaporated when the khedive's creditors began to howl. Moreover, there were serious strategic considerations to take into account: four out of every five ships that passed through the Suez Canal were British, and a secure Egypt was necessary to safeguard the route to India. When Urabi's followers began to massacre the European population of Alexandria, Gladstone dispatched the Royal Navy to bombard the city, and then landed thirty thousand troops to ensure that the revolt caused no further trouble. In September 1882, Urabi's forces were soundly defeated at Tel el-Kebir. Urabi was exiled to Ceylon and Tewfik Pasha was reinstated as khedive.

The situation in the Sudan proved even more difficult to resolve. With Egypt reduced to a puppet state, British politicians wanted only to defend their interests there, not to take on the administration of the Sudan's strategically useless and unprofitable desert wastes. In the early 1880s, however, a revolt against Egyptian rule was launched by a Muslim cleric named Muhammad Ahmed, who claimed to be the 'Mahdi', the long-prophesied descendant of the Prophet Muhammad who had been sent to redeem the Muslim world. The British authorities in Cairo reluctantly acceded to the khedive's demand that the rebellion be suppressed and, in 1883, a force of eight thousand Egyptian soldiers under the command of Colonel William Hicks, a retired Indian Army officer, marched south. Hicks's men were poorly trained, poorly equipped and almost entirely lacking in military discipline. They made it as far as El Obeid in the central Sudan before a forty thousand-strong Mahdist army swept down upon them. Only three hundred Egyptians and two of the twelve European officers survived; Hicks was not among them.

When the news of Hicks's slaughter reached London, Gladstone decided that the time for humouring the khedive on the Sudan had passed. He ordered the authorities in Cairo to carry out an immediate evacuation of all Europeans and Egyptians. Having little choice, Tewfik agreed, but he requested that the British send one of their officers to organize operations; it was thought that the Mahdi would not dare attack the evacuees if they were under direct British authority. It was a dangerous assignment that would require both military and diplomatic skill. In some ways, Major General Charles George Gordon was the ideal candidate. An officer in the Royal Engineers, he had served with distinction in the Crimean War. In the 1860s, during the Second Opium War, he commanded the 'Ever Victorious Army' of Chinese troops who put down the Taiping Revolt against the emperor. Ever since, the British public had seen 'Chinese Gordon' as a hero. In other ways, however, Gordon was less well suited to the job. He was rigid, impulsive and tended to gravitate towards the ideal, whereas the task at hand required flexibility, caution and clear-headed pragmatism. The situation could only be resolved via compromise and negotiation, and neither Gordon nor the Mahdi, who were both inclined to transform purposes into causes, was likely to bend. The difference was that the Mahdi held all the cards, for the forces at his disposal were far superior to anything Gordon could bring to bear.

Gordon arrived in Khartoum in September 1884. Once there, though charged with carrying out an immediate evacuation, he proved extremely reluctant to leave. Gordon may have been unwilling to depart until he felt he could safely take every Egyptian and European with him – a formidable task, as tens of thousands of soldiers and civilians would have to march across hundreds of miles of desert controlled by the Mahdi's forces. He may have feared the consequences of abandoning the Sudanese and may therefore have been attempting to force the British government to take a more active role in the administration of the Sudan. Whatever his reasons, he clearly thought that by remaining in Khartoum he would compel the British government to send a force to relieve him.

Gladstone felt differently. In his eyes, Gordon had agreed to go to Khartoum to carry out an evacuation, and if he disobeyed orders then the consequences were his problem. It was not the responsibility of the British government to send a costly relief force to rescue someone who had exceeded his authority and mission. A tense stalemate resulted, while the Mahdi besieged Khartoum and waited, knowing he could take the city at any time but reluctant to do so because he was aware that Gordon's death might bring a sharp British response. As Gordon continued to hold out, public pressure in Britain mounted; people cared little about the Sudan, but a great deal about Gordon.

Gladstone finally blinked, but too late. In August, the aforementioned relief column was dispatched to rescue Gordon. Its progress up the Nile, however, was slowed by shallow waters, confrontations with the Mahdi's forces, and a decided lack of urgency on Wolseley's part. It reached Khartoum, as we know, two days too late. The news of the fall of Khartoum reached London on the night of 4 February 1885. Wolseley's dispatch to the war secretary, the marquess of Hartington, reported that Gordon's body had not been found and thus his fate was still 'uncertain'.[2] The Cabinet was urgently called back to Westminster for a meeting the next day. It drew up a list of British objectives in the Sudan, the first of which was 'the safety of Gordon if still alive'.[3] Four days later, however, it became clear that Gordon was dead. After a victory over the Mahdi's forces at Kirkbekan, British troops found a letter from the governor of Berber containing a report from the Mahdi that described Khartoum's fall and the death of Gordon, 'the accursed one'.[4]

Gordon's death removed the most pressing reason for the British to remain engaged in the Sudan, and Wolseley's force was quickly brought home, using the excuse of the threat of war with Russia over Afghanistan. The whole adventure had been a disaster from start to finish. The Mahdi died of typhus in June 1885, but his successor, Khalifa Abdallahi ibn Muhammad, ruled the Sudan for the next fourteen years. The episode had shaken British confidence so deeply that it had made Henry Sclater, deputy assistant adjutant general in Cairo, extremely pessimistic about the future of the empire. He wrote to General Goodenough:

> I cannot bear to think of all the ... promises that we have
> made ... Now, all is broken faith, and we are no longer
> the nation out here that we used to be ... One cannot help
> feeling ... that the heart of the Empire and the centre of its life
> is not what it was. Whether it is the commencement of the
> decline of England I know not, but it reminds me much of the
> history of the fall of the Roman Empire.[5]

A disgusted Major Martin concluded: 'What a fiasco the expedition has been! ... Africa keeps up the reputation of being the grave of reputations.'[6]

It would not, however, be the grave of Gordon's reputation. In British memory, he became, as Colonel Butler wrote in his biography in 1889, 'a man as unselfish as Sidney, of courage dauntless as Wolfe, of honour stainless as Outram, of sympathy wide-reaching as Drummond, of honesty straightforward as Napier, of faith as steadfast as More'.[7] The Victorians were good at grief, but the outpouring that resulted from Gordon's death was staggering, even by their standards. The Oxford theologian Benjamin Jowett declared: 'there never has been a public calamity ... affecting so deeply the hearts and minds of England'.[8] Reginald Barnes, the vicar of Heavitree and a friend of Gordon's, wrote: 'When the terrible tidings were made known, England mourned for Gordon as she has seldom mourned even for her heroes. His unworldly temper, his ardent faith, his magnificent energy, his sublime unselfishness – in all this there was something that captivated the heart of the nation; and it needed but the crowning glory of his death to evoke an expression of love and reverence to which there is hardly a parallel in our history.'[9] A day of national mourning was declared for 13 March 1885, with memorial services being held in both Westminster Abbey and St Paul's Cathedral.

Almost immediately, discussions of a national memorial began. Shaped by the wishes of Gordon's brother, Sir Henry William Gordon, for it to be 'for the benefit of young and unfortunate victims of poverty and neglect' rather than a statue or other public monument, the initial proposal was for a hospital in Port Said. When the public deemed this too distant from British shores, it took the new form of the Gordon Boys' Home for impoverished and orphaned young males in Woking.[10] But there would be more traditional monuments as well: a cenotaph in St Paul's Cathedral, a bust in Westminster Abbey, and statues in Trafalgar Square, Gravesend, Chatham, Melbourne and Khartoum. The unveiling of the statue of Gordon at the headquarters of the Royal Engineers in Chatham took place on 19 May 1890.[11] The route through Chatham to the barracks in front of which the statue stood was lined by 'a vast concourse of spectators', who carried signs reading 'Think of Gordon's Life' and 'The Honour of Gordon Ever Remembered'. The importance of the occasion was indicated by the presence of the prince of Wales, who referred to Gordon as 'an Englishman whose name will forever remain memorable in the annals of history for Christian fortitude and heroic courage under unexampled difficulties'.[12]

Some individuals were so moved that they launched their own memorial schemes. C. J. Schofield of Manchester offered £20 for the best design of a stained-glass window to be installed in Manchester cathedral 'in memory of that great and good man who has very truly been called the hero of heroes'.[13] A real-estate developer in Camberwell wished to name 'a block of artizans dwellings' after Gordon; the architect, Ellis Marsland, contacted Sir Henry to ask for an engraving of his brother's arms, which would be emblazoned on 'a heraldic shield in the cornice of the main staircase'.[14] All over Britain and the empire, streets, pubs and buildings were named after Gordon. George William Joy's extremely popular painting *General Gordon's Last Stand* (1893), which depicted him at the top of a staircase in the Governor's Palace at Khartoum, calmly awaiting his fate as a Mahdist soldier aimed a spear at his chest, was reproduced in countless prints and engravings. (See Figure 46.) Poets, novelists and biographers rushed works into print; Tennyson composed the epitaph that was inscribed on his sarcophagus in St Paul's:

Warrior of God, man's friend, and tyrant's foe
Now somewhere dead far in the waste Soudan,
Thou livest in all hearts, for all men know
This earth has never borne a nobler man.

That sarcophagus was empty, for Gordon's body was never recovered.[15] The absence of Gordon's physical remains, however, allowed Britons to fill the empty space with their own conceptions of the heroism that Gordon embodied.[16] These conceptions were contained in the correspondence received by Sir Henry and by Gordon's eldest sister, Augusta, which included hundreds of condolence letters, sent from all corners of the British Isles as well as from America, Europe, Africa, Asia and Australia. Some came from people who knew Gordon or his family well; others were from perfect strangers. They arrived from both prominent and humble people – some of the authors were barely literate – and from all across the political spectrum.

In terms of the views that were expressed about Gordon's death, the correspondence contains a number of themes. There is little on the specifics of the complex geopolitical situation that had led to Gordon being sent to Khartoum, and though there is some criticism of the failure of Gladstone's government to send a relief force earlier, this is far from the most prominent element. Instead, the writers emphasize Gordon's status as a Christian martyr who would now enjoy everlasting fame and who would serve as an example to future generations of Britons.

On the one hand, Gordon was depicted in romantic style as a modern-day knight. The popularity of medieval and chivalric ideals in Victorian Britain has been well documented.[17] But, transposed into an imperial context, the invocation of knightly conduct as a standard for male behaviour took on new and more specific meanings. The last section of Tennyson's long narrative poem *The Idylls of the King*, a retelling of the Arthurian legend, was published in 1885, the year that Gordon died. As the poem neared its conclusion, Tennyson shifted the emphasis from King Arthur's attempt to build a perfect society at Camelot to the quest for the Holy Grail. This could be seen as a metaphor for Britain's view of itself as an imperial nation as it sent its own imperial 'knights' out to distant corners of the world.[18] The qualities of an ideal medieval knight – bravery, loyalty, generosity, modesty, purity and compassion – were all attributed to Gordon. Colonel Butler described him as 'the mirror and measure of true knighthood', adding: 'Doubtful indeed is it if anywhere in the past we shall find a figure of knight or soldier to equal him, for sometimes it is the sword of death that gives to life its real knighthood.'[19] One poet called him 'England's Christian knight', while another preferred 'knight-errant in the cause of right'.[20]

The knightly attribute of chivalry was frequently invoked in descriptions of Gordon's character. 'Ah, Gordon! Thy name was to chivalry sweet,' wrote George O'Byrne of Nottingham. The Reverend Arthur Robins of Windsor declared: 'God who giveth gifts to men, gave the white robe of His Own chivalry to thee.'[21] Addressing an audience in Melbourne, Australia, the Liberal MP Viscount Lymington described Gordon as 'a man who had shown that the golden qualities of English chivalry were not a mere paean and recollection of the past'.[22] Some of Gordon's mourners made these comparisons more explicit by linking him with specific figures from medieval legend. One parallel was the Seigneur de Bayard, the late fifteenth- and early sixteenth-century French knight who was famed for his courtly manners and bravery in battle. In a sermon preached at Scarborough in March 1885, the Reverend Frederick L. Blunt referred to Gordon as 'the Chevalier Bayard *sans peur et sans reproche* ... of this century'.[23] James Moorhouse, the bishop of Melbourne, referred to Gordon as a 'modern Bayard', while Major General Francis Downes, who had just become head of the state of Victoria's Department of Defence, asserted: 'the resemblance between him and Bayard is far closer than most people think ... And, strange to say, his end was like the end of Bayard, for ... Bayard was on the losing side, and the star of his heroism shone out more brightly because ... of the clouds of calamity in which it set.'[24] In *Chinese Gordon* (1884), Archibald Forbes also compared him to Bayard and, in 1898, G. Barnett Smith declared that he was 'well entitled to be styled a modern Bayard':

Like him he died with his face to the foe; and like him, his love of virtue, and especially of that kingliest of virtues, justice, was strong and passionate. It is said that Bayard was wont to declare that all empires, kingdoms and provinces where justice did not rule were mere forests filled with brigands. Could not the same be said of Gordon, who went abroad redressing human wrongs, lifting up the unfortunate and the oppressed and commending the love of that Master whom he served to the whole of the human race?[25]

Bayard was not the only legendary knight to whom Gordon was compared, however. Forbes also likened him to Sir Lancelot, while Moorhouse invoked Sir Galahad, 'whose strength was as the strength of ten, because his heart was pure'.[26] In the introduction to her children's book *The Story of General Gordon* (1906), Jeanie Lang wrote:

> When boys read the old fairy tales, and the stories of King Arthur's Knights of the Round Table, and the Knights of the Faerie Queen, they sometimes wonder sadly why the knights that they see are not like those of the olden days ... But if the boys think this, it is because they do not quite understand. Even now there live knights as pure as Sir Galahad, as brave and true as St George. They may not be what the world would call 'knights'; yet they are fighting against all that is not good, and true, and honest, and clean, just as bravely as the knights fought in days of old. And it is of one of those heroes, who sought all his life to find what was holy, who fought all his life against evil, and who died serving his God, his country and his Queen, that I want to tell you now.[27]

Galahad, the only Knight of the Round Table sufficiently pure to achieve the quest for the Holy Grail, was one of the most popular figures from Arthurian legend in the late nineteenth century because he was seen as a man who elevated moral and spiritual concerns above material and worldly ones. In the 1890s, the artist George Frederic Watts presented a copy of his painting *Sir Galahad* to Eton College, where it was hung in the chapel in an effort to inspire future generations. In 1914, the Presbyterian minister James Burns wrote:

> It should not be difficult for us now to understand the purpose of the great artist. For there are gathered many of the youth of our great Empire who in coming generations are to guide its destinies. In these early and formative days young eyes look out upon life with wistful questionings, and young hearts receive their lasting spiritual impressions. It is then that the great decisions are made, and it is upon the nature of those decisions that the future character and stability of our Empire depend.[28]

Galahad made a perfect parallel to Gordon, whose lonely death at Khartoum echoed the famous knight's solitary, tortuous path to the Holy Grail. Andrew Thompson has written that the late Victorians venerated above all the heroism of 'the ordinary soldier who guarded distant colonial outposts, fought against all the odds and was sometimes rescued but more often overpowered by the enemy ranged against him'.[29] Gordon fitted this ideal perfectly. General Sir Gerald Graham, a friend of Gordon's and fellow Royal Engineer who had been sent to Egypt in 1882, wrote in his memoir of how Gordon and his second-in-command, Colonel John Stewart, had been given the onerous challenge of leading the evacuation of the Sudan:

30 A group of officers and men from the 13th Light Dragoons who survived the Charge of the
Light Brigade (1854). This photograph was taken by Roger Fenton the day after the Battle of
Balaclava. Captain Soame Gambier Jenyns is the bearded figure slightly to the right of centre
directly behind the seated soldier. During the Charge of the Light Brigade, Jenyns was left in
command of the 13th Light Dragoons when the two officers senior to him were killed. Afterwards,
he was among the most prominent survivors of the charge. He later rose to the rank of lieutenant
colonel prior to retiring from the army in 1871.

31 William Simpson's illustration of the Charge of the Light Brigade (1854). Simpson's depiction was a distant, bird's-eye view that reinforced the sense of the charge's nobility, just as it emphasized the orderliness of the British advance as it faced artillery fire from three sides. It was not made on the basis of first-hand knowledge, however, since Simpson only arrived in the Crimea three weeks after the battle. This was evident in his watercolour, which shows the British advancing from east to west rather than west to east.

32 *James Thomas Brudenell, 7th Earl of Cardigan* by Sir Francis Grant (1841). Painted thirteen years before Balaclava, Grant's portrait of Cardigan emphasizes the heroic image of the cavalry officer in the mid-nineteenth century. Cavalry troops like the men of the Light Brigade wore splendid, tight-fitting uniforms that were covered in gold braid. Here, Cardigan is depicted in the uniform of the 11th Hussars, one of the regiments later sent to the Crimea as part of the Light Brigade. They were particularly noticeable in their blue jackets and bright red trousers, which earned them the nickname 'Cherry Bums'.

33 Thomas Jones Barker, *The Charger of Captain Nolan Returning with his Dead Master* (c. 1855). Barker, an Irish artist specializing in historical painting, depicted Nolan's slumped body being carried back to the British lines by his panicked horse. The image shows Nolan as a battlefield casualty and does not assign him any blame for the Charge of the Light Brigade.

34 Lithograph of the room in Blantyre in which David Livingstone was born (c. 1856). The Victorians saw Livingstone's rise from poverty as embodying the virtues of thrift, responsibility and self-help, and the circumstances of his youth were frequently emphasized in retellings of his life story.

35 Silver casket presented to Livingstone (1856). After returning from his transcontinental Zambesi trek, Livingstone was given this casket upon being awarded the freedom of the City of London. The attention and expense that went into its creation attest to the level of fame Livingstone had attained.

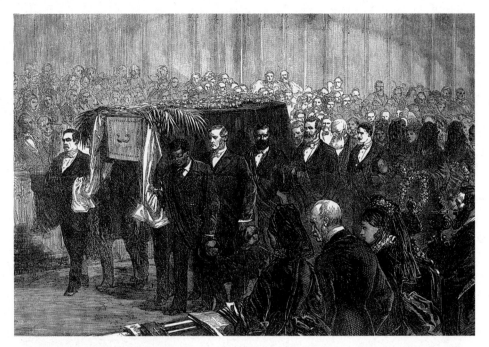

36 This image taken, from the *Illustrated London News*, depicts Livingstone's funeral in Westminster Abbey in April 1874. The Treasury paid the £500 cost. The pallbearers included Henry Morton Stanley and Livingstone's African servant Jacob Wainwright, shown here to the front left of the coffin, who had been deputed to accompany the body back to England because he spoke English.

37 Posthumous print offered for public sale after Livingstone's death. The hagiographic image conveys the saintly reputation Livingstone enjoyed in the years immediately following his death.

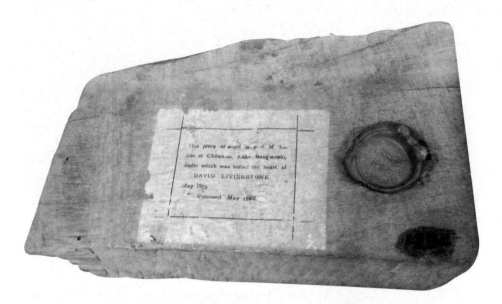

38 Piece of wood from the mvule tree under which Livingstone's heart was buried (c. 1897). After the tree became diseased, it was cut down in 1897 and pieces of it became sacred relics. This example displays the wax seal of Cecil Rhodes's British South Africa Company, showing how Livingstone's heroic reputation as a benevolent presence in Africa was used to legitimize subsequent imperial ventures.

39 and 40 Cartes de visite of Livingstone and Stanley (c. 1872). These cards show the contrasting images that Livingstone and Stanley wished to project as African explorers and imperialists. The differences were encapsulated in their headgear: Livingstone chose a simple peaked cap, similar to those worn by naval officers, because he believed it offered the best protection from the African sun. Stanley's pith helmet with its red tartan cloth band and tassel, in contrast, was the hat of a man looking to cut a dash. Stanley saw Africa as a stage on which his own ambitions could be brought to life, and when they were he would be dressed for the part. The prominent presence of the hats in these photographs produced for public consumption was no accident, as both men regarded them as essential to their public personae.

41 Allan Stewart, *There Were No Survivors* (1895). The men of the Shangani Patrol, with Alan Wilson centre front, stand calmly and bravely as they face the Ndebele onslaught. The Ndebele are visible only as bodies on the ground, but the retreat of the British into a small circle makes their predicament clear.

42 and 43 Sketches from an anonymous soldier's notebook made during the Second Matabele War (c. 1896). With its casual references to the 'terrible execution' caused by the Maxim gun, the drawing on the left illustrates the brutal reality of a conflict in which African casualties were a thousand times greater than those of the British forces. In the drawing on the right, however, the artist perpetuates the myth of the British as underdogs.

44 Charles Edwin Fripp, *The Last Stand at Isandula* (1885). Fripp was a special artist for the *Graphic* who arrived in Zululand four weeks after Isandlwana. He visited the battlefield and saw the numerous British corpses that still lay unburied. His painting, however, largely ignored the brutal reality of the battle; instead, the men in the centre maintain order and discipline as they fight resolutely to the death. Today, this is the most popular painting in the National Army Museum collection.

45 Henry John Nuthall, *The Ground Where the 66th Foot Made their Last Stand at Maiwand* (1880). With its dead horses and mass grave, Nuthall's watercolour provides a vivid contrast to conventional Victorian depictions of 'last stands' in battle.

46 Herbert Thomas Dicksee, etching of General Gordon's death (1897). Based on George William Joy's painting *General Gordon's Last Stand* (1893), Dicksee's etching, and a bevy of imitators, made this extremely popular image of Gordon's martyrdom widely available.

47 and 48 Aftermath of the Battle of Omdurman (1898). Contrasting views of the scene after Major General Sir Herbert Kitchener's victory at Omdurman on 2 September 1898. Above, British soldiers gather for a solemn memorial service for Gordon. Below, the corpses of some of the ten thousand Mahdist troops who died that day. Only forty-seven British soldiers lost their lives.

49 Captain Scott on skis, *Terra Nova* expedition (c. 1911). Though it is frequently Scott's intellectual qualities that are highlighted in assessments of his leadership, he was in fact a hardy Antarctic traveller who often outpaced younger men on sledging journeys.

50 Scott and his companions at the South Pole (1912). Front row, left to right: Birdie Bowers and Edward Wilson; back row, left to right: Lawrence Oates, Robert Falcon Scott, Edgar Evans. This photograph was taken by Birdie Bowers, who pulled a string attached to the camera. The five men reached the Pole a day after finding a flag left by Roald Amundsen, who had been there five weeks earlier. 'We have turned our back now on the goal of our ambition,' Scott wrote in his diary, 'and must face our 800 miles of solid dragging – and good-bye to most of the day-dreams.'

51 Ten Mexican pesos donated to the Scott Memorial Fund (c. 1913). Donated by schoolboys from Mexico, these five-peso notes were forwarded by the British Consulate in Tampico. They illustrate the global nature of the response to Scott's death.

52 Edgar Evans (c. 1911). The death of the working-class petty officer Evans, who was the largest and strongest member of the party, revived fears of national degeneration that had first been awakened when many recruits for the Boer War had turned out to be poor physical specimens.

53 Lawrence Edward Grace Oates (c. 1911). In contrast to that of Edgar Evans, the death of the genteel cavalry officer Oates was pointed to as an example of gentlemanly selflessness and noble self-sacrifice.

54 Daniel Albert Wehrschmidt, *Robert Falcon Scott* (1905). After years in storage, Wehrschmidt's portrait of Scott went back on display in the National Portrait Gallery in early 2013. Its return to public view reflects not only the resilience of Scott's status as a hero, but also the continuing prevalence of heroic failure in British culture.

And this mighty task was to be carried out by two Englishmen, with no army at their back, in a country of vast extent, the greater portion of which was in open revolt under a religious leader who appealed to the ever-present fanaticism of the population, and who had just annihilated the whole available field-force which had been commanded by another Englishman. It seemed a forlorn hope; but one of these two Englishmen bore a mighty name, and was armed with a purer faith and higher spirit than mere fanaticism could inspire, while the other was an officer of tried worth and courage.[30]

In the introduction to a collection of Gordon's letters from the Crimea, Demetrius Boulger described Gordon as 'an almost solitary Englishman surrounded by a wide and ever-widening sea of rebellion and fanaticism'.[31] Colonel Butler recounted 'the amazing spectacle ... of this solitary soldier standing at bay, within thirty days' travel of the centre of Empire, while the most powerful kingdom on the earth – the nation whose wealth is as the sands of the sea, whose boast is that the sun never sets upon its dominions – is unable to reach him'.[32]

But if Gordon was described by some people in intensely romantic form as a modern-day Arthurian knight, others evaluated his achievements in more commonplace and contemporary terms. A word that appears over and over again in the letters of condolence to Gordon's brother and sister is 'duty'; Gordon himself had written in his last letter to his sister: 'I have tried to do my duty.'[33] The Devonian parson S. C. Clarke described Gordon as 'Dead to all love of self, forsaking all for duty!' Peter Gabittass, a poet from Clifton, proclaimed that Gordon 'died at duty's post' and that 'when duty called – was Gordon found'.

Edith Cornwall Leigh of Great Malvern referred to him as 'faithfully doing his duty'.[34] Martin Tupper of Norwood in Surrey proclaimed:

> Gordon is nobler; victorious he stands,
> For life or for death, as stern duty commands;
> Whatever a partisan statesman may plan,
> He works and he worships for God and for man;
> And, let what will happen, this, this is his boast –
> An Englishman dies, as he lives, at his post![35]

The Young Men's Christian Association chapter based at Trinity Church in Dublin wrote: 'We are sure the consciousness that dying as he did at the post of honour and duty, while it evoked the admiration and sympathy of the world, will tend greatly to alleviate the sorrow of those who have lost in him a brother and a friend.'[36] In a sermon preached at St Michael's Church in Chester Square in London in February 1885, the Reverend James Fleming declared that Gordon 'stood like one lashed to the post of duty till he was compelled to say, "No man stood with me, but all men forsook me!"'[37]

Equally important in defining Gordon's heroism was self-sacrifice. Queen Victoria telegraphed Gordon's sister Augusta to console her for the death of 'your dear noble, heroic brother who served his country and his Queen so truly, so heroically, with self-sacrifice so edifying to the world'.[38] An anonymous poet wrote in a similar vein:

> O magnitude of self-denial!
> Magnificence of loss and pain!

Life, glory yielded with a smile
And honour kept without a stain.[39]

Other amateur poets, meanwhile, referred to the 'noble deeds, without one thought of self' of the 'self-sacrificing hero'.[40]

Revenge for Gordon: Kitchener and Omdurman

As the pace and aggression of British imperialism in Africa increased in the final decades of the nineteenth century, Gordon, like Livingstone before him, gave it a benevolent face. In the introduction to the published version of Gordon's journal, Egmont Hake laid out an idealized set of principles for 'those whose lot is thrown in barbarous lands' that Gordon had supposedly embodied:

> To accept government, only if by so doing you benefit the race you rule; to lead, not drive the people to a higher civilisation; to establish only such reforms as represent the spontaneous desire of the mass; to abandon relations with your native land; to resist other governments, and keep intact the sovereignty of the State whose bread you eat; to represent the native when advising Ameer, Sultan or Khedive, on any question which your own or any foreign government may wish solved; and in this to have for prop and guide that which is universally right throughout the world, that which is best for the people of the State you serve.[41]

Similarly, Demetrius Boulger wrote: 'In these pages may be seen the clearness of vision, the promptitude of resolve and action, the steadfast courage, the unswerving devotion to duty, the implicit belief in his own country, which, if remarkable when combined in the person of an individual, are still the essential attributes of a people which as an insignificant minority is charged with and has accepted the task of spreading good government and maintaining peace through a great part of the Eastern world.'[42]

The reality of Britain's role in the Sudan, however, was very different from these idealized visions of empire. After learning of the fall of Khartoum in early February 1885, Captain John Pelham Dalison of the Queen's Own (Royal West Kent) Regiment wrote home to his mother thirsting for a fight:

> I like the cheek of the Mahdi calling on the British to surrender and all become Musselmen. We'll see him at Jericho first. It only shows his utter ignorance of the character and class of people he is dealing with, to think of such a thing, but then he is only a savage. Surrender indeed, I felt as if I should like to run across the desert into Khartoum by myself and run amuck among the Arabs, when I read the telegram.

Dalison complained that 'since the news arrived of the fall of K[hartoum]' the 'niggers here have got much bolder': 'They will actually look you in the face now, and make my fingers itch to knock 'em down, but one has to be very particular and careful not to irritate them, for if they deserted, we should lose all their labour and as there are thousands of them they would considerably increase the numbers of our enemy.' He predicted an easy victory for the British once they reached Khartoum. 'The tables shall be turned and we shall call upon the Mahdi to surrender,' he wrote. 'If he won't I shall be sorry for his army, for he is bound to lose 1000s against our superiority of arms, discipline and morale.'[43]

Here, then, we have all of the darker realities of late nineteenth-century imperialism: the casual racism, the readiness to resort to violence and the assumption of British superiority. Dalison's views present a stark contrast to the language of chivalry and gallantry that surrounded Gordon's death.

Dalison's hoped-for revenge for Gordon had to wait over thirteen years, but it did come eventually. The Sudan had not flourished after the Mahdi's death; the dervish army was demoralized and fractious as a result of being in a constant state of *jihad*, or holy warfare, against Egypt to the north and Abyssinia to the south. The population, meanwhile, had fallen from eight million in 1885 to three million a decade later, as famine, disease and the relentless persecution of supposed apostates took their toll. By the mid-1890s, the British, who retained a belief that the reconquest of the Sudan was inevitable and were awaiting just such an opportunity, determined that the Khalifa's state had been sufficiently weakened to ensure that a successful military campaign would be a relatively simple matter. They now had a strategic interest in the Sudan as well, for by retaking it they could curb the ambitions of the French, who were beginning to press into the region of the Upper Nile. In 1896, Major General Sir Herbert Kitchener, who as a young captain had served on the failed Gordon relief expedition in 1884 and 1885, was made sirdar, or commander, of a new Anglo-Egyptian army.

Initially, his orders were merely to establish a buffer zone along the border with the Sudan in order to protect Egypt, but as the Khalifa's power continued to crumble British ambitions expanded. Kitchener devoted nearly two years to training his troops and building a network of rail and steamship supply lines in preparation for a full-scale reconquest of the Sudan. On 2 September

1898, 25,000 British, Egyptian and Sudanese troops met sixty thousand followers of the Khalifa at Omdurman, a fort on the banks of the Nile that guarded Khartoum. The British Lee-Enfield rifles and Maxim machine guns made for slaughter: in five hours, eleven thousand Mahdists were killed and another sixteen thousand wounded, compared to only forty-seven dead and 382 wounded from Kitchener's force. 'What the fire those dervishes must have been under was like one cannot imagine!' wrote F. E. W. Hervey-Bathurst, an officer in the Grenadier Guards, in his diary. 'Our volleys went off like one shot, and with that, shells and Maxim guns, it must have been hell.'[44] Kitchener, for his part, shrugged and called it 'a thorough dusting'.[45] He left the wounded to die in the desert; afterwards, some reports claimed that he ordered many of them to be shot. He then proceeded to Khartoum, which still lay in ruins, and executed all of the Khalifa's followers he could find. The Mahdi's bones were exhumed from the tomb that had been built just outside the city and hurled into the Nile. Kitchener was presented with his skull as a trophy; the press printed (false) rumours that he used it as an inkwell.[46]

A desire for Gordon to be avenged had lingered in the hearts of many late Victorian Britons, but even so, Kitchener's actions aroused considerable discomfort. The desecration of the Mahdi's remains was seen as barbaric; Winston Churchill, who was at Omdurman as a war correspondent, called it 'a wicked act, of which the true Christian, no less than the philosopher, must express his abhorrence'. Queen Victoria, too, was appalled: she wrote to Kitchener to register her disapproval of 'the destruction of the poor body of a man who, whether he was very bad and cruel, after all was a *man* of certain importance ... The graves of our people have been respected, and those of her foes should, in her opinion, be also.'[47] (Italics in original.) The queen was reminding Kitchener that the British were expected to be magnanimous, not gloating, winners. This was the flip side of the celebration of Gordon's noble death; victory itself was less important than how one behaved in achieving it.

In some ways, the criticism of Kitchener was unfair, for he understood that Omdurman was about confirming Gordon's nobility, not about crushing the Sudanese. Two days after the battle, he gathered his troops for a 'Gordon Memorial Service' in Khartoum. Hervey-Bathurst described the service in his diary:

The troops were drawn up four deep facing the front of the house, Grenadiers on the right, Egyptians and Soudanese on the left, the 1st British Brigade at right angles to us on our right, the front rank fixed bayonets and shouldered. Officers stood in front and the Sirdar [i.e., Kitchener], attaches, generals and staffs stood in the centre . . . The drums of the Grenadiers and Black bands played 'God Save the Queen' and the khedival hymn. While this was being done, the flags, Union flag and Egyptian crescent and star, were hoisted on two flag poles put on top of the wall of the Palace. The British flag was up first and flew first in Khartoum. The gunboat *Melik* fired a salute of 15 guns (the governor's salute), and the troops gave three cheers for Her Majesty and three for the Khedive. Then the gunboat fired 15 minute guns, and while this was going on, the 'Dead March' was played, followed by the Egyptian 'Dead March' and a *pibroch* ('The Flowers of the Forest') by the pipers of the Camerons and Seaforth. Then the Soudanese band played two verses of Gordon's favourite hymn 'Abide with Me' and the Presbyterian [clergyman] read a prayer.

Hervey-Bathurst felt that 'the whole thing was most impressive as usual, and the occasion and surroundings intensified the feeling – English troops standing on the ground, and the flag flying again on the place that had been waiting for it for 13 years, and Gordon's murder avenged. I felt it was a great occasion and so did all of us.'[48] The next day, he toured the Mahdi's tomb and the Khalifa's house at Omdurman. He was plagued by 'the most vile stinks from dead dervishes', as everywhere he went there were 'lots of dead men, women and children'.[49] The contrast between the solemnity of the memorial service and the rotting corpses that littered the battlefield sums up the contradictions of the late Victorian empire, which was motivated by noble ideals but constantly forced to confront brutal and bloody realities. (See Figures 47 and 48.)

These contradictions were clearly visible in Sir Henry Newbolt's poem 'Vitaï Lampada' (1892), which became one of the dominant literary expressions of heroic failure in Victorian Britain:

There's a breathless hush in the Close to-night
Ten to make and the match to win
A bumping pitch and a blinding light,
An hour to play, and the last man in.
And it's not for the sake of a ribboned coat.
Or the selfish hope of a season's fame,
But his captain's hand on his shoulder smote
'Play up! Play up! And play the game!'

The sand of the desert is sodden red –
Red with the wreck of a square that broke
The gatling's jammed and the colonel dead,

And the regiment blind with dust and smoke.
The river of death has brimmed its banks,
And England's far, and Honour a name,
But the voice of a schoolboy rallies the ranks –
'Play up! Play up! And play the game!'

This is the word that year by year,
While in her place the school is set,
Every one of her sons must hear,
And none that hears it dare forget.
This they all with a joyful mind
Bear through life like a torch in flame,
And falling fling to the host behind –
'Play up! Play up! And play the game!'[50]

Today, the poem's link to Gordon is all but forgotten, but it refers to the Battle of Abu Klea in January 1885, in which the advance column of 1,100 men sent across the desert by Wolseley to reach besieged Khartoum fought off an attack by twelve thousand Mahdists. The column's one machine gun was jammed by sand after firing only seventy rounds, but although the Mahdists managed to penetrate the British square, they were pushed back by determined fire from the troops in the rear ranks. In the end, the British lost fewer than a hundred men while 1,100 Mahdists died in the fifteen-minute battle. An anonymous officer who visited the battlefield a month later reported that 'hundreds of rotting corpses of the enemy' were 'lying on the ground so thick in one place that I found myself unable to pick my way on my camel without his brushing up against the bodies'.[51] But these facts were all but forgotten in Newbolt's poem, which made it appear as if the British had *lost* the battle. Here, then, was the ultimate encapsulation of the sentiments that Gordon's death had crystallized: victory truly was irrelevant, as heroic failure was no longer a consolation for defeat, but a positive ideal that helped to conceal the realities of late nineteenth-century imperial warfare.

CHAPTER SEVEN

CAPTAIN SCOTT

IN 1900, A thirty-two-year-old naval lieutenant named Robert Falcon Scott was chosen to lead the National Antarctic Expedition, the first major British attempt to explore the Antarctic since James Clark Ross's venture of 1839–43. Scott had no polar experience and no particular interest in Antarctica, but he saw polar exploration as a means to promotion, something for which there were few other avenues in the peacetime Royal Navy. He also had a widowed mother and an unmarried sister to support. On his first trip south, he proved a capable leader with a natural inclination for scientific research, and as a result the *Discovery* expedition – known like most polar expeditions by the name of ship in which it travelled – achieved impressive results in increasing human knowledge of Antarctica.

Scott's first expedition, however, also demonstrated the limits of the methods of polar exploration that the British had developed over the course of the nineteenth century. These relied on man-hauling, in which men pulled the sledges themselves, as the primary mode of transport. Scott and his men made considerable improvements to the sledging techniques that had been used in the Arctic, but their shortcomings as a mode of polar travel were also revealed. In 1902, a sledging journey undertaken by Scott and two companions, Edward Wilson and Ernest Shackleton, established a new farthest south at 82°17'S. This was only 200 miles (320 km) further than the Norwegian Carsten Borchgrevink had gone in 1900, however, and only a third of the way to the South Pole. The party had sledged for ninety-three days, far longer than the Arctic explorers of the mid-nineteenth century had managed, but at nowhere near the speed it would take to get to the Pole and back before they ran out of food and other vital supplies. Suffering from exhaustion, extreme cold and malnutrition, Shackleton had nearly died.

In recognition of the expedition's achievements, Scott earned a bevy of medals and a promotion to captain, and was made a Commander of the Victorian Order. Far greater heroic stature, however, awaited the conqueror of the South Pole. It was Shackleton who made the next attempt, and very nearly succeeded: in January 1909, he and three companions made it to 88°23'S, only 97 miles (155 km) from the Pole. But he had fallen short, and it was now left to Scott to finish the job. It was a deceptively simple-looking task: follow in Shackleton's footsteps, but go just a bit faster, and the Pole would be his. Scott left nothing to chance: he devised an elaborate system of transport, using newly invented motor-sledges (the precursor to today's Sno-Cats), ponies (in imitation of Shackleton) and dogs. He was beginning to recognize the limits of man-hauling, but even so, it was to be the sole means of transport for the crucial last stages of the journey to the Pole and for virtually the entire journey back. (See Figure 49.)

The task was demanding enough in itself, but at the eleventh hour Scott was surprised to learn that he had competition. The

Norwegian explorer Roald Amundsen, who had led the first expedition to sail through the Northwest Passage from 1903 to 1906, had been intending to try to reach the North Pole first, but after Frederick Cook and Robert Peary both claimed to have got there in 1909, he turned south instead. Because Amundsen had raised the funds for his expedition by stating his intention to go to the Arctic, he feared that if he revealed that he was heading for the opposite end of the globe, his patrons might demand their money back. He therefore kept his new objective a secret until the last possible minute, not even telling his men where they were headed when they set sail. It was not until Scott reached Melbourne in the summer of 1910 that he received a telegram simply stating: 'Am going south Amundsen.'[1] Scott readily understood what this meant: Amundsen was a hardened polar explorer whose abilities were not in doubt. He was, moreover, only trying to reach the Pole, whereas Scott's expedition had an extensive scientific programme to carry out as it made its southern journey. Scott opted not to alter his plans, but he recognized that Amundsen was likely to win the race.

Explaining Defeat

From the time it first became known to the British public, Amundsen's conduct was the subject of debate and criticism. In September 1911, John Scott Keltie, the secretary of the Royal Geographical Society, wrote to Scott: 'It is certainly sad that Amundsen should seem to have done such a low-down thing ... He was deeply in debt and had to make money somehow ... It does seem mean that for such a motive a man should rush in and try to snatch the goal from another who, he knew, has been preparing his way for years ... However it is now a race and I hope with all my heart that you will win.'[2] Scott did not win: in early March 1912, the news that Amundsen had reached the Pole on 14 December 1911 captured headlines around the world. Though they doubtless wanted to, the Royal Geographical Society could not entirely ignore Amundsen's achievement. They did not invite him to come to London to give a lecture, but informed him that, if he was coming to England for other reasons, 'the Society would be glad if he would attend one of our meetings and give an account of his expedition'. Amundsen, though insulted, agreed, and the lecture was scheduled for November 1912. The Royal Geographical Society, however, refused to book the more prestigious Albert Hall for the triumphant explorer, but instead banished him to the smaller Queen's Hall.[3] In a letter that survives in draft form in the Society's archives, Keltie reported on the lecture to Scott's widow, Kathleen. The manuscript retains his numerous alterations and excisions, showing how he could barely contain his wrath:

> Even ... if Amundsen's whole statement is true still it does not exonerate him from doing ~~a thing which no Englishman with a spark of chivalry in him would have dreamt of doing~~ a thing which to say the least shows a lack of chivalry ~~trying to get in front of a man who had practically devoted 12 years of his life to the attainment of his object. What would have been thought and said of an Englishman who had tried to sneak in through the Behring Straits and snatch the victory of the North Pole from poor Peary, who had been working at it stage after stage for some 20 years?~~ However, the thing has been done and I have no doubt that Amundsen actually has been at the Pole.[4]

Already, then, a narrative had taken shape to justify Scott's failure on the grounds that Amundsen had cheated. By not telling Scott, and the world, that he was going for the South rather than the North Pole, he had not played the game fairly and allowed an honest, manly competition to take place.

At the time Keltie wrote the letter, unbeknownst either to himself or to Kathleen, Scott had been dead for eight months. His southern journey, which had begun in October 1911, had been a struggle from the start. The motor-sledges had broken down almost immediately, and the ponies floundered in the soft snow. As they strained to haul their food and supplies up the 110-mile (176 km) Beardmore Glacier, which ascended 10,000 feet (3,048 m), they were making barely 10 miles (16 km) a day, while Amundsen, who had already reached the Pole, averaged 25 miles (40 km) using skis and dogs.[5] Amundsen's men actually gained weight on the polar journey and sometimes left food behind in their supply depots as they went faster than expected, whereas Scott's, who burned more calories due to the physical exertions of man-hauling, were slowly starving to death.

Scott selected four men for the final push to the Pole: his old *Discovery* companion and close friend Edward Wilson; the army officer Lawrence Edward Grace 'Titus' Oates; Henry Robertson 'Birdie' Bowers of the Royal Indian Marine Service; and the naval petty officer Edgar Evans, another *Discovery* veteran. On 16 January 1912, around ten miles from the South Pole, they saw a black flag fluttering in the snow, irrefutable evidence that they had been beaten. They reached the Pole the next day; Scott captured their disappointment when he wrote: 'Great God! this is an awful place, and terrible enough for us to have laboured to it without the reward of priority.'[6] (See Figure 50.)

As they turned north, the temperature began to drop as the Antarctic summer came to an end. This was dangerous, not only because the colder temperatures sapped calories at a faster rate, but because it caused the surface to freeze into ice crystals that impeded the glide of the sledge runners.[7] It was, as Scott recorded, as if they were dragging the sledges 'over desert sand'.[8] Their progress slowed so that they rarely reached their next cache of supplies with food or fuel to spare. Evans, the biggest man of the party and thus the one who needed the most calories, was the first to succumb. By early February, he was, as Scott recorded in a passage that was later excised from the published version of his diary, 'dull and incapable'.[9] On the 17th, Evans collapsed, forcing them to camp. He died that night.

The others carried on, but they were moving very slowly. On 1 March, the thermometer plunged to -40°C; they were all aware that their pace was not sufficient for survival. 'Thing look very black indeed,' Scott wrote two days later.[10] On 16 March, Oates, who had been suffering badly from frostbitten feet and from scurvy which had caused a leg wound that he had received in the Boer War to reopen, declared that he could not continue and begged his companions to leave him in his sleeping bag. They convinced him to limp on for one more day, but that night, in what became one of the defining moments of the tragedy, Oates left the tent and walked out into the snow. Scott recorded that he told his companions: 'I am just going outside and may be some time.' 'We knew,' he said, 'that poor Oates was walking to his death, but though we tried to dissuade him, we knew it was the act of a brave man and an English gentleman.'[11]

Oates's sacrifice, however, could not save them. Two days later, on 19 March, they were pinned in their tent by a blizzard. Scott's feet were now badly frostbitten, and Wilson and Bowers made a desperate attempt to reach One Ton Depot, 11 miles (18 km) away, but were forced back when the weather worsened. As they lay waiting to die, Scott wrote the last entries in his diary, as well as letters to his family and friends, and a final 'Message to the Public':

> For my own sake I do not regret this journey, which has shown that Englishmen can endure hardships, help one another and meet death with as great a fortitude as ever in the past. We took risks, we knew we took them; things have come out against us, and therefore we have no cause for complaint, but to bow to the will of providence, determined still to do our best to the last ... Had we lived, I should have had a tale to tell of the hardihood, endurance and courage of my companions which would have stirred the heart of every Englishman. These rough notes and our dead bodies must tell the tale.[12]

The news of Scott's death did not reach Britain until 10 February 1913. The word 'shock' was frequently employed to describe people's immediate response. One friend of Scott's sister Ettie described being 'so shocked at seeing posted up the awful news', while another reported: 'I had only just come back home when I saw the appalling, shocking news on a poster.'[13] However it was heard, the news produced strong emotions. Another friend of Ettie's, Georgina Francis Dalrymple Gervais, wrote from County Tyrone in the north of Ireland that her husband 'quite broke down when telling me the news'.[14]

In the immediate aftermath of the disaster, the Royal Geographical Society struggled to cope with the barrage of letters of condolence that arrived each day and with the need to satisfy the public's demand for a demonstration of reverence for the dead. 'I never knew anything that created so widespread an impression, not even, I believe, the death of Queen Victoria,' Keltie wrote to Kathleen Scott. The Society was inundated with requests for tickets: first for the memorial service that was held at St Paul's Cathedral on 14 February and then for a special meeting that was held at the Albert Hall in May. Ten thousand people were turned away from the former event; the demand for tickets was so intense that even some 'ex-Inniskillings' – men from Oates's regiment, the Inniskilling Dragoons – were denied entry. A. C. Shawyer of the Old Comrades' Association reported to Oates's mother, Caroline: 'Although Colonel Pennefarther tried hard to get [tickets] . . . I am afraid he and several other old officers did not get in. However, I met eight of the men who loved your son and we made a bold bid to get in and succeeded. We sent in a policeman to say we were a party of ex-Inniskillings and he got permission for us to enter and we were given a good seat just behind the band.'[15] The chaos was such that a friend of Ettie's complained that 'we were terribly hustled at the entrance'. Even so, the attendees found the service very moving. L. L. Morant wrote: 'never before has the death of five men brought forth such a scene, such admiration, such honour, one can *never* forget it.'[16] (Italics in original.) Demand for tickets for the Albert Hall meeting was just as strong. Although ten thousand tickets were given out, Keltie had to deal with numerous complaints about the denial of requests or the location of seats. 'The demand for tickets . . . is unprecedented,' he told one disgruntled fellow of the Society. 'We could have filled [the seats] three times over.'[17] Other memorial services that were held outside London were similarly oversubscribed. S. I. Richardson told Ettie that he had tried to attend the service held at the YMCA in Belfast, but, even though he had 'arrived twenty minutes before the time', he 'could not get in'.[18]

From all across the United Kingdom, people sent condolences, poems and other communications, not only to the Royal Geographical Society but also to the families of the dead. The expressions of sympathy flowed in from all ranks of society: one 'working man' even offered to sell his violin to raise money for the memorial fund.[19] Such was the intensity of the emotion that Scott's death aroused that seemingly everyone who had ever come into even minor contact with him or with a member of his family – ranging from royalty to domestic servants – felt a need to write to express their sorrow. The outpouring threatened to overwhelm the families of the dead. Edward Wilson's mother, Mary Agnes, wrote to Ettie that 'there was so much to read – to reply to'. Kathleen Scott's brother, Rosslyn Bruce, noted that 'we have been almost overwhelmed with letters of sympathy, nearly 400, I think, in all ... Most of them are from friends, but numbers (from all parts of the world) from strangers.'[20]

As had been the case with Franklin's disappearance and Livingstone's death, a few people sought personal advantage and profit from the tragedy. The American Newspaper Publishers Association in New York alerted Keltie that one Frank Morgan-Ash, 'late of Southampton', had published letters in several American newspapers in which he claimed to be the manager of the Scott Memorial Fund and asked for contributions to be sent to his address.[21] The vast majority of people who responded, however, only intended to comfort Scott's friends and relatives, and to share in the outpouring of national grief. Their messages contained many common elements: sympathy for the bereaved families; expressions of Christian religious sentiments;

regret that the men had been so close to safety when they perished; and hopes that the nobility of their actions would provide solace to their relatives. There were also frequent descriptions of the kind of heroism Scott and his companions had represented, which focused on their endurance, fortitude and self-sacrifice. Janet Stirling-Hamilton, who had known the Scott family in Devonport, wrote to Ettie three days after the news reached Britain:

> Since Tuesday my one thought has been of the wild reaches of Antarctic ice and those five heroic lives and their supreme sufferings. On reading of the disaster one marvelled that God should have permitted misfortune after misfortune to overtake those brave souls, but reflection showed how the all-loving Father saw in those four [*sic*] sons the capacity for the most heroic deeds of endurance, self-sacrifice for the sake of their country and of each other, and He tested them to the uttermost. Where others would have gone under, they, enduring to the end, triumphed gloriously, bearing fresh witness to the heroic heights that men can rise to. Each disaster bravely borne was another precious jewel in the immortal crown of glory that is theirs today.[22]

The Sailors' Home, which provided accommodation for seamen while they were in London, wrote: 'their splendid fortitude, courage and self-sacrifice under most arduous circumstances stand out as a noble example to all sailors and Britons.'[23] The London-based Burdett Coutts Lodge of the Royal Antediluvian Order of Buffaloes declared: 'we regard the loss as a national one, but are proud to think that even in their last moments of extremity, the nobility of British endurance and self-sacrifice was so gloriously indicated.'[24] Some organizations employed similar formulations, which suggests that boilerplate expressions of public grief quickly emerged. Both the Northumberland County Association and the Tynemouth Association of the National Union of Teachers, for example, expressed their 'deep appreciation of the self-sacrifice and devotion to duty shown by Captain Scott and his comrades, under circumstances which cannot but appeal most strongly to all who have read of the dangers and difficulties which are cheerfully faced by those who undertake the work of polar exploration'.[25]

Seeking Answers

Almost immediately, Britons began to look for explanations for the disaster. A regular meeting of the Royal Geographical Society happened to be scheduled for the day that the news of Scott's death arrived; a paper on the Balkans was hastily cancelled and instead Vice President Douglas Freshfield gave a brief address about the Antarctic tragedy:

> It is a truism to say that in great adventures of this sort it is always the unexpected that happens. No Arctic or Antarctic party was ... ever sent out better equipped or better fitted by the gallantry and experience of its members, from Captain Scott downwards, to meet with the ordinary perils of the Poles. But Arctic travel would not be what it is, a training ground for the highest qualities of the British race, if those perils were altogether avoidable.

Here, Freshfield placed Scott and his companions in the long tradition of British polar explorers who had tested themselves against the rigours of the polar environment. Their failure was thus a testament to the 'perils' of that environment, and to their courage and hardihood in taking it on. It was the unpredictable Antarctic weather that had caused their demise, not any errors or deficiencies on their part:

> Of all the dangers of the region of snow and ice ... there is none so terrible, so overwhelming as the blizzard. Even on European mountains it has counted its victims by the dozens. I lost a friend in the Alps only last summer in such a storm. And we can imagine how these terrors are multiplied a hundredfold on an icy wilderness in the heart of the Antarctic. In these conditions, unless shelter is at hand, human powers, even of the toughest, cannot long maintain a struggle against the malign forces of Nature – the end must come.

The deaths of Scott and his men were thus a tragic accident that confirmed their noble qualities, not an indication of weakness or failure. They were 'a band of heroes whose names will shine as examples of that endurance which is the highest form of courage, and as a noble evidence of the qualities of Englishmen. Not once or twice in our rough island story have these qualities been shown, and never more conspicuously than by the members of this ill-fated expedition.'[26]

After Scott's death, the idea that Amundsen had 'cheated' gained greater resonance. 'Naturally enough,' declared the London literary journal the *Bookman*, 'we resented in a way the wondrous good fortune of one who ... was a kind of interloper who had snatched the prize from the enclosing grasp of those who had more dearly won it.'[27] Over time, two other points of criticism emerged beyond the fact that Amundsen had failed to inform Scott of his intended destination. First, it was argued that Amundsen had only made a 'dash to the Pole' rather than carrying out a programme of scientific research. 'There was no question of racing,' declared Sir Clements Markham, who as president of the Royal Geographical Society had selected Scott to lead his first expedition in 1900. 'The grand object was very far from that. It was valuable research in every branch of science.'[28] *The Times* echoed this line: 'Nothing in the painful yet inspiring narrative is more touching than the fidelity with which Captain Scott and his comrades, fighting for their very lives with the remorseless force of Nature, clung with ever increasing peril and weakness to scientific records and geological specimens which it was the primary object of their expedition to secure. It is thus that they snatched victory out of the jaws of death.'[29] In reality, this was a postmortem reinvention of events that would never have occurred had Scott won the race. Privately, Keltie admitted that attempts to argue that the Pole had only been an ancillary goal were specious. 'It is no use in the papers saying the Pole was merely a secondary matter,' he wrote to Kathleen in April 1912. 'We know very well that he had set his mind upon it.'[30] It was also misleading to claim a high value for Scott's scientific results. The coastal areas of Antarctica had by 1910 been explored by numerous expeditions, while Scott's trek to the Pole had explored no new ground because it had stuck so rigidly to Shackleton's route. This was pointed out by the Scottish geographer Hugh Robert Mill, who was a friend and supporter of Scott and who had previously praised his scientific work on the *Discovery* expedition, when he was approached by Keltie in April 1912 about writing an article for the Royal Geographical Society's journal:

I would gladly write an article on Scott's results, but from the geographical point of view there are none ... He kept so close to Shackleton's track that he could discover nothing unless Shackleton had never been there ... Even if Scott reaches the Pole he is tied to his line of depots for a return and can accomplish nothing except to bring his party back alive ... Having referred so positively to the certainty of fine results from Scott's expedition I feel rather sold by the turn of events and I really do not know what to do. There is nothing to praise, and to set out the facts in relation to previous explorations would seem to cast a slur on Scott for having done nothing new.[31]

Publicly, however, the argument that Scott had performed valuable scientific research while Amundsen made his mercenary dash to the Pole remained the stance of the British polar establishment.

The second criticism of Amundsen that developed after Scott's death was that he had used dogs rather than man-hauling as his main means of transport. Only foreigners, it was asserted, were willing to rely on dogs for travel in polar regions and then slaughter them for food when their use was at an end. Markham wrote that Scott

disliked the horrible and disgusting practice of comfortably [gliding] along on ski while the dogs do all the work, and then slaughtering them. This was one consideration which biased him on the side of traction by men. After alluding to what he considered the sordid necessity of so treating dogs on a long journey, he wrote that surely it was a finer conception when men set forth, and made important discoveries by their own

206

unaided efforts ... The foreign practice of killing [dogs] is revolting.[32]

This idea was expressed most famously by the Earl Curzon of Kedleston, president of the Royal Geographical Society, who at the banquet after Amundsen's lecture in London in April 1912, declared: 'I almost wish that in our tribute of admiration we could include those wonderful, good-tempered, fascinating dogs, the true friends of man, without whom Captain Amundsen would never have got to the Pole.' Amundsen later claimed that Curzon then asked for the audience to give 'three cheers for the dogs'.[33]

The British exploration and scientific establishment thus sought to frame an appropriate response to, and explanation for, the tragedy. They emphasized Scott's high moral standards and gentlemanly character, in contrast to Amundsen's unsportsman-like and mercenary conduct. Markham wrote to Curzon that 'it is very painful to see their marches compared, as if the man "who did not play the game" was on an equality or on the same plane in any way with a perfect gentleman like Scott'.[34] The maintenance of this line, however, required the avoidance of awkward questions. Three days after the news of Scott's death reached Britain, Freshfield wrote to Curzon: 'There are a lot of questions which will be asked. What became of the fuel? Why [was] not the relief party at one ton hut [*sic*] ten days before the end provisioned to stay on there some time and make sallies along the south road? How come its provisions were cut so fine that delays by bad weather led to starvation? What were the distances between the depots as compared to Amundsen's?[35] The Royal Geographical Society did its best to ensure that such questions were swept under the carpet. Curzon asserted in his address to the Society on

24 February that the disaster had been a tragic accident: 'I think we shall do well to accept the balanced judgment of the Commander of the Expedition himself, recorded in circumstances which render deception impossible. Just as Amundsen was favoured by an extraordinary combination of fine weather, physical health and good luck, so Scott had to battle with the triple foe of climatic conditions, unprecedented and unimagined for their severe and malignant intensity, the breakdown of two of his party and adverse fortune at every turn.'[36] Curzon did, however, propose a private, informal meeting of the Royal Geographical Society at which some of the returned members of the expedition would be questioned. The retired commander-in-chief of the Royal Navy and Fellow of the Society Sir Lewis Beaumont vehemently opposed this idea, 'because for the Society to be on sure ground it would have to probe very deep and would have probably to disapprove of what was done in many particulars – it would be different if good could come of the enquiry, but I fear nothing but controversy would come of it'.[37] In the end, Beaumont's view prevailed, and though a 'memorial meeting' was held at the Society in late February, no thorough questioning of the members of the expedition took place.

That same month, Kathleen Scott returned from New Zealand, where she had gone to welcome her husband upon his return from Antarctica. There had been no indication thus far that she was inclined to cause trouble. In March 1913, shortly after learning of her husband's death, she had written to Keltie from Sydney to ask him to 'see to it that none of the ridiculous reports of dissension, lack of support, tampering with depots or other harmful fabrications of detrimentalists be allowed to have a light. There is no blame anywhere.' Even so, Curzon met with her immediately to ensure that she maintained a consistent public line. He need not have worried: Kathleen was from the outset determined to celebrate her late husband's heroism, rather than apportion blame for his death. A scrawled note in Curzon's hand records their conversation. They ranged over a number of issues, including 'Scott's words in his diary on exhaustion of food and fuel in depots on his return', which he interpreted to mean that the three men of the last supporting party had 'consumed more than their share' on the return journey. Edgar Evans 'gave out at the Pole' because he 'lost heart' when he could no longer 'perform his share of work', while Oates 'no doubt took opium and thus killed himself'; 'had he not failed they would have got through.' In the end, however, they agreed that it was better to maintain the public position that 'they were killed by the weather and ill luck'.[38]

The line that Scott and his companions had perished due to bad luck thus became standard. Sir William Graham Greene, permanent secretary to the Board of Admiralty, wrote to Ettie that 'one might think [that] the powers of nature, while they allowed one party to make a hasty rush to the Pole and back, resented the attempt to wrest from them their secrets and so thwarted Captain Scott's scientific attack. Certainly nothing but ill luck dogged their steps.' A friend of Ettie's added: 'They had dreadful bad luck, such vile weather,' while Jasper More of Winchester echoed: 'They did seem to have the most dreadful bad luck. One or two misfortunes they could have stood, but everything seemed to be against them.' Bevill Towns wrote to Ettie from Perth: 'I cannot tell you how shocked we were to read of all his sufferings and the magnificent way he struggled against the series of misfortunes which attended his journey. It really seemed as if his luck had altogether left him.'[39]

In some ways, the response to Scott's death closely resembled that of Gordon's three decades earlier, as condolences and expressions of sympathy were dispatched from a wide variety of clubs, political organizations, business enterprises and local government bodies. Also as in Gordon's case, these groups extended beyond the British Isles to the empire. The Royal Geographical Society and Scott's family received condolences from Lord Denman, the governor general of Australia; the prime minister of New Zealand; the government of Western Australia; and a multitude of municipalities, clubs and organizations in Australia, New Zealand, Canada and South Africa as they sought to embrace Scott as an imperial hero.[40] Flora Macartney, presumably a relative of Ettie's husband, Sir William Ellison Macartney, wrote to Ettie from Brisbane: 'What a heritage [Scott] has left to the Empire, all the quiet intense heroism needed to write as he did in those last days may scarcely be comprehended by many.'[41] J. T. Lawson, the honourable secretary of the Balmain East Young People's Club in New South Wales, wrote: 'There is no need to fear that the British Empire will decline, when it possesses men of the calibre of the late Captain Scott and those who shared his fate.'[42]

Expressions of sympathy from the empire took various forms. The Lord Mayor of Sydney wrote to Ettie to thank her for returning to him a 'paper and envelope' that Scott had handed him 'the moment before leaving from Port Chalmers (Otago)' in November 1910: 'I always shall treasure them inasmuch as they were handled by a great hero whose name will go down with honour in British history.'[43] Waitaki High School in Oamaru, New Zealand, boasted of being the first place in the dominions to erect a memorial to Scott, in the form of a tablet that quoted his final message in full, then listed the names of the five men who had 'sacrificed their lives for their country's honour'.[44] In Canada, a Ladies' Guild of the British and Foreign Sailors' Society was formed in Scott's memory to 'promote the welfare of British sailors in Canada'.[45] Lieutenant General Sir Reginald Hart, commander-in-chief of the British forces in South Africa, sent a proclamation expressing the army's 'heart-felt sympathy with the wives, parents and other relatives of the brave men who perished on the eve of success, overcome by the most adverse and unprecedented circumstances'. He further announced that on 14 February memorial services would be held in all military churches in South Africa and all military flags would be flown at half-mast.[46] Sympathy was not limited to colonial citizens who were of British heritage. Kathleen Scott received a letter from the Maori residents of the Wairarapa district of New Zealand stating: 'the deeds of your husband and his comrades bring to our memory the deeds of our ancestor "Kupe" who crossed the sea without compass and reached these islands in which we still remain and extend a welcome to our *pakeha* friends'.[47]

If it was similar in terms of the response it generated within the empire, the reaction to Scott's death differed from that to Gordon's in being much more global. As W. A. Bascand of the Christian Endeavour Society in Christchurch wrote: 'It is indeed a catastrophe, not only to the British nation, but to the whole world.'[48] Condolences poured in from individuals, clubs, schools, and scientific and geographical organizations all over Europe, including Austria, Denmark, France, Germany, Hungary, Italy, Malta, Norway, Portugal, Russia, Spain and Sweden. Ethel Herbert wrote to Caroline Oates from Florence: 'the wave of comprehending grief which swept over Italy on that terrible news from New Zealand was extraordinary in a foreign country'.[49] In March 1913, the French polar explorer Jean-Baptiste Charcot organized a meeting in Paris to raise money for the Scott Memorial Fund; he reported to Keltie that it was 'a great success and the Paris public showed its admiration and deep sympathy for your country with over 6000 people being present, including many of our best men'. Charcot circulated a fundraising letter among French schools and gathered money for a memorial plaque to Scott at Col de Lautaret in the French Alps, where he had helped him to test the motor-sledges prior to his departure on his last expedition. The Norwegian Geographical Society also put up a memorial, in the form of a granite obelisk, at Lake Finse, where Scott had worked to improve British skiing and sledging techniques. In the spring of 1914, Commander Edward 'Teddy' Evans, Scott's second-in-command on the expedition, went on a lecture tour of the European continent that included stops in Paris, Rome, Vienna, Budapest and Berlin. It proved very popular. The president of the Hungarian Geographical Society reported that two members of the royal family had attended and described Evans's presentation as 'very thrilling': 'The Hungarian public was deeply moved by the sad fate of the greatest and noblest British Antarctic explorer.'[50]

The United States also responded. The State Assembly of New York passed a resolution of condolence, while a group of citizens of Baltimore, Maryland, wrote to the Royal Geographical Society of their 'grief over the death of Captain Scott and his companions in the Antarctic under circumstances that . . . cause true hearted men all the world over to thank God for the superlative example of true courage and heroism that He enabled them to leave to the world'.[51] In their condolences to Kathleen, the British Schools and Universities Club of New York declared that Scott 'has left us an example of the truest type of manhood inspired by thorough unselfishness to friends, superb endurance in time of peril, uncon-querable patriotism and unswerving devotion to duty'.[52] The American Arctic explorer Adolphus Greeley, the leader of the disastrous Lady Franklin Bay Expedition of 1881–84, praised Scott's men and said: 'their sense of duty, their persistence of action, their endurance of fatigue, their accomplishment of purpose, their acceptance of disaster, their solidarity of spirit and their fearlessness of death, reflect credit not only on their country but also on mankind at large'.[53] The Royal Geographical Society also received condolences from Argentina, Bolivia, Japan and Peru. (See Figure 51.)

This outpouring of grief reflected the global nature of Antarctic exploration. There was a great deal of prestige at stake in the quest to discover and map the frozen southern continent, and above all to win the race to the South Pole. John Kennedy Maclean had written in *Heroes of the Polar Seas* (1910) that 'the honour of being first' to the South Pole 'has now become a matter of international competition'.[54] In the first decade of the twentieth century, Australia, Belgium, France, Germany, Japan, Norway and Sweden had all sponsored Antarctic expeditions. The pressure was partic-ularly intense for the British, who had already lost the race to the North Pole after having done so much work in the Arctic in the nineteenth century. 'There is one Pole left, and it should be our Pole,' Arthur Conan Doyle declared in 1909.[55]

These sentiments were expressed in the context of growing concerns about Britain's ability to withstand the international competition that the race to the South Pole had engendered. The Edwardian period was marked by increasing anxieties about Britain's economic, imperial and military capacities. These concerns were sparked in part by the Boer War, which lasted far longer and cost far more casualties than expected. In the first year of the war, close to a third of army recruits had been rejected as physically unfit, some due to their small stature and others to deficiencies such as heart disease, weak lungs and bad teeth. This gave rise to a campaign for 'National Efficiency', a phrase derived from the economist Sidney Webb's book *A Policy of National Efficiency* (1901). At the core of National Efficiency was the concern that the physical fitness of Britain's citizens had been adversely affected by the unwholesome urban and industrial environment in which many of them lived. This physical decline was undermining the nation's military and economic strength. Movements such as the Boy Scouts and a bevy of patriotic organizations sought to address these problems, but National Efficiency remained a prevalent concern prior to the outbreak of the First World War and beyond.[56]

Scott's defeat brought all of these fears to the forefront, as it confirmed the sense that heroic qualities were becoming increasingly scarce. 'In these days, especially,' wrote Major Frederick Jackson to Scott's mother, Hannah, 'the nation can ill afford to lose such brave and noble souls – England's best.' In a similar vein, a friend of William Ellison Macartney's wrote to him: 'England cannot afford to lose men like him, especially in these times.' Others concurred. 'Men like him can ill be spared'; 'how badly England can spare such splendid men'; 'we can ill afford to lose such men' – these were common sentiments in the letters of condolence.[57]

In assessing the reasons for the disaster, a key issue was whether Scott's men had 'broken down' because of the rigours of the Antarctic environment or because they were physically weaker than their Norwegian rivals. The Welsh petty officer Edgar Evans was a particular concern, as the debate over National Efficiency focused on the working classes, who were seen to have been the most negatively affected by urban and industrial life. (See Figure 52.) This helps to explain why he, among the five men who had died, was more frequently singled out for blame, for there was more anxiety surrounding his 'breakdown' than there was in relation to the others. In his address to the Royal Geographical Society on 24 February, Curzon referred to Evans's 'unaccountable breakdown' as 'the first symptom, and possibly the initial cause, of the ultimate disaster'. Markham, too, blamed Evans: 'The delays caused by his inability to march, had fatally thrown out the calculations.'[58] The press engaged in much speculation about the role of what the *Daily Mail* called Evans's 'sudden breakdown', which it claimed had been a 'disastrous blow and probably fatal'. A headline in the *Daily Express* pointed to 'The Problem of Seaman Evans', while another headline in the *South Wales Echo* proposed to explain why Evans, 'the giant of the party', had 'failed'.[59]

But if the Antarctic disaster engendered fears of national decline, it simultaneously provided a counterbalance to them. Scott's diary provided plenty of useful material. There was the death of Captain Oates, which Markham described as 'one of the finest and most heroic deeds in our annals', while Curzon asked: 'Does history contain a finer picture than this young fellow ... walking out of the tent into the shrieking snowstorm to give up his life for his friends?'[60] (See Figure 53.) Cecil Williams, an acquaintance of Oates's mother, Caroline, wrote in his letter of condolence of 'how splendidly he behaved, and the nation must feel proud today that he was an Englishman'. Similarly, Herbert Whyte, a friend of Oates's, wrote: 'he died as he had lived, to the last, a noble and gallant English gentleman'.[61] Ewing Paterson, a former member of the Inniskilling Dragoons, cited his death as 'an example to every officer of the regiment who now realizes that once a pursuit is taken up it must be gone into even if death looms ahead'.[62]

The manner in which Scott had faced his own death also garnered much praise. Curzon declared:

Can anything be more beautiful than the calm heroism with which he sat down with death staring him in the eyes . . . ? The result is that this plain man, who claimed powers neither of speech nor writing, has left a message which will outlive the highest flights of trained eloquence . . . I find it hard to say whether my impression is more vivid of the hardships and sufferings cheerfully endured, of the patient effort to add to human knowledge, or of the invincible spirit in which the writer faced his task.[63]

His assessment was shared by the British public. 'I never read anything so noble, dignified – so gloriously *strong* as that message to the world,' (italics in the original) wrote a friend of Ettie's. 'It made one's heart swell to know one had lived in the same age as such fine souls as these.' Similarly, Flora Colhoun wrote to Ettie from Germany: 'What a hero's letter. Knowing no human help was possible – what thought for others.' James T. Canton declared: 'there can be no soul, however sordid, which did not thrill at the reading of your glorious brother's last message, and generations yet unborn will read in those words an encouragement to the loftiest patriotism'.[64]

The way that Scott and his companions died had thus proved that British greatness remained intact. A letter of condolence to Ettie stated that Scott's death was 'a thing to be proud of, for real men are few and far between these days', while others declared:

'how splendid to think that England still produces such heroes' and 'it should make everyone feel proud of their country . . . that it can produce such men.' Georgina Francis Dalrymple Gervais wrote: 'in this money-seeking and self-advertising age it is a joy to note the Empire has still such heroes worthy of the greatest days of Elizabeth'. Sir William's relative General Sir Gerald Francis Ellison wrote: 'chiefly one is thankful that the heart and mind of the nation is still so sound that it can readily appreciate at its true worth real greatness when brought face to face with it'.[65] Scott was compared to British heroes of old, as if to reassure a nervous nation that its strength and character still endured. 'He and Franklin stand in the first rank of men,' wrote one friend of Sir William Ellison-Macartney's, while another asserted: 'it is Nelson in the moment of victory over again.' General Ellison wrote: 'his name will go down to future generations of Englishmen associated with the names of Wolfe and Nelson as one of the great Englishmen who died nobly in the hour of victory'.[66] The poet Everard Digby concluded from the manner of Scott's death:

British pluck still lives again,
Endurance both with heart and brain;
Inherent in our Island race.
Courage to do, and Death to face.[67]

These claims, however, veiled fears lurking just beneath the surface that Britain was no longer capable of producing heroes of the same quality as in days of yore. Keltie told the Swedish explorer Sven Hedin: 'it is some little comfort to know that the human race, and even Englishmen, have still some of the noble qualities of their ancestors'.[68] Similarly, he wrote to the French polar explorer Charles Rabot: 'We are often taunted in England with being a degenerate race, but when such deeds as these are possible still among us, I think we may cherish the belief that after all our degeneration has not proceeded very far.'[69] These anxieties were on full display in a poem by Coulson Peart that was issued in pamphlet form as part of the 'Patriotic Verses Series':

Are there yet 'Men' in Britain? Are *all* land lubbers now?
O! who will face the long last race, the biting frost and snow?
There is *one* place of mystery, but *one* more post to win,
To open out, to tell about, for country and for King.
O! who will dare the iceberg's glare, the Southern Pole to find,
And add the glory of the deed to future sons of all mankind?
O who will volunteer to steer, by sun, by moon,
By stars, through fear, into the ghastly Southern sphere?
Where cold will freeze and tempest blast, and blizzard wreck,
    starvation track?
Lives there a man who dares the deed? who with his life may
    ne'er come back,
Shall other nations find the man and Britain be the one to lack?
Arouse ye heroes? Hear the call? Up men of England! Scotland!
    All!
Shall honour fly? Shall Glory fall?

Scott provided a reassuring answer to these questions:

Out spake a young Devonian, a Captain by degree,
'O I will brave the Southern wave and take a crew with me,
Give but the ship, right to equip, and men who fear no foe,
I will uphold through heat or cold, the honour of my country, so

That other nations seeing, say "Old England still can shew
   the way
To deeds as brave as in the past, to acts that evermore shall
   last." '[70]

As we have seen, the global response to Scott's death reflected the fierce competition among a variety of nations to win the race to the South Pole. Losing to the Norwegians was bound to raise questions in Britain about the reasons for their defeat. But because the race took place at a time when other nations, Germany and the United States in particular, had caught up to and even surpassed Britain's industrial productivity and were challenging the supremacy of the Royal Navy, these questions went beyond the context of Antarctic exploration and hinted at broader anxieties about Britain's status as a world power. In this sense, Scott was the first twentieth-century heroic failure. It is premature to describe him, as Roland Huntford has suggested, as a 'suitable hero for a nation in decline', for Britain did not truly begin to slip from great-power status until after the First World War.[71] But it is accurate to say that his failure necessitated his transformation into a hero for somewhat different reasons than Sir John Franklin's or General Gordon's had. Britons needed Scott's heroism not to show them that their empire was benevolent, just and moral, but rather to reassure them that their empire, and their nation, were just as strong and powerful as they had been a few decades earlier.

CONCLUSION

THE SCOTT MEMORIAL Fund Committee was established soon after the news of the deaths of Captain Scott and his four companions in the Antarctic reached Britain in February 1913. It swiftly amassed a massive £75,000, which the Committee's leading lights decided to use for four purposes: £5,100 went to pay the expedition's debts, £34,000 went to the families of the dead and £17,500 went to the publication of the scientific results. That left £18,000 to be used for a memorial to Scott in London. In July 1913, Lord Curzon, the chair of the subcommittee that had been charged with designing the memorial, contacted the Office of Works about obtaining a site in Hyde Park directly across from the Royal Geographical Society. Lionel Earle, permanent secretary to the Office of Works, informed him that 'it is perfectly impossible for the First Commissioner [of Works] to give his approval to any statue being erected in any of the royal parks which would diminish the open space by even one blade of grass'. Earle reminded Curzon that the First Commissioner, Lord Beauchamp, had stated to the House of Commons in April 1912 that he would 'oppose any scheme which is brought before him for the erection of any statue in any royal park'. It was, as William Soulsby, the secretary of the Memorial Fund Committee, wrote to Curzon thus 'hopeless to expect that the government will accord any position in any of the parks' for a statue of Scott.[1] The subcommittee then considered a range of alternative sites, including Greenwich, Battersea Park, Shadwell Park, the Chelsea Embankment and a recessed space on the side of the Foreign Office building on Whitehall, none of which was suitable. By this point, Soulsby was fed up with the whole thing:

> Personally I think a modest memorial in St Paul's would be quite ample, without any further statue or commemorative group elsewhere. If you were to take a census of London statues, you would find that nine-tenths of the subjects are quite forgotten and their achievements obsolete. At Guildhall we have busts and statues of politicians . . . who are out of all recollection nowadays, and I conclude from this that the public have a very short memory and that in a few years Captain Scott and his companions will have drifted into the same obscurity as many more distinguished men.[2]

Soulsby was wrong: a century later, Scott's heroic stature endures. To be sure, there was a time when Scott seemed in danger of disappearing from the pantheon of British heroes. In 1979, in his book *Scott and Amundsen*, Roland Huntford denigrated him as an inept bungler; the damage to Scott's reputation was lasting and severe. In recent years, however, Scott has rebounded: the explorer Sir Ranulph Fiennes published a hagiographic biography in 2003, and the centennial of his death was marked in March 2012 by a memorial service in St Paul's Cathedral.

The recovery of Scott's reputation was confirmed in January 2013, when, in slightly belated commemoration of the centennial of his death, his portrait by Daniel Albert Wehrschmidt returned to public view in the National Portrait Gallery after decades in storage.[3] (See Figure 54.) It remains there at the time of writing, a testament to Scott's continuing status as a hero, and to the enduring presence of heroic failure in British culture.

Heroic failure endures because, as the place of the British nation in the world has evolved over the last century, it has proven adaptable to a variety of circumstances. In the Second World War, it provided a comforting myth of resilience in the face of adversity. In 1941, George Orwell wrote in his essay 'England your England':

In England all the boasting and flag-wagging, the 'Rule Britannia' stuff, is done by small minorities. The patriotism of the common people is not vocal or even conscious. They do not retain among their historical memories the name of a single military victory. English literature, like other literatures, is full of battle-poems, but it is worth noticing that the ones that have won for themselves a kind of popularity are always a tale of disasters and retreats. There is no popular poem about Trafalgar or Waterloo, for instance. Sir John Moore's army at Corunna, fighting a desperate rearguard action before escaping overseas (just like Dunkirk!), has more appeal than a brilliant victory. The most stirring battle-poem in English is about a brigade of cavalry which charged in the wrong direction. And of the last war, the four names which have really engraved themselves on the popular memory are Mons, Ypres, Gallipoli and Passchendaele, every time a disaster. The names of the great battles that finally broke the German armies are simply unknown to the general public.[4]

In keeping with this view, Dunkirk is today frequently included in lists of Britain's heroic failures; the phrase 'Dunkirk spirit' refers to the way in which the British people, at least according to popular mythology, banded together and persevered despite the overwhelming odds against them as they faced the Germans alone. Dunkirk, however, was emphatically *not* a failure, or if it was, it was only one on the part of the German military command, who for reasons that are still debated halted their attack long enough to permit large numbers of Allied troops to escape. Its inclusion thus shows an eagerness to embrace heroic failure as a national ideal, even when the events do not support such an interpretation.

In the 1960s, heroic failure was adapted once again, this time as a symbol of Britain's changing imperial values in an era of decolonization. This was exemplified by some of the most prominent films of the period. In Cy Endfield's *Zulu* (1964), the Anglo-Zulu War, with Isandlwana prominently featured in the opening scenes, is used to address the moral ambiguities of empire. At Rorke's Drift, rather than being full of patriotic enthusiasm, the soldiers openly question why they are fighting, but this makes their stand against the odds more rather than less heroic. The Zulus, meanwhile, are depicted as courageous and noble warriors, a portrayal with clear political implications in a film released only two years after South Africa had left the Commonwealth due to its refusal to end apartheid. Basil Dearden's *Khartoum* (1966) is in some ways a more conventional film, but it strips any sense of imperial mission away from Britain's activities in the Sudan in the 1880s and transforms General Gordon's intervention into a largely individual and purely moral effort, a recognition that empire was no longer fashionable. Finally, Tony Richardson's *The Charge of the Light Brigade* (1968) most blatantly repurposes heroic failure for a postimperial era. A complex combination of epic and satire, the film was, as Jeffrey Richards writes, 'anti-war and anti-military, a direct response to the Vietnam War which dominated the thinking of many of the creative and the young, who saw it as an affront to the new age of freedom, peace and love, as a reminder of great-power politics and of archaic imperialism'.[5]

In more recent decades, as was discussed in the Introduction, heroic failure has come to serve as a metaphor for British decline, and has sometimes even been blamed for it. As the comic actor and writer Tim Brooke-Taylor put it in 1983:

> When it comes down to it, the British aren't honestly that fussed about winning. Better a gallant loser than an outright victor in most of our eyes, and if we do have to win, it has to be by the narrowest margin. What makes British heroism so impressive is the way we lose, going down with all guns blazing, fighting to the last man, rallying around the standard. These are the ideals and examples that raise a lump in every good British throat – and which are partially responsible for the loss of the Empire.[6]

Here, Brooke-Taylor links the celebration of heroic failure to Britain's loss of its colonies and world-power status. Other commentators have also endorsed this argument; in reviewing a new edition of the diaries of Scott and Amundsen that has been edited by Scott's most vocal critic, Roland Huntford, John Crace wrote in the *Guardian*: 'Decline and fall is a paradigm of British life over much of the last hundred years. Perhaps we get the national heroes we deserve.'[7]

The evolution of heroic failure to serve a variety of national purposes over the course of the twentieth century, however, should not be permitted to conceal the reasons for which it first emerged in the nineteenth. It has too often been interpreted in the present without an understanding of its roots in the past. The one constant in the changing uses of heroic failure in British culture has been its continuing relationship to the British Empire. The empire, as historians have increasingly come to recognize, has been a pervasive presence in British life since the late eighteenth century. As A. G. Hopkins observed: 'images of empire and the imperial ideal ... entered the British soul and influenced its character'.[8] The empire, however, was throughout its history an extremely complex entity, not only in terms of its geographical and ethnic diversity, its administrative structure and its economic value, but also in terms of its moral character. It could be imagined as a zone in which cultural enlightenment and Christianity were promoted, but there were always moments in which these ideals were challenged. Slavery was not abolished until the 1830s, and the massive military presence that was required to maintain the security of existing colonies and to conquer new territory made it difficult to see the empire consistently as based on consent rather than coercion.

In order to render the complexity of the empire comprehensible in a metropolitan context, Britons created a variety of narratives. These served different purposes at the specific points at which they were brought into being, but in general they were intended to ensure that the empire could be perceived in a positive light.[9] They persisted well into the twentieth century as a means of dealing with the uncomfortable realities of decolonization.

In recent years, however, the notion that the British extracted themselves from empire with minimal bloodshed and upheaval has been challenged. Malaya, for example, was long held up as an example of a successful counterinsurgency effort in contrast to the American failure in Vietnam in subsequent years. The British military and police action that began in the late 1940s, the argument goes, managed to win the 'hearts and minds' of the population and therefore prevented a communist regime from coming to power when the country gained independence in 1957. Historians now, however, point to the brutality of the British methods used in this effort, including the killing and torture of thousands of suspected communist insurgents and the detention and resettlement of around 500,000 Malayans in euphemistically named 'New Villages'.[10] Similarly, the Mau Mau rebellion that began in Kenya in 1952 was long seen as an uprising of blood-crazed savages who engaged in bizarre, bestial rituals and ruthlessly massacred the colony's white population.[11] In recent years, however, historians have brought the brutality of the British campaign against the Mau Mau to light.[12]

In a nineteenth- rather than a twentieth-century imperial context, heroic failure performed a similar function to the stories of the success of the counterinsurgency in Malaya and the horrors of the Mau Mau uprising: it made it possible for Britons to see their empire in a positive and moral light, particularly at moments when the reality was quite different.[13] The prominence of heroic failure in the nineteenth century derived from its capacity to transform Britain's heroes of armed conflict and exploration into carriers of the nation's moral virtues and cultural ideals.

This process was made easier by the dire circumstances in which their actions occurred. Lost in the jungles of Africa and the

frigid polar regions or overwhelmed by the enemy on the battlefield, they made it possible for the British to see themselves as
selfless and self-sacrificing in an era in which they nakedly pursued
national aggrandizement via imperial conquest with the aid of
technology and weaponry that was often far superior to that
possessed by their opponents. Heroic failure, it should be noted,
never seriously threatened Britain's national security. Though they
were often on the wrong end of individual battles, none of the
military heroic failures discussed in this book occurred in a war
that the British lost, and those involving exploration took place
in contexts – the Arctic, the Antarctic and the interior of Africa
– that were not vital to the nation's strategic interests.

Will heroic failure remain a British cultural ideal? In 2013,
after Andy Murray became the first British man to win the
Wimbledon Championship since 1936, the *Sunday Telegraph*
columnist Matthew d'Ancona suggested that its appeal is fading:

The paradigm of the plucky loser had its high season with
Eddie the Eagle, Frank Spencer, and the *Book of Heroic Failures*.
It was part of a post-war, post-colonial Britishness – the idea
that all we had left was a sense of irony about inevitable decline.
But that has been challenged repeatedly – by Thatcher, especially after the Falklands, by Blair's 'Cool Britannia' and, most
recently, by the spectacular success of the Olympics ... What
sort of nation are we? What's certain is that, against all proph-
ecies, we aren't content to be a country of cuddly losers.[14]

Perhaps, as d'Ancona suggests, the British nation has evolved in a
way that will soon render heroic failure irrelevant. If, after all, it
has been closely linked to empire over the last two centuries, it

stands to reason that the disappearance of that empire might mean its disappearance from British culture as well. But, on the other hand, since 1800, it has proved a supremely adaptable ideal. This author, for one, would not bet against its finding a place in post-imperial Britain.

NOTES

Introduction

1. In 2010, a statue of Sir Keith Park, air chief marshal during the Battle of Britain, was added.
2. John Cleese, *So Anyway . . .* (London: Random House, 2014), pp. 56–57.
3. University of Cambridge, Scott Polar Research Institute, MS 1453/31.
4. Rudyard Kipling, *Something of Myself and Other Autobiographical Writings* (Cambridge: Cambridge University Press, 1991), p. 111.
5. Ben Parsons, 'England's Footballers "Doomed to Heroic Failure"', *Argus*, 16 June 2010. The team did not even manage heroic failure, as it was drubbed by Germany 4–1 in the quarter-finals.
6. Nick McGrath, 'Eddie the Eagle: "I Went from £6,000 a Year to £10,000 an Hour"', *Daily Telegraph*, 19 February 2012.
7. http://www.channel4.com/news/andy-murray-tennis-australian-open-plucky-loser-paradigm.
8. Roland Huntford, *The Last Place on Earth: Scott and Amundsen's Race to the South Pole* (New York: Random House, 1999), p. 543.
9. Correlli Barnett, *The Collapse of British Power* (New York: William Morrow & Company, 1972).
10. Martin Wiener, *English Culture and the Decline of the Industrial Spirit, 1850–1980* (Cambridge: Cambridge University Press, 1981).
11. For a critique of declinism as a political issue, see David Cannadine, 'Apocalypse When?: British Politicians and British "Decline" in the Twentieth Century', in Peter Clarke and Clive Trebilcock, eds, *Understanding Decline: Perceptions and Realities of Britain's Economic Performance* (Cambridge: Cambridge University Press, 1997), pp. 261–84; and Jim Tomlinson, 'Thrice Denied: "Declinism" as a Recurrent Theme in British History in the Long Twentieth Century', *Twentieth-Century British History* 20 (2009), pp. 227–51.
12. The scholarship on British decline is extensive. See in particular Peter Clarke and Clive Trebilcock, eds, *Understanding Decline: Perceptions and Realities of Britain's Economic Performance* (Cambridge: Cambridge University Press, 1997); Nicholas

Crafts, 'Forging Ahead and Falling Behind: The Rise and Relative Decline of the First Industrial Nation', *Journal of Economic Perspectives* 12 (1998), pp. 193–210; Bernard Elbaum and William Lazonick, eds, *The Decline of the British Economy* (Oxford: Oxford University Press, 1986); Aaron Friedberg, *The Weary Titan: Britain and the Experience of Relative Decline 1895–1905* (Princeton: Princeton University Press, 1988); Gordon Martel, 'The Meaning of Power: Rethinking the Decline and Fall of Great Britain', *International History Review* 13 (1991), pp. 662–94; Keith Neilson, '"Greatly Exaggerated": The Myth of Decline in Great Britain before 1914', *International History Review* 13 (1991), p. 696; Sidney Pollard, *Britain's Prime and Britain's Decline: The British Economy 1870–1914* (London: Hodder Arnold, 1989); and Barry Supple, 'Fear of Failing: Economic History and the Decline of Britain', *Economic History Review* 47 (1994), pp. 441–58.

13. Jack P. Greene, *Evaluating Empire and Confronting Colonialism in Eighteenth-Century Britain* (Cambridge: Cambridge University Press, 2013), p. 99.

14. David Armitage, *The Ideological Origins of the British Empire* (Cambridge: Cambridge University Press, 2000), p. 8.

15. Thomas Metcalf writes that 'as Britain became, during the course of the nineteenth century, a society shaped by the ideals of liberalism and, in time, of democracy, the existence of an autocratic rule over India stood in sharp contrast with the presumption, ever more deeply embedded in the British constitution, that the people, through election and representation, possessed the right to choose those who were to rule over them'. Thomas R. Metcalf, *Ideologies of the Raj* (Cambridge: Cambridge University Press, 1994), p. x.

16. Ibid.

17. 'Ideologically, the proconsular instinct for authority challenged a significant spectrum of liberal opinion, whose roots ran deep.' Bill Schwarz, *Memories of Empire, Volume I: The White Man's World* (Oxford: Oxford University Press, 2011), p. 24.

18. Schwarz writes: 'The stories told in the metropole, emphasising adventure and heroism, rarely conformed to the brute realities of everyday life in the empire.' Ibid., p. 68.

19. John MacKenzie has written that 'imperial heroes developed instrumental power because they served to explain and justify the rise of the imperial state, personified national greatness and offered examples of self-sacrificing service to a current generation. They were the pathfinders who entered geographical and ethnic space, preparing the way for moral conquest. They were used as the embodiment of the collective will, stereotypes of a shared culture and promoters of unity in the face of fragmentation.' John M. MacKenzie, 'Heroic Myths of Empire', in John M. MacKenzie, ed., *Popular Imperialism and the Military, 1850–1950* (Manchester: Manchester University Press, 1992), pp. 114–15. Similarly, Berny Sèbe writes: 'Imperial heroes embodied the symbolic implementation of the colonial project and performed a highly mythologized meeting between conquerors and conquered ... These exemplary figures led local soldiers, braved indigenous resistance and an inhospitable environment to carry out their explorations or to convert native populations, playing the role of pathfinders propagating the ideals of Christian service and sacrifice, progress, republican universalism, patriotism or its more acute forms, jingoism or chauvinism ... Above all, the moral paradigm that they conveyed could easily be turned into a justification for colonial conquest and rule.' Berny Sèbe, *Heroic Imperialists in Africa: The Promotion of British and French Colonial Heroes, 1870–1939* (Manchester: Manchester University Press, 2013), p. 2.

20. Stefan Collini writes that character 'enjoyed a prominence in the political thought of the Victorian period that it had apparently not known before and that it has, arguably, not experienced since'. Stefan Collini, *Public Moralists: Political and Intellectual Life in Britain 1850–1930* (Oxford: Clarendon Press, 1991), p. 94.

21. See, for example, Linda Colley, *Britons: Forging the Nation, 1707–1837* (New Haven and London: Yale University Press, 1992); Peter Mandler, *The English National Character: The History of an Idea from Edmund Burke to Tony Blair* (New Haven and London: Yale University Press, 2006); and Gerald Newman, *The Rise of English Nationalism: A Cultural History 1740–1830* (New York: St Martin's, 1987).
22. See Paul Langford, *Englishness Identified* (Oxford: Oxford University Press, 2000), pp. 148–57. This was from an early date a key distinction that Britons drew between themselves and Americans. 'Rank bad sportsmanship was one of the commonest complaints against Americans,' writes Langford, as they had evolved their 'tradition of sport in a spirit quite foreign to English ways, as a cynically mercenary form of competition in which the manner of winning counted for nothing'. Langford, *Englishness Identified*, p. 151.
23. See Mark Girouard, *The Return to Camelot: Chivalry and the English Gentleman* (New Haven and London: Yale University Press, 1981).
24. Langford, *Englishness Identified*, p. 150.
25. Collini adds that 'the constant invocations of the virtues of character' in the Victorian era 'presuppose an agreed moral code'. Collini, *Public Moralists*, p. 100.
26. Samuel Smiles, *Character* (London, 1871), p. vi.
27. Max Jones, 'What Should Historians Do with Heroes?: Reflections on Nineteenth- and Twentieth-Century Britain', *History Compass* 5:2 (2007), p. 440.
28. Gott continues: 'The British understandably try to forget that their Empire was the fruit of military conquest and of brutal wars involving physical and cultural extermination ... A self-satisfied and largely hegemonic belief survives in Britain that the Empire was an imaginative civilising enterprise, reluctantly undertaken, that brought the benefits of modern society to backward peoples ... There is a widespread opinion that the British Empire was obtained and maintained with a minimum degree of force and with maximum cooperation from a grateful indigenous population.' Richard Gott, *Britain's Empire: Resistance, Repression and Revolt* (London: Verso, 2012), p. 1.
29. Jeanne Morefield writes that these imperial narratives 'rely not merely upon historical omission but, rather, upon prolonged and creative forms of deflection that consistently ask the reader to avert her eyes, away from colonial violence and economic exploitation, and back toward the liberal nature of the imperial society'. Jeanne Morefield, *Empire without Imperialism: Anglo-American Decline and the Politics of Deflection* (Oxford: Oxford University Press, 2014), pp. 1 and 3.
30. The Indian Rebellion of 1857, the most searing military trauma of the nineteenth century, produced plenty of heroic martyrs – Henry Havelock, Henry Lawrence, John Nicholson – who died while securing victories, but no heroic failures.
31. See John Darwin, *The Empire Project: The Rise and Fall of the British World-System 1830–1970* (Cambridge and New York: Cambridge University Press, 2009).
32. See John M. MacKenzie, 'On Scotland and the Empire', *International History Review* 15 (1993), pp. 714–39.
33. National Library of Scotland, John Murray Archive, MS 40219.
34. Graham Dawson writes that 'within nationalist discourse, martial masculinity was complemented by a vision of domestic femininity, at home with the children and requiring protection'. Graham Dawson, *Soldier Heroes: British Adventure, Empire and the Imagining of Masculinities* (London and New York: Routledge, 1994), p. 2.
35. The country that most closely rivals Britain in celebrating heroic failure is probably Japan, which has a strong cultural tradition of embracing 'heroes who were unable to achieve their concrete objectives'. See Ivan Morris, *The Nobility of Failure: Tragic Heroes in the History of Japan* (Fukuoka, Japan: Kurodahan Press, 2013).

36. As Patricia Limerick has written, in American history 'conquest took another route into national memory. In the popular imagination, the reality of conquest dissolved into stereotypes of noble savages and noble pioneers struggling quaintly in the wilderness.' That struggle, most influentially in the 'frontier thesis' of Frederick Jackson Turner, became the 'central story of American history', one that 'turned Europeans into Americans'. Patricia Limerick, *The Legacy of Conquest: The Unbroken Past of the American West*, new edn (London and New York: W.W. Norton, 1988), pp. 19–20.

37. Jeffrey Richards, *Film and British National Identity: From Dickens to Dad's Army* (Manchester: Manchester University Press, 1997), p. 53.

38. Sir John Seeley, *The Expansion of England: Two Courses of Lectures* (London: Macmillan, 1883), pp. 8 and 43.

Chapter 1: Heroic Failure in Britain prior to 1850

1. John MacKenzie writes that 'nineteenth-century heroism derived particular potency from exotic backgrounds'. John M. MacKenzie, 'Heroic Myths of Empire', in John M. MacKenzie, ed., *Popular Imperialism and the Military 1850–1950* (Manchester: Manchester University Press, 1992), p. 113.

2. Benton Rain Patterson, *The Generals: Andrew Jackson, Sir Edward Pakenham and the Road to the Battle of New Orleans* (New York and London: New York University Press, 2005), p. 215.

3. G. R. Gleig, *A Narrative of the Campaigns of the British Army at Washington and New Orleans* (London: John Murray, 1821), p. 326.

4. Patterson, *Generals*, pp. 247–50.

5. Gleig, *A Narrative of the Campaigns of the British Army*, pp. 332–33.

6. News of the treaty did not reach New Orleans until 10 February.

7. Historic New Orleans Collection, William C. Cook War of 1812 in the South Collection, MS 557, Folder 86.

8. *Ibid.*, Folder 110.

9. Barbara Groseclose, *British Sculpture and the Company Raj: Church Monuments and Public Statuary in Madras, Calcutta, and Bombay to 1858* (Newark, DE: University of Delaware Press, 1995), ch. 3.

10. Linda Colley, *Britons: Forging the Nation, 1707–1832* (New Haven and London: Yale University Press, 1992), p. 192.

11. Scott Hughes Myerly, *British Military Spectacle: From the Napoleonic Wars through the Crimea* (Cambridge and London: Harvard University Press, 1996), p. 10. The navy, because even in peacetime its power was deployed at sea and not at home, was largely immune from such suspicions. Horatio Nelson's funeral in January 1806, for example, was used by government ministers to promote a view of the post-Nelson Royal Navy as the inheritor of his 'tactical genius and inspired courage'. Timothy Jenks, 'Contesting the Hero: The Funeral of Admiral Lord Nelson', *Journal of British Studies* 39 (2000), p. 428.

12. Allan R. Skelly, *The Victorian Army at Home* (London and Montreal: Croom Helm, 1977), p. 243.

13. Myerly, *British Military Spectacle*, p. 150.

14. Charles Mitchell, 'Benjamin West's *Death of General Wolfe* and the Popular History Piece', *Journal of the Warburg and Courtauld Institutes* 7 (1944), p. 33. Peter Harrington writes that West 'laid the foundation for future history paintings'. Peter Harrington, *British Artists and War: The Face of Battle in Paintings and Prints, 1700–1914* (London: Greenhill, 1993), p. 35.

15. George Landmann, *Historical, Military and Picturesque Observations on Portugal* (London: T. Cadell and W. Davies, 1818), p. 515.

16. National Army Museum, Templer Study Centre, 2002–07–286.

17. Ibid., 1971–02–33–528.

18. Ibid., 1982–03–39.

19. Christopher Hibbert, *Corunna* (New York: Phoenix, 2003), p. 189.

20. Diego Saglia writes of how Wolfe's omission of Moore's name from the text of his poem and the use of 'we' as a first-person subject 'cements the nation': 'Celebrating a dead and retreating commander is then not such a misplaced operation as it may first appear . . . Failure and the defeat of Corunna become emblematic of Britain's unflinching determination to pursue the war as well as of a cohesive national community.' Diego Saglia, *Poetic Castles in Spain: British Romanticism and Figurations of Iberia* (Amsterdam: Rodopi, 2000), p. 162.

21. *Martial Achievements of Great Britain and her Allies*, sections on the Battle of Corunna and the death of Sir John Moore [no page numbers], National Army Museum, Templer Study Centre, 1983–03–6.

22. John Pemble, *Britain's Gurkha War: The Invasion of Nepal, 1814–16* (London: Frontline, 2008), p. 146.

23. Ibid., p. 148.

24. Ibid., p. 152.

25. Ibid., p. 163.

26. *A Memoir of Major-General Sir R.R. Gillespie* (London, 1816), dedication and p. 3.

27. Ibid., pp. 231 and 238–39.

28. Ibid., pp. 243–44.

29. http://www.irishmasonichistory.com/sir-rollo-gillespie-and-his-monument-by-wbro-aiken-mcclelland.html.

30. Felix Driver writes: 'Acres of print space – in books, tracts, periodicals and newspapers – were devoted to celebrating distant feats of exploration beyond the known horizon. The figure of the explorer seemed to draw together the most cherished national ideals in an age of supreme confidence about the virtues of the British: a fearless sense of adventure, selfless dedication, heroic valour and technological mastery.' Felix Driver, 'David Livingstone and the Culture of Exploration in Mid-Victorian Britain', in John M. MacKenzie, ed., *David Livingstone and the Victorian Encounter with Africa* (London: National Portrait Gallery, 1996), p. 112. See also Beau Riffenburgh, *The Myth of the Explorer: The Press, Sensationalism and Geographical Discovery* (Oxford and New York: Oxford University Press, 1994).

31. Tim Jeal, *Stanley* (New Haven and London: Yale University Press, 2007), p. 91.

32. A. G. Hopkins writes that 'heroes who die while enduring are especially valuable because their mythological status can be manipulated to provide an economical and effective way of symbolizing individual and national ideals'. A. G. Hopkins, 'Explorers' Tales: Stanley Presumes – Again', *Journal of Imperial and Commonwealth History* 36 (2008), p. 671. Similarly, Felix Driver writes that 'martyrdom . . . was of course fundamental to the heroic reputation of explorers from Mungo Park to Livingstone'. Felix Driver, 'The Active Life: The Explorer as Biographical Subject', *Oxford Dictionary of National Biography* (Oxford University Press): http://www.oxforddnb.com/view/theme/94053, accessed 25 April 2014.

33. Dane Kennedy, *The Last Blank Spaces: Exploring Africa and Australia* (Cambridge, MA: Harvard University Press, 2013), p. 88.

34. Ibid., p. 64.

35. Ibid., p. 5.

36. Ibid., p. 258.

37. See Frank T. Kryza, *The Race for Timbuktu: In Search of Africa's City of Gold* (New York: Harper Collins World, 2006); and Anthony Sattin, *The Gates of Africa: Death, Discovery and the Search for Timbuktu* (New York: St Martin's, 2004).

38. Kenneth Lupton, *Mungo Park the African Traveler* (Oxford: Oxford University Press, 1979), p. 34.
39. Scottish Borders Archive, box of uncatalogued museum materials on Park, letter of 9 May 1795.
40. John Wishaw, 'Life of Mungo Park', in *The Journal of a Mission to the Interior of Africa, in the Year 1805* (London, 1815), p. xv.
41. Richard B. Sher, *The Enlightenment and the Book: Scottish Authors and their Publishers in Eighteenth-Century Britain* (Chicago: University of Chicago Press, 2006), pp. 185–87 and 217; and Charles W. J. Withers, 'Geography, Enlightenment and the Book: Authorship and Audience in Mungo Park's African Texts', in Miles Ogborn and Charles W. J. Withers, eds, *Geographies of the Book* (Farnham, Surrey: Ashgate, 2010), p. 192.
42. Anthony Sattin, 'Afterword to the First Journey', in Mungo Park, *Travels into the Interior of Africa* (London: Eland, 2003), p. 290.
43. Scottish Borders Archive, SC/S/56.
44. Martyn proved to be an irascible and violent character. In the postscript to what turned out to be his last letter in November 1805, he wrote: 'My head a little sore this morning – was up late last night drinking ale in company with a Moor who has been at Gibraltar & speaks English. Got a little tipsy. Finished the scene by giving the Moor a damned good thrashing.' The casual brutality of Martyn's alcohol-soaked description differs greatly from typical public modes of representing African exploration in the nineteenth century. British Library, Add MS 37232 K, f. 63.
45. Scottish Borders Archive, SC/S/56.
46. British Library, Add MS 37232 K, ff. 67–69.
47. Scottish Borders Archive, SC/5/16/1/3.
48. Ibid.
49. British Library, Add MS 37232 K, f. 63.
50. Scottish Borders Archive, SC/5/16/1/3.
51. See Charles W. J. Withers, 'Memory and the History of Geographical Knowledge: The Commemoration of Mungo Park', *Journal of Historical Geography* 30 (2004), pp. 316–39.
52. Wishaw, 'Biographical Sketch', p. lxxxvi.
53. *The Life and Travels of Mungo Park* (Edinburgh, 1838), p. 81.
54. British Library, Add MS 42954, f. 384.
55. Oudney died in Africa, and Clapperton made a case that he should receive his salary of £300. The government agreed to pay him the higher amount for the period after Oudney's death. National Archives, Long Papers, Bundle 3, Africa: Hugh Clapperton, Dixon Denham and Richard Lander, Explorations in North and West Africa (1812–1831), Letters of 30 July 1825 and 13 August 1825, T 1/3413.
56. National Archives, Letters from the Secretary of State: African Exploration, Entry Books (1825–32), CO 392/1, ff. 15–16 and 24.
57. Denham got £700, and Oudney's family £100. National Library of Scotland, John Murray Archive, MS 40056, f. 111.
58. Jamie Bruce Lockhart, *A Sailor in the Sahara: The Life and Travels in Africa of Hugh Clapperton, Commander R.N.* (London and New York: I.B. Tauris, 2008), p. 188.
59. *Edinburgh Review* XLIV (1826), pp. 173–74.
60. National Archives, Letters from the Secretary of State: African Exploration, Entry Books (1825–32), CO 392/1, f. 21.
61. Ibid., f. 26.
62. National Archives, Letters from the Secretary of State: African Exploration, Entry Books (1825–32), CO 392/1, f. 22.

63. Ibid., Long Papers, Bundle 3, Africa: Hugh Clapperton, Dixon Denham and Richard Lander, Explorations in North and West Africa (1812–1831), Letter of 18 July 1826, T 1/3413.

64. Ibid., Letters from the Secretary of State: African Exploration, Entry Books (1825–32), CO 392/1, ff. 107–08. Lander, too, went to Africa well armed. He was issued '2 fowling pieces' and '2 brace pistols', along with 'bullet moulds', 'powder flasks', 'shot belts', 'flints pistol', 'balls for guns' and 'balls for pistols' from the Tower of London, and cartridges, powder and 'shot in bags' from the military depot at Woolwich. National Archives, Long Papers, Bundle 3, Africa: Hugh Clapperton, Dixon Denham and Richard Lander, Explorations in North and West Africa (1812–1831), Letters of 28 December 1829 and 29 January 1830, T 1/3413.

65. The lack of respect for Lander clearly related in part to his social status; whereas the vast majority of nineteenth-century explorers were from the upper ranks of society or at least, like David Livingstone, well educated, he was the son of a Truro innkeeper and was barely literate. Lander thus lacked the literary abilities to shape his own myth, and others did not see him as worthy of having it shaped for him.

66. Even with the existence of the Panama Canal, the Passage makes the voyage from New York to Tokyo 3,000 miles (4,800 km) shorter.

67. P. L. Simmonds, *Sir John Franklin and the Arctic Regions: A Narrative, Showing the Progress of British Enterprise in the Accomplishment of the North-West Passage*, 6th edn (London, 1855), p. 4.

68. This was true, at any rate, until the summers of 2007 and 2008, when due to global warming the Passage was sufficiently clear of ice that vessels other than icebreakers could navigate it.

69. Charles Richard Weld, *Arctic Expeditions: A Lecture* (London: John Murray, 1850), p. 3.

70. Anthony Brandt writes that the British 'pursued an enterprise that met with repeated and often deadly failure over a period not just of years but of centuries, persisting in tempting fate until fatality became inevitable . . . Yet tragedy can be the scene of heroism as well as arrogance and folly . . . To behave nobly and heroically in an obviously hopeless cause is a kind of folly, but it can also constitute a kind of greatness. Despite the wrongheadedness of the enterprise, an air of transcendence arises from their sufferings. It was in vain that they died, but their deaths raised them up . . . and made them emblems of whatever it is in human beings that can seem sublime.' Anthony Brandt, *The Man Who Ate his Boots: The Tragic History of the Search for the Northwest Passage* (London: Jonathan Cape, 2011), p. 6.

71. Ibid., p. 35.

72. Sherard Osborn, *The Career, Last Voyage and Fate of Captain Sir John Franklin* (London, 1860), pp. 29–30.

73. 'Tapping into the romantic myth of sublime ice, Arctic exploration was deemed an example of British civilisation at its best, the responsibility and pride of the British Navy . . . representing not simply a physical but an ethical test.' Catherine Lanone, 'John Franklin and the Idea of North: *Narrative of a Journey to the Shores of the Polar Sea in the Years 1819–1822*', in Frédéric Regard, ed., *British Narratives of Exploration: Case Studies of the Self and Other* (London: Pickering and Chatto, 2009), p. 124.

74. Osborn, *Career, Last Voyage and Fate of Captain Sir John Franklin*, p. 46.

75. Later in life, Ross did not demur when he was introduced as having been wounded thirteen times during the war with France. Certainly, he was seriously injured while taking on the batteries of Bilbao as a lieutenant on HMS *Surinam* in 1805.

76. *Quarterly Review* 21 (1819), p. 214. Barrow would later write that Ross's promotion to captain was undeserved, as it had been 'obtained by a few months' voyage of pleasure round the shores of Davis's Strait and Baffin's Bay, which had been performed centuries

ago, and somewhat better, in little ships of thirty to fifty tons. It is a voyage which any two of the Yacht Club would easily accomplish in five months.' John Barrow, *Voyages of Discovery and Research within the Arctic Regions, from the Year 1818 to the Present Time* (New York: Harper and Brothers, 1846), pp. 47–48.

77. Glyn Williams, *Arctic Labyrinth: The Quest for the Northwest Passage* (Berkeley: University of California Press, 2009), p. 180.

78. Pierre Berton, *The Arctic Grail: The Quest for the North West Passage and the North Pole, 1818–1909* (New York: Viking, 1988), p. 34.

79. *Description of the Vase Presented to Captain Parry, in Pursuance of the Resolutions of a Public Meeting of the Inhabitants of Bath, Held on the 28th Day of February, 1821* (Bath, 1821).

80. In 1826, Captain John Frederick Dennett of the Royal Navy published a volume tracing the various Arctic expeditions of the era (as well as, somewhat oddly, Giovanni Belzoni's archaeological excavations in Egypt). His descriptions are revealing of the standard for polar heroism in this era. At the conclusion of his chapter on Parry's first voyage, for example, he wrote: 'The perseverance and steadiness of purpose manifested by Captain Parry, are deserving the highest praise, and all that human effort could accomplish was effected by him.' John Frederick Dennett, *The Voyages and Travels of Captains Parry, Franklin, Ross and Mr Belzoni* (London, 1826), p. 62.

81. 'The last two expeditions undertaken by Captain Parry have been particularly unfortunate,' pronounced the *Gentleman's Magazine* in 1826. 'Literally nothing has been accomplished connected with the primary object of these expeditions – the extension of geographical knowledge.' *Gentleman's Magazine* 96 (1826), p. 233.

82. The use of steamships for ocean travel was in its infancy in the 1820s. Ross's steamship, the *Victory*, which was powered by paddle wheels on both sides, sailed so slowly under steam that the engine was removed and dumped on the shore during the first winter. The vessel proceeded under sail for the rest of the voyage.

83. *Athenaeum* (21 July 1832), p. 474.

84. Hugh Wallace has noted 'the paradoxical fact that in Arctic discovery the humanitarian aim to find a lost expedition might be a much stronger incentive to explore than was exploration itself'. Hugh N. Wallace, *The Navy, the Company and Richard King: British Exploration in the Canadian Arctic, 1829–1860* (Montreal: McGill-Queen's University Press, 1980), p. 19. Back later tried to get through the Northwest Passage himself by allowing his ship to be frozen in the ice and then drift with the pack. He failed, but earned a knighthood for his trouble.

85. Sir John Ross, *Narrative of a Second Voyage in Search of a North-West Passage, and of a Residence in the Arctic Regions during the Years 1829, 1830, 1831, 1832, 1833* (London, 1835), p. 132.

86. Brandt, *Man Who Ate his Boots*, p. 256; and National Library of Scotland, John Murray Archive, MS. 40057, f. 84.

87. Booth was also granted a baronetcy.

88. M. J. Ross, *Polar Pioneers: John Ross and James Clark Ross* (Montreal and Kingston, Ontario: McGill-Queen's University Press, 1994), p. 165.

89. *Description of a View of the Continent of Boothia, Discovered by Captain Ross, in his Late Expedition to the Polar Regions, Now Exhibiting at the Panorama, Leicester Square* (London, 1834), p. 12.

90. Berton, *Arctic Grail*, p. 120.

91. *Narrative of the Second Voyage of Captain Ross to the Arctic Regions in the Years 1829–30–31–32–33* (London, 1834), p. 105.

92. *Edinburgh Review* 63 (1836), p. 287.

93. *Narrative of the Second Voyage of Captain Ross*, p. vi.

94. Ibid., pp. 67–68 and 85.
95. Ibid., p. 88.
96. Ross, *Narrative of a Second Voyage in Search of a North-West Passage*, p. 89.
97. Ibid., p. 119.
98. Ibid., p. 135.
99. 'Sir John Ross's Narrative of his Arctic Expedition', *The Times*, 13 May 1835.

Chapter 2: Sir John Franklin

1. Derbyshire Record Office, Papers of the Gell Family of Hopton, D3311/61.
2. Anthony Brandt, *The Man Who Ate his Boots: The Tragic History of the Search for the Northwest Passage* (London: Jonathan Cape, 2011), p. 7.
3. John Franklin, *Narrative of a Journey to the Shores of the Polar Sea in the Years 1819–20–21–22* (London: Conway Maritime Press, 2000), pp. 249–50.
4. The journal was also issued in a cheaper octavo edition and translated into French and German.
5. Catherine Lanone, 'John Franklin and the Idea of North: *Narrative of a Journey to the Shores of the Polar Sea in the Years 1819–1822*', in Frédéric Regard, ed., *British Narratives of Exploration: Case Studies of the Self and Other* (London: Pickering and Chatto, 2009), p. 124.
6. William Henry Davenport Adams, *Neptune's Heroes; or, The Sea-Kings of England* (London, 1860), p. 424.
7. National Library of Scotland, John Murray Archive, MS 40056, f. 101.
8. His first wife, Eleanor, had died of tuberculosis in 1825.
9. The *Erebus* and *Terror* had previously been used on George Back's attempt to rescue John Ross in the 1830s and on James Clark Ross's Antarctic expedition of 1839–43. Bomb ships were built to carry mortars and used to bombard targets on land. Their hulls and decks were reinforced to withstand the recoil from the mortar launches. The *Terror* had also participated in the bombing of Fort McHenry during the War of 1812, making it quite possibly the vessel responsible for the 'bombs bursting in air' line of the American national anthem.
10. Invented in France as a way to feed soldiers during the Napoleonic Wars, canning was patented in the United Kingdom in 1810. A laborious and expensive process in the first half of the nineteenth century, it was used primarily by the army and navy.
11. John Brown, *The North-West Passage, and the Plans for the Search for Sir John Franklin: A Review* (London: Stanford, 1858), p. 47.
12. Derbyshire Record Office, Papers of the Gell Family of Hopton, D3311/51/1.
13. Mary Richardson, whose husband, the naval surgeon Sir John Richardson, was a close friend of Franklin's, wrote to Eleanor Gell in 1849 about the 'fraud and cunning' of one psychic. She told her that he had told one of her friends that Franklin 'had died early in the voyage' and then told another that 'he was well and all the crew in good spirits'. That same year, Gell received another report from a clairvoyant claiming that Franklin was 'alive' and 'with three or four companions somewhere inland'; they were 'endeavouring to get to England'. Her friend Rose Beaufort, however, told her that her father, the hydrographer Sir Francis Beaufort, 'has no belief in clairvoyance and no admiration for the present sample of it, which he thinks both false and very clumsy'. Ibid., D3311/56/6, D3311/81/1 and D3311/122/25.
14. The only rescue expedition that might have saved some of Franklin's men was that led by Sir John Ross in 1848. It explored the vicinity of North Somerset Island at a time when the survivors were making their desperate journey from King William Island to the Great Fish River.

15. P. L. Simmonds, *Sir John Franklin and the Arctic Regions: A Narrative, Showing the Progress of British Enterprise in the Accomplishment of the North-West Passage*, 6th edn (London, 1855), p. 253.

16. William Kennedy, *A Short Narrative of the Second Voyage of the Prince Albert, in Search of Sir John Franklin* (London, 1853), p. ii.

17. Brown, *The North-West Passage, and the Plans for the Search for Sir John Franklin*, p. 424.

18. James A. Browne, *The North-west Passage and the Fate of Sir John Franklin* (Woolwich, 1860), pp. iv–v.

19. Sherard Osborn, *Stray Leaves from an Arctic Journal; or Eighteen Months in the Polar Regions, in Search of Sir John Franklin's Expedition, in the Years 1850–51* (London, 1852), p. 210.

20. Ibid., p. 272.

21. James Mangles, ed., *Papers and Despatches Relating to the Arctic Searching Expeditions of 1850–51* (London, 1851), pp. 13–14.

22. National Archives, Letters to James Clark Ross from Leopold McClintock (1851), BJ 2/11, ff. 18–19.

23. Derbyshire Record Office, Papers of the Gell Family of Hopton, D3311/57/3.

24. National Archives, Relief of Sir John Franklin, ADM 7/608.

25. Ibid., Petitions as to the Search for Sir John Franklin (1851–52), ADM 7/611.

26. Francis Leopold McClintock, one of Belcher's officers and an experienced Arctic sailor, wrote to James Clark Ross in June 1852: 'the want of experience is very evident in our chiefs and Sir Edward will not be told anything and has made himself unpopular in a variety of ways already.' Ibid., Letters to James Clark Ross from Leopold McClintock (1851), BJ 2/11, f. 44.

27. The *Investigator* was subsequently trapped in the ice, and McClure's men had themselves to be rescued by the *North Star*, the only vessel to survive Edward Belcher's expedition of 1852. McClure did not return to England until October 1854, though reports of his discovery preceded him. This was the first of three potential routes for the Northwest Passage that were found during the search for Franklin. See Hugh N. Wallace, *The Navy, the Company and Richard King: British Exploration in the Canadian Arctic, 1829–1860* (Montreal: McGill-Queen's University Press, 1980), pp. 115–41.

28. The following year, Bellot fell into a crack between two ice floes in the Wellington Channel and died; he was memorialized by a granite obelisk that still stands on the banks of the Thames in Greenwich.

29. Kennedy, *Short Narrative of the Second Voyage of the Prince Albert*, p. 173.

30. 'The Northwest Passage', *Nautical Magazine* 22 (1853), pp. 577 and 616.

31. Simmonds, *Sir John Franklin and the Arctic Regions*, p. 249.

32. Ken McGoogan, *Fatal Passage: The Untold Story of Scotsman John Rae, the Arctic Adventurer Who Discovered the Fate of Franklin* (London and New York: Bantam Books, 2001), p. 186.

33. Ibid., p. 193.

34. The engraver had mistakenly inscribed a 'B' rather than an 'H'.

35. *The Great Arctic Mystery* (London: Chapman and Hall, 1856), pp. 6–7.

36. Derbyshire Record Office, Papers of the Gell Family of Hopton, D3311/57/3.

37. Ibid., D3311/122/25.

38. *Great Arctic Mystery*, p. 9.

39. Though liberal in his attitudes to social reform, Dickens was less broad-minded when it came to race. He voiced strong support for the harsh punishment of the Indian rebels in 1857 and fiercely defended the draconian actions of Governor Edward Eyre in putting down a rebellion among Jamaica's black population in 1865.

40. Charles Dickens, 'The Lost Arctic Voyagers', *Household Words* 10 (2 December 1854), p. 361.

41. *Repton School Prize Poems* (Derby, 1860), found in Derbyshire Record Office, Papers of the Gell Family of Hopton, D3311/85/13, p. 13. For the remainder of the nineteenth century, the accusations of cannibalism were usually eliminated from Franklin's story. For example, when the National Portrait Gallery created an 'Arctic Room' to display its collection of portraits of Arctic explorers in 1899, the description read simply: 'In 1854, whilst employed by the Hudson Bay Company on a surveying expedition with sledge and boat, Dr John Rae heard from the Eskimos of Boothia Felix that a party of about forty white men had been met on the west coast of King William's Island, on their way to the Great Fish River, where they had all perished of starvation. From these natives he also obtained some relics of the ill-fated party. For this discovery he received the Government reward of £10,000.' National Portrait Gallery, Heinz Archive and Library, RP1208, NPG 46/13/9.

42. Derbyshire Record Office, Papers of the Gell Family of Hopton, D3311/122/3.

43. Ibid., D3311/122/1.

44. McClintock's case demonstrates how the motives for the search for Franklin were not solely humanitarian or emotional, for he had told James Clark Ross in a letter of December 1851 'how very anxious' he was 'to obtain Arctic employment'. 'I cannot help feeling that the present is the *all important* moment which will determine whether I am to rise in my profession or be placed upon the shelf,' he wrote. (Italics in original.) He need not have worried, as he would, largely thanks to his success in obtaining evidence of Franklin's fate, rise to the rank of rear admiral. He came to be known as the father of British polar sledging technique; this letter already shows evidence of his efforts in this area, as it refers to his 'proposed equipment for travelling parties'. He later gave Ross a detailed report of the 700-mile (1,120 km) sledging journey he and his party undertook on Austin's rescue expedition of 1850. McClintock praised his men for their 'spirited perseverance and patient endurance of fatigue and privation', showing once again how these qualities were coming to be seen as the litmus test of heroism in the context of British exploration. National Archives, Letters to James Clark Ross from Leopold McClintock (1851), BJ 2/11, ff. 2–3, 23 and 38–39.

45. Brandt, *The Man Who Ate his Boots*, p. 377.

46. Ibid., p. 378.

47. Modern forensic analysis of the bodies suggests that they perished of tuberculosis or pneumonia. See Owen Beattie and John Geiger, *Frozen in Time: The Fate of the Franklin Expedition* (New York: Dutton, 1987).

48. 'Fate of Sir John Franklin's Expedition', *The Times*, 23 September 1859.

49. Expeditions to learn more about Franklin's fate continued into the 1870s. They confirmed Rae's findings, cannibalism included. Modern forensic analysis of the skeletons of Franklin's men has shown that their bones are scarred with knife-cuts consistent with butchery.

50. James Parsons, *Reflections on the Mysterious Fate of Sir John Franklin* (London, 1857), p. 110.

51. Owen A. Vidal, *A Poem upon the Life and Character of Sir John Franklin* (Oxford: T. and G. Shrimpton, 1860), Derbyshire Record Office, Papers of the Gell Family of Hopton, D3311/85/6.

52. It quickly became apparent that the public was not treating his memorial with reverence. Instead, 'the unprotected state' of the statue was making it 'liable to injury from mischievous boys and others'. Various ideas were contemplated as to how to remedy the problem, including the installation of a 'fender or railing' around the base of the statue and moving it to another site altogether, but it was determined that the best course was

to move the pedestal 3 feet (91 cm) further back. Noble, who charged £45 to perform this service, expressed his regret that 'the unreflecting among the public render the removal desirable'. National Archives, Statue of Sir John Franklin (1861–1914), WORK 20/85.

Chapter 3: The Charge

1. These figures come from the count taken the day after the battle. The exact number of men who participated in the charge remains a point of debate, as do the casualty figures. See Terry Brighton, *Hell Riders: The Truth about the Light Brigade* (London: Penguin, 2004), pp. 290–94.
2. Donald Thomas, *Charge! Hurrah! Hurrah!* (London: Routledge & Kegan Paul, 1974), p. 269. The Battle of Chillianwallah, which is described in detail below, took place during the Second Anglo-Sikh War in 1849. The British claimed victory, but the high number of casualties caused serious concern back home. Particularly notorious was the charge of the 24th Foot against the Sikh guns, which resulted in a casualty rate of over 50 per cent for the regiment.
3. Ian Fletcher, *Galloping at Everything: The British Cavalry in the Peninsular War and at Waterloo, 1808–15* (Staplehurst, Kent: Spellmount, 1999), pp. 27–28 and 30.
4. Ibid., p. 105.
5. Ibid., p. 169.
6. Edward Cotton, *A Voice from Waterloo: A History of the Battle Fought on the 18th June 1815* (London, 1849), p. 58.
7. See Stephen Badsley, *Doctrine and Reform in the British Cavalry, 1880–1918* (Farnham, Surrey: Ashgate, 2008).
8. Nigel Jones, *Peace and War: Britain in 1914* (London: Head of Zeus, 2014), pp. 238–9.
9. Amarpal S. Sidhu, *The First Anglo-Sikh War* (Stroud, Gloucestershire: Amberley, 2010), p. 22.
10. George Bruce, *Six Battles for India: The Anglo-Sikh Wars, 1845–6, 1848–9* (London: Arthur Barker, 1969), p. 170.
11. *Despatches and General Orders Announcing the Victories Achieved by the Army of the Sutlej over the Sikh Army at Moodkee, Ferozeshah, Aliwal & Sobraon* (London, 1846), pp. 58 and 72.
12. Campbell later explained that he had admired the 24th for a similar feat during the Peninsular War and wished to see it duplicated. Edward Joseph Thackwell, *Narrative of the Second Sikh War in 1848–49*, 2nd edn (London, 1851), p. 45.
13. Saul David, *Victoria's Wars: The Rise of Empire* (London: Penguin, 2007), p. 129.
14. Ibid., p. 130.
15. National Army Museum, Templer Study Centre, 1967–11–1–5.
16. 'The War in the Punjab', *The Times*, 5 March 1849.
17. Major General Edward Joseph Thackwell, who was in command of the cavalry division, had harsh words for Campbell, and noted that 'the annals of British warfare present few such losses by a single corps as were sustained by the 24th Foot, in this action'. Thackwell, *Narrative of the Second Sikh War*, p. 54.
18. Sir Colin Campbell, *Memorandum on the Part Taken by the Third Division of the Army of the Punjab, at the Battle of Chillianwala* (London: James Ridgway, 1851), pp. 12–13.
19. http://www.ukniwm.org.uk/server/show/conMemorial.39/fromUkniwmSearch/1.
20. Grant later rose to the rank of lieutenant and served as quartermaster and interpreter for the 35th Bengal Native Infantry. He died in Agra in 1854 at the age of twenty-eight.
21. Tyne and Wear Archives, B81.

22. David Buttery observes: 'The fame of this charge reveals an unusual trait in the British psyche. Almost any other country in the world would have emphasized the other famous incidents during the Battle of Balaclava in preference. Considering that the Heavy Cavalry Brigade mounted a highly successful charge almost immediately before the incident, this is strange. The charge had little strategic or tactical influence on the outcome of the campaign and historians' concentration on this event reveals a national passion for glorious and spectacular failure.' David Buttery, *Messenger of Death: Captain Nolan and the Charge of the Light Brigade* (Barnsley: Pen & Sword Military, 2008), p. ix.

23. The rank of general could not be purchased and could only be attained through promotion.

24. Brighton, *Hell Riders*, p. 29.

25. Ibid., p. 108.

26. Ibid., p. 113.

27. Tyne and Wear Archive, B81.

28. Ibid.

29. Ibid., B57.

30. Captain Arthur Tremayne, 'Letters from the Crimea', Tyne and Wear Archive, B46.

31. Ibid., p. 21.

32. National Army Museum, Templer Study Centre, 1968–08–8.

33. Terry Brighton estimates that fewer than two hundred of the British casualties were caused by Russian artillery fire: 'The losses inflicted on such a closely packed enemy riding directly at the muzzles of their guns to the front and offering an easy target for their guns on each flank – less than one man killed or wounded per round – were for the Russian artillery an astonishing failure.' Brighton, *Hell Riders*, p. 299.

34. Russell is often referred to as the first war correspondent, but in fact the *Morning Post* had dispatched C. L. Grüneisen to cover the Carlist Wars in Spain in the 1830s. Russell was, however, the first reporter to cover from the front lines a war in which the British fought.

35. For Russell's account of the Battle of Balaclava, see Nicholas Bentley, ed., *Despatches from the Crimea* (London: Frontline, 1966), pp. 119–29.

36. Tennyson's underestimation of the number of participants in the charge derived from Russell's account, which referred to '607 sabres'. He was dismayed to learn that the figure was incorrect and had to be consoled by his wife that, if he had known the correct number, it would have ruined the metre.

37. *The Adventures of 'Our Own Correspondent' at the Seat of War in the Crimea, by Himself* (London, 1855).

38. George Brackenbury, *The Campaign in the Crimea: An Historical Sketch* (London, 1855), pp. 37–40.

39. Peter Harrington, *British Artists and War: The Face of Battle in Paintings and Prints, 1700–1914* (London: Greenhill, 1993), p. 133.

40. *Athenaeum*, 17 February 1855, p. 207.

41. A. N. Wilson, *The Victorians* (London: Norton, 2002), p. 192.

42. Donald Thomas, *Lord Cardigan: The Life of Cardigan of Balaclava* (London: Routledge & Kegan Paul, 1974), p. 253.

43. Ibid., p. 254.

44. Ibid., pp. 260–61.

45. Saul David, *The Homicidal Earl: The Life of Lord Cardigan* (London: Abacus, 1997), p. 435.

46. George Ryan, *Our Heroes of the Crimea* (London, 1855), p. 58. Cardigan's stature as a hero in fact became so great that it later provoked a backlash. He would be accused of abandoning his men after reaching the Russian guns by Major Somerset Calthorpe, who had been a member of Raglan's staff, and by Alexander Kinglake, who had been a witness at Balaclava and became MP for Bridgewater.

47. Several reports claim that he dashed forward as the charge began, either out of eager-ness to reach the battery at the end of the valley or because he realized that Lucan had misinterpreted Raglan's order and was trying to stop the disaster. Some witnesses saw him throw his right arm in the air before he died, possibly indicating that he was pointing towards the redoubts on the heights on the right, where Raglan had intended the brigade to attack. But if Nolan was trying to halt the charge, he did so too late.
48. *The Times,* 2 March 1855.
49. *Morning Chronicle,* 14 November 1854.
50. *Illustrated London News,* 30 October 1875, p. 420; and Buttery, *Messenger of Death,* p. 163.
51. M. J. Trow, *The Pocket Hercules: Captain Morris and the Charge of the Light Brigade* (Barnsley: Pen & Sword Military, 2006), p. 92.
52. Ibid., p. 99.
53. Ibid., p. 108.
54. Ibid., p. 129.
55. Morris had been promoted to brevet lieutenant colonel after his return to the Crimea in 1855.
56. Trow, *Pocket Hercules,* pp. 137–38.

Chapter 4: David Livingstone

1. See Mira Matikkala, *Empire and Imperial Ambition: Liberty, Englishness and Anti-imperialism in Late Victorian Britain* (London: I.B. Tauris, 2011).
2. Robert MacDonald writes: 'Had Britain the right to impose her will on other countries and other races? Social Darwinism theories suggested that might was indeed right, that "clean breeding" proved in a fight who was best, that "successful" nations alone survived a trial of strength, liberal ideas of progress argued that the benefits of civilisation should be shared. Yet the facts of conquest were often ugly, and the imperialist's version of the schoolmaster's warning, "this hurts me more than it hurts you", rang as false as it always did to the victim receiving the punishment. In metaphorical terms, the life of the hero served its purpose: it was a distraction from the harsh facts.' Robert H. MacDonald, *The Language of Empire: Myths and Metaphors of Popular Imperialism, 1880–1918* (Manchester: Manchester University Press, 1994), p. 81.
3. Martin Dugard, *Into Africa: The Epic Adventures of Stanley and Livingstone* (New York: Broadway, 2003), p. 73.
4. As his biographer Tim Jeal writes: 'Livingstone can be said to have failed in all he most hoped to achieve.' Tim Jeal, 'David Livingstone: A Brief Biographical Account', in John M. MacKenzie, ed., *David Livingstone and the Victorian Encounter with Africa* (London: National Portrait Gallery, 1996), p. 13.
5. Ibid., pp. 13–14.
6. Livingstone did not discover the rapids on his first journey because he failed to take elevation measurements during a crucial portion while he was not on the river. He thus did not realize that the Zambesi dropped 600 feet (183 m).
7. David Livingstone Centre, J/3/2, K/3/2 and M/4/2.
8. Tim Barringer, 'Fabricating Africa: Livingstone and the Visual Image 1850–74', in John M. MacKenzie, ed., *David Livingstone and the Victorian Encounter with Africa* (London: National Portrait Gallery, 1996), p. 179. Livingstone took an active role in ensuring that the journal presented him in the way that he wanted, vehemently protesting when he felt that Whitwell Elwin, the editor of the *Quarterly Review,* whom John Murray had supplied to assist him in preparing the journal for publication, was subjecting his prose to a 'process of emasculation'. Livingstone told Murray in no

uncertain terms: 'I really cannot afford to appear as he would make me.' http://www.Livingstoneonline.ucl.ac.uk/view/transcript.php?id=LETT581.

9. Adrian S. Wisnicki, 'Interstitial Cartographer: David Livingstone and the Invention of South Central Africa', *Victorian Literature and Culture* 37 (2009), p. 257.

10. Gregory Fremont-Barnes, *The Indian Mutiny 1857–58* (Botley, Oxford: Osprey, 2007), p. 82.

11. In the early 1860s, an attempt to establish a mission at Linyanti using the overland route from the Cape Colony failed miserably, resulting in the deaths of six Europeans.

12. Tim Jeal, *Livingstone*, revised edn (New Haven and London: Yale University Press, 2013), p. 223.

13. 'The East African Mission', *The Times*, 1 January 1863.

14. John M. MacKenzie, 'David Livingstone and the Worldly After-Life: Imperialism and Nationalism in Africa', in John M. MacKenzie, ed., *David Livingstone and the Victorian Encounter with Africa* (London: National Portrait Gallery, 1996), p. 206.

15. The precise date of the meeting is unclear, as both Livingstone and Stanley had lost track of the days of the month.

16. Clare Pettitt, *Dr Livingstone, I Presume?: Missionaries, Journalists, Explorers and Empire* (London: Profile, 2007), p. 10.

17. See Clare Pettitt, 'Livingstone: From Fame to Celebrity', in Sarah Worden, ed., *David Livingstone: Man, Myth and Legacy* (Edinburgh: National Museums of Scotland, 2012), pp. 83–99.

18. Cameron reported to the Royal Geographical Society that Livingstone's 'servants have disembowelled the corpse and filled it with salt and put brandy into the mouth &c so as to preserve it and are bringing it along with them'. Royal Geographical Society, David Livingstone Collection, DL/5/1/1.

19. Cameron went on to carry out a series of independent explorations and to complete the first crossing of equatorial Africa. He received a hero's welcome when he returned to Britain in 1876.

20. Royal Geographical Society, David Livingstone Collection, DL/5/1/5.

21. Ibid., DL/5/1/3.

22. Pettitt, *Dr Livingstone, I Presume?*, p. 135.

23. National Portrait Gallery, Heinz Archive and Library, RP 386.

24. David Livingstone Centre, Lib H6 1414 and H6 1415.

25. Ibid., Lib G/1/2 and D/3/1. 'In life,' writes Felix Driver, 'Livingstone had been an unreliable and frequently disappointing hero; in death he had become a saint.' Felix Driver, 'David Livingstone and the Culture of Exploration in Mid-Victorian Britain', in John M. MacKenzie, ed., *David Livingstone and the Victorian Encounter with Africa* (London: National Portrait Gallery, 1996), p. 111. John MacKenzie adds that Livingstone's 'posthumous reputation transformed him into an archetype, a public property displayed and used through countless biographies, heroic hagiographies and other publications. He became a Protestant saint whose cult operated at a variety of different levels, imperial, British and Scottish. Like all cults it was bent to suit the requirements of the age.' John M. MacKenzie, 'Heroic Myths of Empire', in John M. MacKenzie, ed., *Popular Imperialism and the Military, 1850–1950* (Manchester: Manchester University Press, 1992), p. 122. See also Chris Wingfield, 'Remembering David Livingstone 1873–1935: From Celebrity to Saintliness', in Sarah Worden, ed., *David Livingstone: Man, Myth and Legacy* (Edinburgh: National Museums of Scotland, 2012), pp. 115–29; and Justin D. Livingstone, 'A "Body" of Evidence: The Posthumous Presentation of David Livingstone', *Victorian Literature and Culture* 40 (2012), pp. 1–24.

26. As Angus Calder writes, Livingston proved 'a completely edifying hero . . . because he persevered after the failure of his great Zambesi expedition and ended his days without

European companions, chasing a geographical chimera through foul country and [confronting] dangerous beasts despite his piles and fevers. He was Will personified.' Angus Calder, 'Livingstone, Self-Help and Scotland', in John M. MacKenzie, ed., *David Livingstone and the Victorian Encounter with Africa* (London: National Portrait Gallery, 1996), p. 88.

27. Livingstone, 'A "Body" of Evidence', p. 7. The term 'van' derives from medieval warfare. In the Middle Ages, armies were divided into three 'battles' or 'wards': the van, or front; the main, or middle; and the rear. To be chosen to lead the van was a great honour.

28. See Adam Hochschild, *King Leopold's Ghost: A Story of Greed, Terror and Heroism in Colonial Africa* (New York: Houghton Mifflin, 1998).

29. Driver, 'David Livingstone and the Culture of Exploration', p. 132.

30. Tim Jeal, *Stanley* (New Haven and London: Yale University Press, 2007), p. 155.

31. Dugard, *Into Africa*, p. 239.

32. MacKenzie, 'David Livingstone and the Worldly After-Life', p. 208.

33. Jeal writes: 'Livingstone's fame had been due not so much to what he had done, as to what he had come to represent in *moral* terms [author's italics]. By praising a man who was said to have died on his knees in Africa while saving the heathen, the British public could feel pride without any nagging guilt over their country's wealth and power.' Jeal, *Stanley*, p. 473.

34. Jeal, *Livingstone*, p. 231.

35. Royal Geographical Society, David Livingstone Collection, DL/5/2.

36. National Portrait Gallery, Heinz Archive and Library, RP 1040, NPG 46/11/40. The portrait is now at Bodelwyddan Castle in Wales, where the National Portrait Gallery displays many of its Victorian works.

Chapter 5: The 'Last Stand'

1. In the 1820s, the Ndebele, under their king, Mzilikazi, had migrated northwards as they sought first to get out from under Zulu authority and then to get away from the Boers who arrived in the Transvaal after 1837. The name 'Matabele' was given to the Ndebele by the Basotho people, who had come into conflict with them after their move north. The Ndebele adapted the term for themselves and transformed it into 'Ndebele'.

2. Stafford Glass, *The Matabele War* (London: Longmans, 1968), p. 8. When nervous BSAC officials inquired about the advisability of giving so many rifles to Africans, Rudd assured them that the Ndebele were inexperienced in their employment and thus would make little use of them.

3. Ibid., p. 83.

4. 'The Shangani Patrol', *Canadian Magazine* 32 (1904), p. 474.

5. National Army Museum, Templer Study Centre, 1999–08–6–6 and 1999–08–6–7.

6. Ibid., 1999–08–6–9.

7. Graham Dawson writes that 'images of British soldier heroes and stories of their colonial adventures assumed a new importance' in the late nineteenth century. Graham Dawson, *Soldier Heroes: British Adventure, Empire and the Imagining of Masculinities* (London and New York: Routledge, 1994), p. 145.

8. Mike Snook, *Into the Jaws of Death: British Military Blunders, 1879–1900* (London: Frontline, 2008), pp. 15–16.

9. Ian Knight, *Zulu Rising: The Epic Story of Isandlwana and Rorke's Drift* (London: Macmillan, 2010), p. 195.

10. Little definitive knowledge exists about Shaka and the early history of the Zulu kingdom, and some historians argue that Zulu society may have been organized along military lines prior to his coming to power. See Carolyn Hamilton, *Terrific Majesty: The*

Powers of Shaka Zulu and the Limits of Historical Invention (Cambridge, MA: Harvard University Press, 2009).

11. War had already broken out between the Boers and the Zulus, resulting in a victory for the former, in 1838.

12. Mzinyathi means 'home of the buffalo' in the Zulu language, and so the British called the river the Buffalo.

13. Saul David, *Zulu: The Heroism and Tragedy of the Zulu War of 1879* (London: Penguin, 2004), p. 25.

14. Ibid., p. 40.

15. Knight, *Zulu Rising*, p. 217.

16. National Army Museum, Templer Study Centre, 1971–12–38–5.

17. David, *Zulu*, p. 140.

18. For an analysis of the Battle of Isandlwana in purely military terms, see Adrian Greaves, *Isandlwana: How the Zulus Humbled the British Empire* (Barnsley: Pen and Sword, 2011).

19. Cetshwayo had ordered his men not to cross the Natal border, but his half-brother Prince Dabulamanzi had not participated in the victory at Isandlwana and was eager to claim a piece of the day's glory for himself by taking Rorke's Drift.

20. Knight, *Zulu Rising*, p. 474.

21. Ron Lock and Peter Quatrill, eds, *The 1879 Zulu War through the Eyes of the Illustrated London News* (Kloof, kwaZulu-Natal: Q-Lock, 2003), pp. 4–5.

22. National Army Museum, Templer Study Centre, 1984–09–33.

23. Moynan's work is, as Ian Knight writes, 'a wonderfully evocative painting, full of the self-confident martyrdom inherent in a good deal of late nineteenth century imperial ideology – the white man's sacrificing his life in the cause of civilised progress'. Knight, *Zulu Rising*, p. 490.

24. Ibid., p. 673. It was not until March 1879 that the British were able to conduct a reconnaissance of the Isandlwana battlefield, and the small British patrol that carried out the examination was fired on by local Zulus. The officer in charge, Major Wilsone Black, recommended waiting for 'at least another month' before making any attempt to bury the dead. Ian Knight, *Companion to the Anglo-Zulu War* (Barnsley: Pen and Sword, 2008), p. 46. It was not until May, four months after the battle, that the first military burial parties were dispatched. At that time, Archibald Forbes of the *Daily News* visited the battlefield, where most of the bodies, including Durnford's, still lay unburied. Corroborating the story of a 'last stand', he reported: 'Durnford had died hard – a central figure of a knot of brave men who had fought it out around their chief to the bitter end. A stalwart Zulu, covered by his shield, lay at the Colonel's feet. Around him, almost in a ring, lay about a dozen dead men, half being Natal Carbineers, riddled by assegai stabs . . . Clearly they had rallied round Durnford in a last despairing attempt to cover the flank of the camp, and had stood fast when they might have essayed to fly for their horses.' It would be the end of June before the last bodies were buried, and not until 1883 that the shallow graves of the British dead were replaced with stone cairns. David, *Zulu*, p. 307.

25. In October 1879, the saved colour was presented to Queen Victoria, who placed a wreath of dried flowers, or *immortelles*, on it to represent the 'immortal bravery' of the 24th Foot. Ever since, the regiment's Queen's Colour has borne a silver wreath around the crown that tops the pole, and the regiment also features a wreath as its badge. Knight, *Companion to the Anglo-Zulu War*, pp. 67–68.

26. National Army Museum, Templer Study Centre, 1971–12–38–6.

27. The colour was carried by the regiment until the 1930s, when it was put on display in Brecon cathedral, where it remains today.

28. National Army Museum, Templer Study Centre, 1984–09–33.
29. Knight, *Zulu Rising*, p. 638.
30. Despite the fact that the Fine Art Society solicited photographs and first-hand accounts in order to ensure the accuracy of the paintings, they contain a number of errors. The colour shown is the Regimental rather than Queen's Colour, and in the second painting the soldier who discovers the bodies is from the 17th Lancers, who had not left England at the time they were found. Melvill and Coghill are shown clinging to the colour even in death, when in reality they had been forced to release it as they struggled to cross the river. De Neuville never visited Africa and painted all of his depictions of the Anglo-Zulu War using Parisian models as stand-ins for British soldiers and Zulus. Knight, *Companion to the Anglo-Zulu War*, p. 154.
31. 'Oleographs from de Neuville', *Spectator*, 10 June 1882, p. 24.
32. At the time of their deaths, Queen Victoria issued a special 'Memorandum Procedure' declaring that they would have received the VC had they survived. Whether Melvill and Coghill deserved one has long been a matter of debate. See Adrian Greaves, 'Saving the Colour: Events Surrounding the Deaths of Lieutenants Coghill and Melvill', in Adrian Greaves, ed., *Redcoats and Zulus: Selected Essays from the Journal of the Anglo-Zulu War Historical Society* (Barnsley: Pen and Sword, 2004), pp. 41–54.
33. Knight, *Companion to the Anglo-Zulu War*, pp. 149–50.
34. David, *Zulu*, p. 184.
35. David, *Zulu*, p. 275.
36. National Army Museum, Templer Study Centre, 1984–09–33.
37. Alexander Wilmont, *History of the Zulu War* (London: Richardson and Best, 1880), p. v.
38. Holditch Mason, *The Zulu War: Its Causes, and its Lessons* (London: William Poole, 1879), p. 3.
39. John Noble, *British South Africa and the Zulu War* (London: Edward Stanford, 1879), pp. 29–30.
40. Frances E. Colenso, *History of the Zulu War and its Origin* (London: Chapman and Hall, 1880), p. ix.
41. Robert Spence Watson, *The History of English Rule and Policy in South Africa* (Newcastle: J. Forster, 1879), pp. 1, 29–30 and 32.
42. This view of Isandlwana persists into the present. Ian Knight writes: 'For the British today ... the invasion of Zululand is largely remembered for the heroism of the ordinary soldiers who took part. There are few things more profoundly pointless than attempting to apply contemporary morality to historical events, but it is nevertheless true that the policies and attitudes which produced the Anglo-Zulu War are deeply unfashionable in Britain nowadays, and uncomfortable truths are buried beneath a veneer of Boy's Own derring-do, of stories of courage, self-sacrifice and Victoria Crosses awarded.' Knight, *Zulu Rising*, p. 4.
43. J. Ewing Ritchie, *Imperialism in South Africa* (London: James Clarke & Co., 1879), pp. 3, 19 and 25.
44. R. W. Leyland, *A Holiday in South Africa* (London: Sampson, Low, Marston, Searle and Rivington, 1882), p. 1.
45. Bertram Mitford, *Through the Zulu Country: Its Battlefields and its People* (London: Kegan, Paul, Trench & Co., 1883), pp. v–vi.
46. Ibid., pp. 81–82.
47. Imperial War Museum, War Memorials Archive, http://www.ukniwm.org.uk/server/show/conMemorial.49538/. Other memorials to soldiers killed at Isandlwana can be found in St Margaret's Church in Chipstead, Surrey (Lance Corporal Nelson Kempsell); St John's Church in Stoke-on-Trent in Staffordshire (Private William Hickin); St John the Baptist Church in Kirby Wiske, North Yorkshire (Lieutenant

Colonel Burmester Pulleine); St Gwynno's Church in Llanwynno in Glamorgan (Private Thomas Chester); Rochester Cathedral in Kent (Colonel Anthony Durnford); and Charterhouse School in Godalming, Surrey (Lieutenant Arthur Gibson). Surgeon-Major Peter Shepherd got two memorials, one in the parish church at Leochel-Cushnie in Grampian and one at the Royal Victoria Military Hospital at Netley in Hampshire. Not surprisingly, given their prominence as heroes after the battle, Lieutenants Melvill and/or Coghill were the subjects of several memorials. Melvill was commemorated by his alma mater, Harrow School in London, while Coghill was celebrated along with Lieutenant George Hodson, who also died at Isandlwana, at Haileybury College in Hertford. Melvill and Coghill were memorialized together at St Winnow Church in St Winnow, Cornwall. Holy Trinity Church in Aldershot, Hampshire, displays a book rest engraved 'To the Glory of God and in Memory of the Officers and Men who Fell at Isandula [*sic*].'

48. Even at Isandlwana, Zulu casualties were double those of the British.
49. With a death rate of close to 90 per cent, the retreat from Kabul remains the worst disaster in British military history.
50. Robert Blake, *Disraeli* (London: Eyre & Spottiswoode, 1966), p. 659.
51. Edmund Yorke, *Maiwand 1880* (Stroud, Gloucestershire: Spellmount, 2013), p. 64.
52. Sir Frederick Roberts, *Forty-One Years in India* (London: R. Bentley & Son, 1898), p. 388.
53. William Trousdale, ed., *War in Afghanistan 1879–80: The Personal Diary of Major-General Sir Charles Metcalfe MacGregor* (Detroit: Wayne State University Press, 1985), p. 108.
54. Sir Percy Sykes, *Sir Mortimer Durand* (London: Cassell, 1926), p. 103.
55. National Army Museum, Templer Study Centre, 1982–02–25.
56. Ibid.
57. Ibid., 1980–04–41.
58. Ibid.
59. Ibid., 1982–02–25.
60. Ibid., 1980–04–41.
61. Ibid., 1982–02–25.
62. Richard J. Stacpoole-Ryding, *Maiwand: The Last Stand of the 66th (Berkshire) Regiment in Afghanistan, 1880* (Stroud: History Press, 2008), p. 104.
63. For an analysis of Maiwand and its military context, see Leigh Maxwell, *My God – Maiwand!: Operations of the South Afghanistan Field Force, 1878–80* (London: Leo Cooper, 1979).
64. Stacpoole-Ryding, *Maiwand*, p. 76.
65. The original of Feller's painting has been lost, but it survives in the form of numerous prints that were issued.
66. National Army Museum, Templer Study Centre, 1961–12–560–1.
67. After the Battle of Tofrek in the Sudan in 1885, the regiment was granted 'royal' status and became the Princess Charlotte of Wales's (Royal Berkshire) Regiment.
68. Bobbie found the streets of England more dangerous than Afghanistan: a year later, he was accompanying the regiment on a march through Gosport when he was run over and killed by a hansom cab carrying a wedding party. The men were so distraught that an officer had to prevent one of them from clubbing the driver with the butt of his rifle. Bobbie was sent to a taxidermist, who preserved him for eternity wearing the Afghan campaign medal that a member of the regiment had given him. He can still be seen today in the Regimental Museum in Salisbury. Stacpoole-Ryding, *Maiwand*, pp. 143–44. Bobbie was not the only regimental pet to receive public attention after surviving a disastrous battle in the late nineteenth century. After Isandlwana, Lion, the

canine companion of Lieutenant James Patrick Daly of the 24th Foot (who perished), limped back to the British lines with two serious assegai wounds. Lion's gravestone at Kilkenny Barracks in Ireland was inscribed: 'This faithful creature followed the fortunes of the Battalion through the Kafir and Zulu wars of 1877–78–79 and was severely wounded at the battle of Isandlwana.'

69. Stacpoole-Ryding, *Maiwand*, pp. 179–80. A memorial listing the names of the officers of the 66th who fell was installed in the church of St John the Evangelist in Bombay. There are also a number of memorials to individual soldiers; Stacpoole-Ryding lists them on pp. 181–86.

70. Arthur Conan Doyle, *The Complete Sherlock Holmes* (New York: Bantam, 1986), pp. 15 and 18.

Chapter 6: General Gordon

1. Durham University Library, Special Collections, Sudan Archive, SAD 723/2/4.
2. National Archives, Overseas: Sudan (Code 0(AJ)): Nile and Suakin Expeditions: Intelligence Reports on Fall of Khartoum and Death of General Gordon, WO 32/6121.
3. Ibid.
4. Ibid.
5. Durham University Library, Special Collections, Sudan Archive, SAD 723/2/25.
6. Ibid., SAD 723/2/14.
7. Sir William F. Butler, *Charles George Gordon* (London: Macmillan, 1889), p. 252.
8. [Anonymous] *Pictorial Records of the English in Egypt: With a Full and Descriptive Life of General Gordon, the Hero of Khartoum* (London: Frederick Warne, 1885), p. 386.
9. Reginald H. Barnes and Charles E. Brown, *Charles George Gordon: A Sketch* (London: Macmillan, 1885), pp. 94–95.
10. British Library, Add MS 52401, f. 59. More Gordon Boys' Homes were later established in other parts of the country.
11. The decision of the artist, William Onslow Ford, to depict Gordon on a camel was considered extremely novel, but the result generally met with the approbation of the art world and the military establishment.
12. 'Unveiling the Royal Engineers Gordon Statue', *Royal Engineers Journal* XX (1890), pp. 123–26.
13. British Library, Add MS 51301, f. 167.
14. Ibid., Add MS 52401, f. 87.
15. The failure to secure his remains was a source of regret for many Victorians, so much so that some sought to locate them long after his death. In 1895, Horace Lyne Squires, head of the Rich and Evans coalmining firm, received information from an unnamed source regarding the disposition of Gordon's head. Squires wrote to General Sir Francis Reginald Wingate, director of military intelligence in Egypt and the Sudan, to inquire about the possibility of recovering it. Squires reported that a member of his church's congregation, 'one of our best known medical men', was on his way to Cairo: 'I asked him *particularly* to see you and explained to him my ideas as to Gordon's remains.' (Italics in original.) Durham University Library, Special Collections, Sudan Archive, SAD 261/1/25.
16. For other discussions of Gordon as a Victorian hero, see Cynthia Behrman, 'The After-Life of General Gordon', *Albion* 3 (1971), pp. 47–61; Denis Judd, 'Gordon of Khartoum: The Making of an Imperial Martyr', *History Today* 35 (1985), pp. 19–25; Stephanie D. Laffer, 'Gordon's Ghost's: British Major-General Charles George Gordon and his Legacies, 1885–1960' (PhD dissertation, Florida State University, 2010); James Rattue, 'The "Cult" of Gordon', *Royal Engineers Journal* 112 (1998), pp. 182–89; Miles Taylor, 'Gordon of Khartoum: Reluctant Son of Southampton', in Miles Taylor, ed.,

Southampton: Gateway to the British Empire (New York: I.B. Tauris, 2007), pp. 83–94; and John Wolffe, *Great Deaths: Grieving, Religion and Nationhood in Victorian and Edwardian Britain* (Oxford: Oxford University Press, 2000), pp. 145–53.

17. See, in particular, Mark Girouard, *The Return to Camelot: Chivalry and the English Gentleman* (New Haven and London: Yale University Press, 1981).

18. Stephanie Barczewski, *Myth and National Identity in Nineteenth-Century Britain: The Legends of King Arthur and Robin Hood* (Oxford: Oxford University Press, 2000), pp. 220–23.

19. Butler, *Charles George Gordon*, pp. 252 and 255.

20. British Library, Add MS 52404, ff. 121 and 202.

21. Ibid., ff. 116 and 150.

22. Ibid., Add MS 52405, f. 214.

23. Ibid., f. 206.

24. Ibid., ff. 210 and 216.

25. Archibald Forbes, *Chinese Gordon: A Succinct Record of his Life* (London: George Routledge and Sons, 1884), p. 1; and G. Barnett Smith, *General Gordon: The Christian Soldier and Hero* (London: S.W. Partridge & Co., 1898), pp. v–vi.

26. British Library, Add MS. 52405, f. 215.

27. Jeanie Lang, *The Story of General Gordon* (London: T.C. and E.C. Jack, 1906), pp. vii–viii.

28. James Burns, *Sir Galahad: A Call to the Heroic* (London, [1914]), pp. 20–21.

29. Andrew Thompson, *The Empire Strikes Back?: The Impact of Imperialism on Britain from the Mid-Nineteenth Century* (Edinburgh: Pearson Education, Ltd., 2005), p. 51.

30. Sir Gerald Graham, *Last Words with Gordon* (London: Chapman and Hall, 1887), p. 5.

31. Demetrius C. Boulger, *General Gordon's Letters from the Crimea, the Danube and Armenia* (London: Chapman and Hall, 1884), p. xiii.

32. Butler, *Charles George Gordon*, p. 253.

33. Anthony Nutting, *Gordon: Martyr and Misfit* (London: Constable, 1966), p. 301.

34. British Library, Add MS. 52404, ff. 36, 65 and 90.

35. Ibid., f. 180.

36. Ibid., Add MS. 51301, f. 13.

37. Ibid., Add MS. 52403, ff. 192–93.

38. Nutting, *Gordon: Martyr or Misfit*, p. 314. Victoria claimed to have been so upset by the news of Gordon's death that she became ill. She later acquired what was supposedly a piece of the staircase on which Gordon had died from the Governor's Palace in Khartoum; it can be seen today in the Royal Engineers Museum in Gillingham in Kent.

39. British Library, Add MS. 52404, f. 4.

40. Ibid., ff. 30 and 42.

41. A. Egmont Hake, ed., *The Journals of Major-General C.G. Gordon, C.B., at Kartoum* (London: Kegan Paul, Trench & Co., 1885), p. x.

42. Boulger, *General Gordon's Letters*, pp. x–xi and xii.

43. Durham University Library, Special Collections, Sudan Archive, SAD 866/6/1.

44. Ibid., SAD 126/7/36.

45. Henry Keown-Boyd, *A Thorough Dusting: The Sudan Campaigns 1883–1899* (Barnsley: Pen and Sword, 1986), p. 236.

46. In truth, Kitchener did not know what to do with the skull and stashed it in a warehouse in Cairo. It was subsequently buried in an unmarked grave in a Muslim cemetery in Wadi Halfa in the northern Sudan.

47. Dominic Green, *Three Empires on the Nile: The Victorian Jihad 1869–1899* (New York: Simon and Schuster, 2007), p. 268.

48. Durham University Library, Special Collections, Sudan Archive, SAD 126/7/44–45. The scene was later depicted by the prominent military artist Richard Caton-Woodville, whose painting showed a stoical and dignified group of British and Egyptian soldiers, with Kitchener at the forefront, watching as four chaplains read the service from their prayerbooks.
49. Durham University Library, Special Collections, Sudan Archive, SAD 126/7/46–47.
50. Sir Henry Newbolt, *Admiral's All and Other Verses* (London: Elkin Mathews, 1898), p. 21.
51. Durham University Library, Special Collections, Sudan Archive, SAD 723/2/34.

Chapter 7: Captain Scott

1. Scott and Amundsen never met, although during a visit to Christiania (today Oslo) in 1910, Scott tried to make contact with Amundsen. Some polar historians have speculated that Amundsen deliberately avoided Scott because he did not want to have to lie about his change in plans.
2. Royal Geographical Society, Robert Falcon Scott Special Collection, File 4.
3. An offended Amundsen initially threatened to cancel the lecture, but was persuaded to go ahead by King Haakon of Norway, who did not wish to spark an international incident.
4. Kathleen Scott has often been interpreted as having led the charge against Amundsen. In her correspondence with the Royal Geographical Society, however, she was far less critical than Keltie. She wrote to him soon after learning the news that Amundsen had reached the Pole: 'if it must be another country I'd sooner Norway than any other'. Royal Geographical Society, Correspondence Block 1911–20, R. F. Scott, File A.
5. Amundsen's journey to the South Pole and back took ninety-nine days; Scott's, which covered a lesser distance because he and his companions did not make it all the way back, 140.
6. Robert Falcon Scott, *Scott's Last Expedition* (London: Wordsworth Editions, 2011), p. 380.
7. At warmer temperatures, the friction created by the runners would have generated enough heat to cause the top layer of crystals to melt, therefore providing lubrication. See Susan Solomon, *The Coldest March: Scott's Fatal Antarctic Expedition* (New Haven and London: Yale University Press, 2002).
8. Scott, *Scott's Last Expedition*, p. 401.
9. Ibid., p. 392.
10. Ibid., p. 407.
11. Ibid., p. 413.
12. Ibid., p. 426.
13. In 1897, Ettie married the Liberal Unionist politician William Grey Ellison-Macartney. He retired from politics in 1903, but went on to serve as deputy master of the Royal Mint. At the time of Scott's death, he had recently been knighted (making Ettie Lady Ellison-Macartney) and appointed to the governorship of Tasmania, despite objections from Irish nationalists in the colony. In her farewell letter to her sister-in-law in January 1913 as she prepared to embark for New Zealand (and before she knew of her husband's death), Kathleen Scott wrote: 'I'm sure they'll like you so much when you get out there that they'll drop all their protests.' Sir William's friend Francis Peter Gervais, a landowner in County Tyrone, linked Scott's death to the cause of Ulster Unionism when he added the postscript to his letter of condolence: 'Pray for us that we may remember him in any risks we take for the cause of Ulster.' The condolence letters to Sir William include one from the Ulster Unionist leader Sir Edward Carson. The government of Tasmania, meanwhile, immediately dispatched condolences to their new governor. University of Cambridge, Scott Polar Research Institute, MS 1464/23.

14. Ibid.
15. An obviously miffed (retired) Lieutenant Colonel Pennefarther also wrote to Mrs Oates to express his frustration at not being admitted: 'Several [men from the Inniskillngs] came to town to attend the service at St Paul's today, and I had tried to make arrangements that they should have special seats, and so as a body, but unfortunately the Cathedral authorities did not see their way to acceding to my request, for which I need not say, I am sincerely sorry.' Ibid., MS 1016/391–419.
16. Ibid., MS 1464/23.
17. Royal Geographical Society, Correspondence Block 1911–20, R. F. Scott, File I (ii).
18. Scott Polar Research Institute, University of Cambridge, MS 1464/23.
19. British Library, Asia, Pacific and Africa Collections, India Office Private Papers, MSS Eur F112/51.
20. University of Cambridge, Scott Polar Research Institute, MS 1464/23.
21. Royal Geographical Society, Correspondence Block 1911–20, R. F. Scott, File I (iv).
22. University of Cambridge, Scott Polar Research Institute, MS 1464/23.
23. Royal Geographical Society, Correspondence Block 1911–20, R. F. Scott, File H (vi).
24. Ibid., File H (ii) and H (vi).
25. Ibid., File H (ii).
26. 'The Antarctic Disaster', *Geographical Journal* 41 (March 1913), p. 205.
27. Edward Larson, *An Empire of Ice: Scott, Shackleton and the Heroic Age of Antarctic Science* (New Haven and London: Yale University Press, 2011), p. 22.
28. Ibid., pp. 22–23.
29. 'Scott's Message', *The Times*, 12 February 1913.
30. Royal Geographical Society, Correspondence Block 1911–20, R. F. Scott, File A.
31. Ibid., File D. Mill was generally a friend and supporter of Scott, so his opinions here can be taken as lacking ulterior motives.
32. British Library, Asia, Pacific and Africa Collection, India Office Private Papers, MSS Eur F112/51.
33. Larson, *Empire of Ice*, p. 24.
34. British Library, Asia, Pacific and Africa Collections, India Office Private Papers, MSS Eur F112/51.
35. Ibid.
36. 'Antarctic Disaster', p. 212.
37. British Library, Asia, Pacific and Africa Collections, India Office Private Papers, MSS Eur F112/51.
38. Royal Geographical Society, Correspondence Block 1911–20, R. F. Scott, Files G and H. Curzon also recorded another conversation with Edward Wilson's wife, Oriana, which focused on 'a passage in her husband's diary which spoke of the "inexplicable shortage of fuel and provisions on the return journey"'. But she, too, was not inclined to cause to public difficulty; Curzon added: 'she proposes to show [the passage] to no one and keep [it] secret.' British Library, Asia, Pacific and Africa Collections, India Office Private Papers, MSS Eur F112/51.
39. University of Cambridge, Scott Polar Research Institute, MS 1464/23.
40. Royal Geographical Society, Correspondence Block 1911–20, R. F. Scott, File H (iii); ibid., File H (iv); and University of Cambridge, Scott Polar Research Institute, MS 1453/162 D.
41. University of Cambridge, Scott Polar Research Institute, MS 1453/31.
42. Royal Geographical Society, Correspondence Block 1911–20, R. F. Scott, File H (iv).
43. University of Cambridge, Scott Polar Research Institute, MS 1453/31.
44. Ibid., MS 1464/23.

45. Ibid., MS 1453/31.
46. Ibid., MS 1453/162 D.
47. Ibid.
48. Ibid.
49. Ibid., MS 1016/391–419.
50. Royal Geographical Society, Correspondence Block 1911–20, R. F. Scott, File E. Evans's public prominence was not looked upon with favour by everyone. In May 1913, Oriana Wilson complained to Curzon: 'I see that once more Commander Evans has been honoured by the King, though he had already received promotion for his one year's service in the Antarctic.' Similarly, Keltie asked Kathleen Scott in February 1914: 'What do you think of all the honours that have been conferred upon Evans on the continent and here about his lecture tournaments?' Kathleen later complained that Evans had donated a number of items to the Royal Geographical Society that were rightfully hers, writing to Keltie: 'Commander Evans made curious use of his association with the expedition which is my excuse for ejaculations of annoyance when I see his name on my husband's property.' British Library, Asia, Pacific and Africa Collection, India Office Private Papers, MSS Eur F112/51; and Royal Geographical Society, Correspondence Block 1911–20, R. F. Scott, File A.
51. Royal Geographical Society, Correspondence Block 1911–20, R. F. Scott, File H (i).
52. University of Cambridge, Scott Polar Research Institute, MS 1453/31.
53. Royal Geographical Society, Correspondence Block 1911–20, R. F. Scott, File H (iii).
54. John Kennedy MacLean, *Heroes of the Polar Seas* (London: W. & R. Chambers, 1910), p. 378.
55. Larson, *Empire of Ice*, p. 166.
56. See G. R. Searle, *The Quest for National Efficiency: A Study in British Politics and Political Thought, 1899–1914* (Berkeley: University of California Press, 1971).
57. University of Cambridge, Scott Polar Research Institute, MS 1464/23.
58. 'Antarctic Disaster', pp. 212 and 219.
59. Max Jones, *The Last Great Quest: Captain Scott's Antarctic Sacrifice* (Oxford: Oxford University Press, 2003), p. 111.
60. British Library, Asia, Pacific and Africa Collection, India Office Private Papers, MSS Eur F112/51; and 'Antarctic Disaster', p. 212.
61. University of Cambridge, Scott Polar Research Institute, MS 1016/391–419.
62. Ibid.
63. 'Antarctic Disaster', p. 211.
64. University of Cambridge, Scott Polar Research Institute, MS 1464/23.
65. Ibid.
66. Ibid.
67. Ibid., MS 1453/31.
68. Royal Geographical Society, Correspondence Block 1911–20, R. F. Scott, File H (v).
69. Ibid., File H (i).
70. Scott Polar Research Institute, University of Cambridge, MS 1453/31.
71. Roland Huntford, *Scott and Amundsen* (London: Hodder and Stoughton, 1979), p. 560.

Conclusion

1. British Library, Asia, Pacific and Africa Collection, MSS Eur F112/53.
2. Ibid. Ultimately London was abandoned altogether, and the memorial was erected in Devonport in Scott's native town of Plymouth. It was not unveiled until 1925, over a decade after Scott's death.

3. The National Portrait Gallery unfortunately missed the centennial of Scott's death in March 2012, as the portrait did not go on display until January 2013. The history of Scott's appearances there parallels the ebb and flow of his reputation. In 1914, the gallery acquired a portrait of Scott by Charles Percival Small. As Small was a friend of Scott's rather than a skilled artist, it was not a good likeness, but few portraits of Scott existed, and the National Portrait Gallery was eager to put one on display given the scale of the response to his death. In contemplating its acquisition, Charles Francis Bell, one of the gallery's trustees, opined that despite its poor quality it should not be rejected 'on the chance of something better being eventually secured'. In 1924, it obtained the Wehrschmidt portrait, which was of considerably better quality than Small's, on loan from Scott's family, and immediately put it on display. Apart from being taken down along with the rest of the gallery's collection to protect it from bomb damage in the Second World War, the portrait remained on view until at least 1961. At some point between then and 1997, however, it was removed, in keeping with the decline of Scott's reputation in this period. As recently as a decade ago, when I was conducting the research for my book *Antarctic Destinies*, I was told by the keepers of the gallery's storage facility that it was unlikely that Scott's portrait would return to public display in the foreseeable future. National Portrait Gallery, Heinz Archive and Library, RP 1726, NPG 46/18/35 and RP 2079.
4. George Orwell, *The Lion and the Unicorn: Socialism and the English Genius* (London: Penguin, 1982), p. 42.
5. Jeffrey Richards, *Films and British National Identity: From Dickens to Dad's Army* (Manchester and New York: Manchester University Press, 1997), p. 158. See also Jeffrey Richards, 'Imperial Heroes for a Post-Imperial Age: Films and the End of Empire', in Stuart Ward, ed., *British Culture and the End of Empire* (Manchester: Manchester University Press, 2001), pp. 128–44.
6. Tim Brooke-Taylor, *Rule Britannia: The Ways and World of the True British Gentleman Patriot* (London: Littlehampton, 1983), p. 109.
7. http://www.theguardian.com/world/2010/sep/27/captain-scott-antarctic-amundsen-south-pole.
8. A. G. Hopkins, 'Back to the Future: From National History to Imperial History', *Past and Present* 164 (1999), p. 214.
9. John MacKenzie writes: 'Empires … have always been realms of fantasy. The outer regions where empires are created and controlled is a fantastical world where larger-than-life events take place, where great victories may be achieved and where fortunes and reputations can be made.' John MacKenzie, 'General Editor's Introduction', in Berny Sèbe, *Heroic Imperialists in Africa: The Promotion of British and French Colonial Heroes, 1870–1939* (Manchester: Manchester University Press, 2013), p. xiii.
10. See in particular Christopher Hale, *Massacre in Malaya: Exposing Britain's My Lai* (Charleston, SC: History Press, 2013).
11. For the various uses of the Mau Mau myth in both Kenyan and European contexts, see Carl G. Rosberg, Jr. and John Nottingham, *The Myth of Mau Mau: Nationalism in Kenya* (New York: Praeger, 1966); A. S. Cleary, 'The Myth of Mau Mau in its International Context', *African Affairs* 89 (1990), pp. 227–45; Dane Kennedy, 'Constructing the Colonial Myth of Mau Mau', *International Journal of African Studies* 25 (1992), pp. 241–60; John Lonsdale, 'Mau Maus of the Mind: Making Mau Mau and Remaking Kenya', *Journal of African History* 31 (1990), pp. 393–421; and David Maughan-Brown, *Land, Freedom and Fiction* (London: Zed, 1985).
12. See David Anderson, *Histories of the Hanged: The Dirty War in Kenya and the End of Empire* (London: W.W. Norton, 2013); and Caroline Elkins, *Imperial Reckoning: The Untold Story of Britain's Gulag in Kenya* (New York: Holt, 2004).

13. MacKenzie describes how the maintenance of imperial ideals depends on 'the comforting notion that the violence through which empires are created is justified by the cargoes of good things that are delivered with them'. MacKenzie, 'General Editor's Introduction', p. xiii.
14. http://www.channel4.com/news/andy-murray-tennis-australian-open-plucky-loser-paradigm.

ARCHIVAL SOURCES AND SUGGESTIONS FOR FURTHER READING

Archival Sources

The research for this book utilized the following archival and museum collections:

British Library
David Livingstone Centre, National Trust for Scotland
Derbyshire Record Office
Durham University Library, Special Collections, Sudan Archive
Historic New Orleans Collection
National Archives
National Army Museum, Templer Study Centre
National Library of Scotland
National Portrait Gallery, Heinz Archive and Library
Royal Engineers Museum and Library
Royal Geographical Society
Scottish Borders Archive
Tyne and Wear Archives
University of Cambridge, Scott Polar Research Institute

Suggestions for Further Reading

Introduction

Berenson, Edward, Heroes of Empire: Five Charismatic Men and the Conquest of Africa (Berkeley: University of California Press, 2002).

Jones, Max, 'What Should Historians Do with Heroes?: Reflections on Nineteenth- and Twentieth-Century Britain', *History Compass* 5:2 (2007), pp. 439–54.

MacKenzie, John M., 'Heroic Myths of Empire', in John M. MacKenzie, ed., *Popular Imperialism and the Military, 1850–1950* (Manchester: Manchester University Press, 1992), pp. 109–38.

Riffenburgh, Beau, *The Myth of the Explorer: The Press, Sensationalism and Geographical Discovery* (London and New York: Bellhaven, 1993).

Sèbe, Berny, *Heroic Imperialists in Africa: The Promotion of British and French Colonial Heroes, 1870–1939* (Manchester: Manchester University Press, 2013).

Chapter 1

Berton, Pierre, *The Arctic Grail: The Quest for the North West Passage and the North Pole, 1818–1909* (New York: Viking, 1988).

Fleming, Fergus, *Barrow's Boys: The Original Extreme Adventurers* (New York: Grove, 1998).

Hibbert, Christopher, *Corunna* (New York: Phoenix, 2003).

Kennedy, Dane, *The Last Blank Spaces: Exploring Africa and Australia* (Cambridge, MA: Harvard University Press, 2013).

Lockhart, Jamie Bruce, *A Sailor in the Sahara: The Life and Travels in Africa of Hugh Clapperton, Commander R.N.* (London and New York, I.B. Tauris, 2008).

Lupton, Kenneth, *Mungo Park the African Traveler* (Oxford: Oxford University Press, 1979).

Patterson, Benton Rain, *The Generals: Andrew Jackson, Sir Edward Pakenham and the Road to the Battle of New Orleans* (New York and London: New York University Press, 2005).

Pemble, John, *Britain's Gurkha War: The Invasion of Nepal, 1814–16* (London: Frontline, 2008).

Ross, M. J., *Polar Pioneers: John Ross and James Clark Ross* (Montreal and Kingston, Ontario: McGill-Queen's University Press, 1994).

Sattin, Anthony, *The Gates of Africa: Death, Discovery and the Search for Timbuktu* (New York: St Martin's, 2004).

Williams, Glyn, *Arctic Labyrinth: The Quest for the Northwest Passage* (Berkeley: University of California Press, 2009).

Chapter 2

Beattie, Owen, and Geiger, John, *Frozen in Time: The Fate of the Franklin Expedition* (New York: Dutton, 1987).

Brandt, Anthony, *The Man Who Ate his Boots: The Tragic History of the Search for the Northwest Passage* (London: Jonathan Cape, 2011).

Lambert, Alex, *The Gates of Hell: Sir John Franklin's Tragic Quest for the Northwest Passage* (New Haven and London: Yale University Press, 2009).

McGoogan, Ken, *Fatal Passage: The Untold Story of Scotsman John Rae, the Arctic Adventurer Who Discovered the Fate of Franklin* (London and New York: Bantam Books, 2001).

Sandler, Martin W., *Resolute: The Epic Search for the Northwest Passage and Sir John Franklin, and the Discovery of the Queen's Ghost Ship* (New York: Sterling, 2008).

Chapter 3

Brighton, Terry, *Hell Riders: The Truth about the Light Brigade* (London: Penguin, 2004).

Buttery, David, *Messenger of Death: Captain Nolan and the Charge of the Light Brigade* (Barnsley: Pen & Sword Military, 2008).

David, Saul, *The Homicidal Earl: The Life of Lord Cardigan* (London: Abacus, 1997).

——, *Victoria's Wars: The Rise of Empire* (London: Penguin, 2007).

Sidhu, Amarpal S., *The First Anglo–Sikh War* (Stroud, Gloucestershire: Amberley, 2010).

Thomas, Donald, *Cardigan: The Hero of Balaclava* (London: Routledge & Kegan Paul, 1974).

Trow, M. J., *The Pocket Hercules: Captain Morris and the Charge of the Light Brigade* (Barnsley: Pen & Sword Military, 2006).

Chapter 4

Jeal, Tim, *Livingstone*, revised edn (New Haven and London: Yale University Press, 2013).
——, *Stanley* (New Haven and London: Yale University Press, 2007).
MacKenzie, John M., ed., *David Livingstone and the Victorian Encounter with Africa* (London: National Portrait Gallery, 1996).
Pettit, Claire, *Dr Livingstone, I Presume?: Missionaries, Journalists, Explorers and Empire* (London: Profile, 2007).

Chapter 5

David, Saul, *Zulu: The Heroism and Tragedy of the Zulu War of 1879* (London: Penguin, 2004).
Greaves, Adrian, *Isandlwana: How the Zulus Humbled the British Empire* (Barnsley: Pen and Sword, 2011).
Ian Knight, *Zulu Rising: The Epic Story of Isandlwana and Rorke's Drift* (London: Macmillan, 2010).
Snook, Mike, *Into the Jaws of Death: British Military Blunders, 1879–1900* (London: Frontline, 2008).
Stacpoole-Ryding, Richard J., *Maiwand: The Last Stand of the 66th (Berkshire) Regiment in Afghanistan, 1880* (Stroud: History Press, 2008).
Yorke, Edmund, *Maiwand 1880* (Stroud, Gloucestershire: Spellmount, 2013).

Chapter 6

Asher, Michael, *Khartoum: The Ultimate Imperial Adventure* (New York and London: Penguin, 2008).
Green, Dominic, *Three Empires on the Nile: The Victorian Jihad 1869–1899* (New York: Simon and Schuster, 2007).
Keown-Boyd, Henry, *A Thorough Dusting: The Sudan Campaigns 1883–1899* (Barnsley: Pen and Sword, 1986).
Pollock, John, *Kitchener: The Road to Omdurman* (London: Constable, 1999).

Chapter 7

Barczewski, Stephanie, *Antarctic Destinies: Scott, Shackleton and the Changing Face of Heroism* (London: Continuum, 2006).
Crane, David, *Scott of the Antarctic: A Life of Courage and Tragedy* (New York: Knopf, 2006).
Jones, Max, *The Last Great Quest: Captain Scott's Antarctic Sacrifice* (Oxford: Oxford University Press, 2003).
Larson, Edward, *An Empire of Ice: Scott, Shackleton and the Heroic Age of Antarctic Science* (New Haven and London: Yale University Press, 2011).

INDEX

ILLUSTRATION CREDITS

1 Leonard Bentley; 2 Yale Center for British Art; 3 Bridgeman Images; 4 *Memoirs of the Bernice Pauahi Bishop Museum*, Vol. VII (Honolulu, 1918); 5 Spixey; 6, 7 and 10 Courtauld Images; 8 Royal Ontario Museum; 9, 12, 16, 22, 34, 36, 37, 40, and 46 Wellcome Images; 11 Comber Historical Society; 13 Scottish Borders Archive; 14 Kim Traynor; 15 British Library, London; 17, 32 and 54 National Portrait Gallery, London; 18 and 19 The National Archives; 20 Library and Archives Canada; 21 clevelander96; 23, 24, 25, 26, 27, 28, 29, 41, 42, 43, 44 and 45 National Army Museum, London; 30, 31, 49; 50; 52 and 53 Library of Congress; 33 National Gallery of Ireland; 35 and 38 David Livingstone Centre, National Trust for Scotland; 39 Smithsonian Institution; 47 and 48 Durham University Library, Archives and Special Collections; 51 University of Cambridge, Scott Polar Research Institute

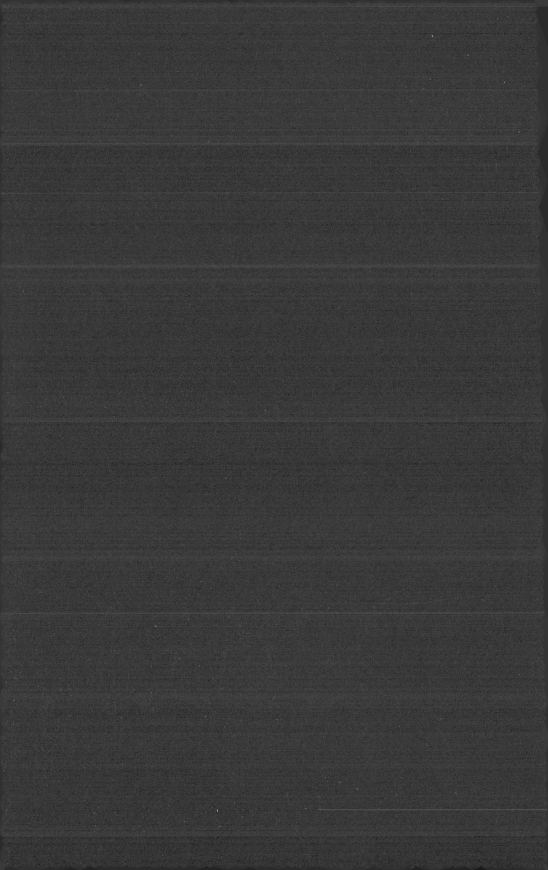